Where
the
Body
Meets
Memory

An
Odyssey
of
Race,
Sexuality,
and
Identity

Anchor Books
A Division of
Random House, Inc.
New York

Where the Body Meets Memory

DAVID
MURA

Copyright © 1996 by David Mura

All rights reserved. Published in the United States by Anchor Books,
a division of Random House, Inc., New York, and in Canada by
Random House of Canada Limited, Toronto. Originally published
in hardcover in the United States by Anchor Books in 1996.

ANCHOR BOOKS and colophon are registered trademarks of Random House, Inc.

The Library of Congress has cataloged the Anchor hardcover edition as follows:
Mura, David.
Where the body meets memory: an odyssey of race, sexuality,
and identity / David Mura.
p.   cm.
1. Mura, David.   2. Mura, David—Sexual behavior.   3. Japanese Americans—Race
identity.   4. Japanese Americans—Cultural assimilation.   5. Japanese Americans—
Sexual behavior.   6. Japanese Americans—Biography.   7. United States—Race
relations.   I. Title.
E184.J3M7844   1995
305.895´6073—dc20   95-40950
CIP

ISBN 978-0-385-47184-8

Book design by Jennifer Ann Daddio

www.anchorbooks.com

147687453

FOR SAMANTHA, NIKKO, AND TOMO

CONTENTS

*Where
the
Body
Meets
Memory*

"Defense is for times of insufficiency,
attack is for times of surplus."

—SUN TZU,
THE ART OF WAR

Prologue: Silences

"My body was given back to me sprawled out, distorted, recolored, clad in mourning in that white winter day."

—Frantz Fanon,
Black Skin, White Masks

I WAS BORN on a sweltering summer day in June 1952.

Early that morning, two white MPs drove my mother the fifty miles from the South Side of Chicago to the Great Lakes Naval Training Center Hospital. My father was half a world away, stationed in Germany. Of course, he didn't want to miss the birth of his son—he didn't see me until I was six months old—but better to be in Germany than in Korea, that terrible forgotten Asian war.

When I think of my mother taking that drive to Great Lakes, it seems strange and poignant. She was just twenty, still a girl really. Eight years earlier she'd been living in a concentration camp in the mountains of Idaho, and here she was driving an hour and a half with two white men she'd never seen before even as her contractions sharpened and quickened, and I pushed harder to enter this world.

"I suppose I was so young," she says now, "I didn't really think about it. I just got in the car and went."

The MPs drove along Lake Shore Drive, then took Sheridan Road, winding through the rich northern suburbs of Winnetka and Kenilworth. Beyond was farmland until you reached the industrial city of Waukegan. They talked about the Cubs, the heat, their pain-in-the-ass superiors. There were long lapses into silence, the boredom of the drive. Except for occasionally asking if she was all right, they didn't talk to my mother, this tiny beautiful young Japanese American in the backseat, her stomach bloated to bursting. It was awkward for them, driving this pregnant woman; perhaps her race made it more so. My mother closed her eyes and tried to sleep. One of the MPs lit a cigar. My mother said nothing, but opened the window wider. Sweat beads slipped down her furrowed brow. Slowly, her breaths grew shorter. They were almost there.

This was her second trip to the base in a week; two days before she had taken the same drive on a false alarm. This time she knew for certain. She wondered what her husband was doing at the moment. She realized he was probably going to bed. When he wakes up, she thought, he'll be a father.

In his letters to my Aunt Yo at the time, my father spoke of someday taking "Terry and the 'kids' to Europe," now that Europe was no longer the faraway continent of wishful dreams. His sense of the future was filled with bright promise and plenty; he felt himself part of an "era of change," of fantasies becoming reality. On his leaves, he was traveling to Munich, Bonn, and Cologne; in Paris, he gazed on *Mona Lisa*, rowed in the pond behind Versailles, ate bouillabaisse and coq au vin; later, he saw Buckingham Palace and the Indian temple in the British Museum, walked along the Thames beneath Big Ben. He was a gardener's son from the streets of Los Angeles, a Nisei—second generation Japanese American—and, like my mother, just a few years from the camps, and here he was buying champagne and fine wines, buoyed by the high price of the dollar and the flush of the postwar boom. And he was going to have a child. He was certain it would be a boy, whom he'd name David, which means beloved, an old biblical name of a great king, the composer of psalms of devotion.

Still, my father worried about my mother, pregnant and alone. He wondered if her plight was some indication of his own restless ways, even though it was the draft and not his own choice which brought him to Germany: "With this letter," he wrote my Aunt Yo, "I'm enclosing a money order for $10.00 and also a card for Terry. Will you please see that Terry does get some flowers and this card after the blessed event? How I wished that I could be there with her, but I guess I just can't be. I do hope that everything will be perfect for Terry and that she will have an easy time. Loving Terry as much as I do, I seem to have gotten her into one predicament after another. I'll really have to settle down and make her a good home after I get back . . . and you can believe me when I say, I'll really try!"

As it turned out, things did go well for my birth, and my father's certainty about having a firstborn son proved true. All that remained was for the six months of his tour to pass quickly, and for my parents to be reunited, so they could start their life as a family in that city beside the great lake in which my father loved to swim.

MINNEAPOLIS. Late at night, in the marriage bed. Early spring, the scent of lilacs wafting in from the backyard. The children, at last, asleep. My wife, Susie, is reading an article in *Cancer*, a bit of research squeezed in at day's end. I ferret through my father's high school yearbook—1944, Denson High, the Jerome, Arkansas, camp—and think about how, when I was younger, I wanted nothing to do with my Japanese American past.

I pick up the newsletter for my father's fiftieth high school reunion. In one of the articles, my father writes of his teacher Marie Cash, who prepared "all of us for 'life after camp' . . . by strengthening our faith in the principles underlying America." She is the one who taught him how to shake hands, how to grasp firmly and look into the other person's eyes ("Whenever I shake anyone's hand, Marie Cash is there"). She told him that outside of camp there would be more good people than bad, and over the years, my father claims, "she proved to be right."

"Look at this," I say. "It's like the whole complexity of the camps has been reduced to the fact that this woman showed him how to shake hands. The camps as a course in Dale Carnegie."

"What do you expect?" Susie says. "It sounds like your father."

"But it makes me feel crazy. There's nothing here about the losses the Issei suffered, nothing about the fights between the Kibei and the JACLers and the No-No Boys. It just sounds like a public relations campaign for the camps."

"Well, that's what he does. He's a professional PR man."

Susie turns back to her magazine. She's heard much of this before; her knowledge of the camps goes deeper than most non-Japanese Americans.

She knows that Executive Order 9066, which set up the camps in 1942, was fueled by racism, wartime hysteria, and a desire for the property of Japanese Americans. She knows some forces in the community, like the Japanese American Citizens League, urged people to go along with the order, to cooperate with the government. Others felt furious, resentful, betrayed. She knows all about the loyalty oath for Japanese Americans, with its two crucial questions: Do you forswear allegiance to the emperor and swear allegiance to the United States? And will you serve in the armed forces of the United States? She knows three of my uncles answered yes to both questions; one was wounded in Europe. She knows there were young men, No-No Boys, who answered in the negative. Some were Kibei, Nisei who'd been educated in Japan. Others saw their no as a form of protest. She knows the Issei, or first generation, my grandparents, were forbidden by law to become citizens.

In short, she knows the camps were more complicated than my parents say. She knows also how obsessive I can be about the past.

"Do you have to read that magazine?" I ask.

"I've got to keep up a little bit." Pause. "What do you want to talk about?"

She senses I'm gearing up. I get like this just before we go to bed. Some train of thought pops into my head, and I've got to process it before I sleep. I become like a partygoer strung out on Dexedrine who won't allow anyone around him to slip off to sleep. Usually, this is just about the time Susie has become bone-weary and wants to retire.

"You know your father is like that. All high school yearbooks are like that."

"But not all high school yearbooks are produced in the middle of a war in a concentration camp. Listen to this: 'Typically American are Denson High students. We use slang, chew gum, go on dates, wear bobby socks and dirty saddles, and jitterbug. We're almost sentimental in our honor of Old Glory.' "

"So write your own version."

"That's what I'm trying to do. But they never talked about it when I was growing up, and now, when they talk about it, it's like the camps were nothing."

My mother says she was too young to remember the camps. My father said he had to work in his father's nursery in L.A. before the war; when they got to the camps, he could go out and play baseball after school.

"They have their view. You have yours. What's the problem?"

"It's just that I'm still concerned about writing about all this."

"You'll be fine. You've done it before." Pause. "Now can I go back to my magazine?"

A few minutes pass. Susie looks up.

"You know what the real problem is?"

"What?"

"You're going to write about me again, aren't you?"

IN MY STORY of Japanese American identity, it's hard to avoid dealing with my marriage and the fact that my wife is white. Three-quarters WASP. One-quarter Austrian Hungarian Jew. We met more than two decades ago, when she was eighteen and I was twenty. "Susie has ancestors all the way back to the Pilgrims," my mother said to someone recently, her tone imparting both pride and astonishment at her daughter-in-law. She sees our marriage as a mark of assimilation. Sometimes I feel like that too. At other times it's much more complicated.

In 1985, after having shunned connections with Japan for most of my life, I won a grant to live in Tokyo for a year. Susie interrupted her medical school training to be with me. After we returned to the States, I wrote *Turning Japanese*, a book about our year there, how Japan had forced me to confront certain questions of identity I'd long avoided, how it changed the ways Susie and I looked at ourselves and each other. In the book I was fairly candid about our various arguments during the course of the year, and I recounted the tensions that arose when I became attracted to a German woman artist there, though that attraction never crossed into infidelity.

When the book was published, Susie felt certain misgivings about it. Some readers wondered why she put up with me; one reviewer dubbed her a saint. Other readers felt from the book that they knew who she was. A friend of ours came up to her at my publication reading, leaned forward in a mock-riveting stare, and said, "I'm reading *Turning Japanese*." Pause. "I just wanted to prepare you for people's reactions."

Susie's standard response now is: "All the good parts are true, and the rest he made up."

No one, of course, believes her.

We have a daughter who is four now and a son who is four months. Children for the next century. When Susie was pregnant, Samantha wanted to call her new brother Prince Charming, or Prince for short. We named him Nikko David Sencer-Mura. Nikko isn't a common Japanese name, but is a Japanese word whose characters mean "sunlight."

When Samantha was born, Susie had wanted to give her a Japanese middle name. I protested that this would make her seem too different from her classmates, and so we named her Samantha Lyn Sencer-Mura. In the time since, I've come to realize that Susie was right in wanting to mark the presence of Sam's Japanese background in her name. Sam's classmates are going to be children of many colors and backgrounds; as the demographics tell us, the faces of America are becoming more and more diverse. This is the world we ought to prepare our children for.

My parents had four children: me, Susan, John, and Linda. My sister Susan is two years younger than I, and we form one generation. We grew up in Chicago and Morton Grove, a middle-class suburb. John is eight years younger, Linda ten. They grew up in Northbrook, an upper-middle-class neighborhood, with parents that seemed less driven than the ones I grew up with. Once, when I was visiting home in my twenties, I was telling a friend how my father used to hit me when I was a child, and my sister Linda, twelve at the time, said indignantly, "My father would never hit anyone."

She was right; the father she knew was quite different from the one I knew. Her father had achieved his dreams, was living in a five-bedroom house that would have seemed a mansion to him as a child; he had gone through certain battles with me he would never go through again.

On the other hand, my sister Susan probably suffered both by being a girl and by not achieving the academic success I had. Susan was the tomboy, the one who babysat the younger ones when we were on vacation. I was the dreamer, the moody, introspective one.

My Aunt Ruth and Aunt Baye think that Susan was never given room to blossom; she was always too reliable and helpful, the second fiddle. "You may have had your problems with your father," Ruth says, "but Susan was treated like a handmaiden. Nobody fussed over her." To them, my father's constant pressures about grades were a form of attention, marked me as special. My sister never received such admonitions.

When my mother heard all this, she said, "They don't have children. How do they know what it's like to raise a child? It's easy to do it part-time, on vacations. You'll see when you have kids of your own."

My aunts are probably right about my sister, but so is my mother. If you don't have children, you can't imagine how difficult it is to raise them, how little control you have over who they are, who they will become. You can never know what effect you're having. You can do something that seems right at the time, then later wrong, then later it seems right again. At what age do you judge whether you've been successful as a parent? In high school, one child may be a star, the other engaged in constant rebellion and hell raising, sneaking drugs, staying out late, skipping school. In college, they reverse roles. Later, divorce, children, a failure in business, can change the whole picture once more.

Today, my sister works at Allstate insurance, is a whiz with computers, but her real passion is charity work, and for months at a time, she's consumed with organizing a silent auction or a walkathon or a dinner dance for some foundation for cancer or spina bifida. She's a born-again Christian, though quiet in her religion; she doesn't proselytize. In many ways, she has the strongest moral sense of anyone in the family, is the best of us in the depth of her generosity. How would my parents compare her life with mine? How would they determine which of us has traveled farther from the family?

ONE NIGHT a few years ago, I was working on a poem about my daughter, trying to take in her presence, trying to link her life with the past—my father and mother, the internment camps, my grandparents. In the poem I pictured myself serving her sukiyaki, a dish I shunned as a child, and her shouting for more rice, brandishing her *hashi* (a word for chopsticks which I never used as a child, and only began to use after my trip to Japan). As I described her running through the garden, scattering petals, squashing tomatoes, I suddenly thought of how someone someday will call her a "gook," that I knew this with more certainty than I knew she'll find happiness in love.

Later, I talked to Susie about moving out to the West Coast or Hawaii, to a place where there would be more Asian Americans. Samantha, I said, would meet more children there like her (in Hawaii, almost half the children are *hapa*—the Hawaiian term for mixed race; she'd be the norm not the minority). I spoke of the need to spend more time living in an Asian American community. My writing comes out of that community, is addressed to that community. I can't tell its stories if I'm not a part of it.

As I talked about moving, Susie started to feel uneasy. "I'm afraid you'll cross this bridge and take Sam with you, and leave me here," she said.

"But I've lived all my life on your side of the bridge. At most social gatherings, I'm constantly the only person of color in the room. What's wrong with living a while on my side of the bridge? What keeps you from crossing?"

Susie, a pediatric oncologist, works with families of all colors. Still, having a hybrid daughter has changed her experience. When Sam was younger and Susie took her to the grocery store, someone would always come up and say, "Oh, she's such a beautiful little girl. Where did you get her?" This happened so often, Susie swore she was going to teach Sam to say, "Fuck you, my genes came all the way over on the *Mayflower*, thank you."

These incidents marked one of the first times Susie experienced something negative over race that I haven't. When I'm with Sam, no one asks me where she came from. For Susie, the encounters were a challenge to her position as Samantha's biological mother, a negation of an arduous pregnancy and the labor of birth and motherhood. For me, they stirred an old wound. Those who mistake Sam for an adopted child can't picture a white woman married to an Asian man.

I'M SPEAKING ON MULTICULTURALISM at a conference for high school teachers. It's a speech I give frequently, half on the psychological barriers in dealing with racism, half on the various stages of my Japanese American identity. At the end of the speech I ask for questions.

"You've talked about how your parents didn't teach you much about Japanese culture," says one of the teachers. "How are you going to change that for your children?"

I hear this question almost every time I speak.

"I'm trying to do things differently. I read them Japanese fairy tales, show them Japanese art; they've got some videos of Japanese folk tales, like Momotaro. I'd like them to live a while in Japan. But it isn't easy. As a parent now, I realize how hard it would have been for my parents to teach me about Japanese culture, given the cultural climate around us. And I probably would have hated it if they had tried to send me to Japanese school."

This answer usually suffices. But then I add, "What seems more important to me than teaching my children about Japanese culture is to teach them about what it means to be a Japanese American and a person of color in this country."

I don't let out, though, my misgivings toward the initial question, however sincere. I feel audiences often ask me about Japanese culture because haiku and *The Tale of Genji* aren't as threatening to our images of America as the history of Japanese America. Those traditional cultural artifacts go down easier than the internment camps, the Asian exclusion laws, or the racial stereotypes perpetuated by our media.

What can I teach my daughter of the past? My Japanese American identity comes from my own experience, something I know. But I am still trying to understand that experience. I am still struggling to find languages to talk about the issues of race. It's simpler to pretend multiculturalism means teaching her *kanji* and how to conjugate Japanese verbs.

I know every day my daughter will be exposed to images which tell her that Asian bodies are marginalized: The women are exotic, sensual, and submissive; the men are houseboys or Chinatown punks, kung fu warriors or Japanese businessmen, robotlike and powerful or robotlike and comic. I know that she will face constant pressures to forget she is part Japanese American, to assume a basically white middle-class identity. When she reaches adolescence there will be powerful messages for her to conform to an unspoken norm, to disassociate herself from the children of recent Asian immigrants. She may find herself wanting to assume a privilege and status which comes from not calling attention to her identity, or from playing into the stereotype that makes Asian women seem so desirable to certain white men. And I know I will have no power over these forces.

The difficulties are caused by more than a lack of knowledge; there's the powerful wish not to know, to remain silent. How, for instance, can I talk to my daughter about sexuality and race? My own experience is so filled with shame and regret, is so filled with incidents I would rather not discuss, it seems much easier to opt for silence. Should I tell her of how, when I look at her mother, I know my desires for her cannot be separated from the way the culture has inculcated me with standards of white beauty? Should I tell her of my own desires for a "hallucinatory whiteness," of how such a desire fueled in my twenties a rampant promiscuity and addiction to pornography, to the "beautiful" bodies of white women? These elements of my story are all too much to expect her to take it in. They should not even be written down. They should be kept hidden, unspoken. Better to claim the forces that shaped me do not exist.

In the end, what I want to give to my daughter are not my answers, but the courage to ask her own questions and to keep asking them, no matter how confusing, frightening, or threatening they may be. I keep reminding myself there is too much to know, too many questions I can't solve. All I can give her are the tools to find her own answers.

IN HER AUTOBIOGRAPHY, the daughter of Marlene Dietrich writes that one day in 1942, a few months after Pearl Harbor, the lawns and gardens in Hollywood began to wilt and fester, and the intricate symmetry brought to them by the Japanese gardeners was no more. This vanishing seemed mysterious to her; she knew nothing about the internment camps. Afterward, the Japanese gardeners were replaced by Mexican gardeners, but the landscaping was not the same. It was for her the end of an era of magic in childhood in Hollywood. I see this child, lonely, forlorn, less lovely than her mother, standing at the veranda out back, saddened like the little girl in Hopkins' poem over "Goldengrove unleaving," mourning "the things of man" and the mortality of Hollywood and herself. I see her quickly turning the page to some other, more glamorous matter.

History is a matter of perspective. There are at least as many tales as there are participants. Some do the telling, some the listening; some hold center stage, some are walk-ons or stagehands behind the wings or, like the *kurokata* in Kabuki or No, black-hooded figures without faces, whom no one is to notice or acknowledge.

FIFTY YEARS AFTER THE CAMPS, Susie and I come out of a darkened theater where, in *Rising Sun*, Wesley Snipes and Sean Connery have just been chased through Los Angeles by Japanese thugs. Snipes eases to a corner, calls out the homeboys, who recognize him as a former high school basketball star from the 'hood. A few frames later, the Japanese thugs are surrounded by black faces and chattering in terror. The audience cheers. To the homeboys, the white cop, Connery, sitting with Snipes, isn't nearly the enemy that the Japanese are.

Michael Crichton and this movie would have us believe the Japanese are buying up America, worming their way into our economy with their robotlike precision and amoral cunning; they are behind the scenes controlling the politicians and businesspeople, the police, even the universities. They accuse Americans of racism to thwart any attempt to stop them. They cheat at business, blackmail, murder, and expect not to be caught or called to account because they are the superior race, they are Japanese.

Such portrayals work like shell games or three-card monte; they divert our critical attention from the workings of our own economy and government. Of course, American businesspeople never engage in such dubious practices, just as Americans never take over property and resources elsewhere on the globe. It's the Japanese who are running this country into the ground, not Americans.

Susie and I went to see *Rising Sun* on Cape Cod, where we vacation every year with my in-laws. After the movie, on the drive home, she waited apprehensively. Often, after films with racist stereotypes of Asians or Asian Americans, I begin to bubble up wave after wave of anger and diatribe, resentment and analysis, a roiling ride of emotions that will strike at the nearest target, which is often her. *Rambo, Sweet 16, Year of the Dragon, Showdown in Little Tokyo,* it's a familiar list to many Asian Americans.

"It was better than the book in certain ways, but it was still awful," I tell her.

"That's all?"

"You're expecting something more?"

"Yes. Usually after films like this you go ballistic. And you hated the book."

"I don't know. These days I just feel less inclination to go around

14

picketing and yelling and screaming. It takes too much energy, and where does it get you? I'd rather just write about it."

I pull the car into the driveway of our cottage, shut off the engine. "Actually, I'd rather not have to write about it. And I'm angry about that, as much as the movie itself. I feel I always end up focusing on what whites are doing, they're setting the agenda. That's one reason why protest art is so boring after a while, even if I do it myself, even if I do think it's necessary. It's just responding to stupidity and ignorance, the callousness of people with power."

"You're just getting old," Susie says. "Old and mellow."

THE NEXT DAY at the Cape, Susie's sister Annie and her husband, Frank, told us they fell asleep during *Rising Sun*. They preferred Clint Eastwood's *In the Line of Fire*.

"There just wasn't anything happening in *Rising Sun*," said Frank. "The book was more interesting."

I thought for a moment about saying something, but didn't. I'm on vacation, I said to myself. Frank's on vacation. We're all on vacation. This is family. I don't want to get up on a soapbox. I'd rather hit the beach and look for shells with Samantha.

In Minnesota, where I've lived for some twenty years, I'm sometimes perceived as a hard-liner about issues of race, quick to anger, part of the PC crowd. One critic has written, "To white liberals other than his wife, he is unforgiving." This is not, of course, how I see myself. Though I may be fueled by a certain moral earnestness, I'm much less rigid than the caricatures created by conservative critics. I may sometimes think I ought to be on unstinting vigilance, but that's hardly the way I live my life or want to live my life. There are times I just need to let go, to let things rest.

And yet, even as I chose to say nothing to my brother-in-law, images in *Rising Sun* began to crop up in my mind. In one scene, the Japanese playboy Eddie Sakumura cavorts with two white party girls; he picks up a sushi off the belly of one, then drips sake over the nipple of the other and licks her clean. Harvey Keitel, a cop, peers in at the window and mutters, "He's plundering our natural resources." I thought of how my wife and I made love earlier that morning, when the children were with their grandparents. I thought of how her body looked in the mirror beside the bed, her skin contrasting with the darker tan of my own, how the images and phrases, the movies and my desires, have melded into each other, despite any attempts I make to keep them separate. What would the Harvey Keitel character say if he were to see me with my wife? What did the other people who saw the movie with us—Caucasians all, this was Cape Cod—think of us? Why did I feel this vague sense of anxiety as I left the theater? What part of that anxiety had to do with Japan bashing and what part with the specter of miscegenation, the proof of which lies in the faces of our daughter and son? What will our daughter and son make of movies like this? What images will form the backdrop for their questions of identity?

IT IS EASIER FOR MEN to express anger than grief. That's one of the problems with men. When something hurts or insults us, when we're punished or pushed aside by more powerful forces, when our humanity has been assaulted, we don't feel anger *and* sadness; all our feelings convert to anger, which then becomes rage. We don't know how to grieve, to cave in, to allow another person to enter what we're feeling. Sadness threatens our image of ourselves as males. And there are so many threats. Which ones are real? It's too difficult, too dangerous to assess.

And what if you are a man of color? You begin to think you can never let down your guard. Whatever my anger can accomplish, it can never destroy what the world around me is telling me: there are those with more power than I who say I am not a man, who can enforce this message in myriad ways. Most often, as an individual, I'm helpless against this power. And my helplessness evokes a towering rage. Not thought. Not strategy. Not avenues of coalition. But rage. Visions of revenge.

Do I keep these emotions in check? Or do I change the structures through which I define myself as a male? Do I say to myself, who cares if I am a man according to the definitions of the culture? And if I try to alter the ways I see myself as a man, will that change the forces which say I am not a man? Or those voices which tell me such forces do not exist, that I am hallucinating, that what I see arrayed against me is only my paranoia, my failure to adjust?

A friend, the Japanese American actor Marc Hayashi, once said to me, "Every culture needs its eunuchs. And we're it. Asian American men are the eunuchs of America."

When he said this, I felt this instant shock of recognition. I knew I'd been fueled by a fury over this my whole life. It's part of what led me into so much trouble.

WHEN I VISIT MY PARENTS in the suburbs of Chicago, it's often in the summer. I walk in, I'm greeted by modest hugs, and we go to the living room to talk. In years past, our talk was usually about my brother in L.A. and his newest girlfriend, his searches to get a film script produced or to make it as a rock-and-roll star; it was about my sister in Boston and her poor-paying job at a public relations firm, her newest boyfriend; or my other sister's search for a new job. Rarely does the conversation float to my writing, a silence which is both comfortable and discomfiting. I look out the back window at the immaculate lawn, and beyond to the golf course where men in plaid pants and white shirts stalk off into the early evening sun, irons flashing in their hands, their bags trailing behind them, a world made more silent and peaceful by the pneumatic seal of the glass. I listen to the air conditioner's hum and long for the hot and sticky summer air, the city streets my parents escaped from years ago.

And if I search in this image of my parents for a story? There seems to be none. Their calm suburban world is without history. Time is refused admittance at the entrance to this subdivision; nothing happens here. Sometimes the past, their past, seems to have existed on a plane so eccentric it has nothing to do with the present. It involved fictional creatures who have no connection to my mother or father.

I am left with this split: there's the sense of some almost legendary long ago, where real events occurred, where people argued, lost homes, had accidents, lost lives, and there's the sense of my parents' suburban life, inhabited by golf courses and tennis games, watching the Masters or Wimbledon on television, the latest video from Blockbuster, shopping at the mall.

Where would I start investigating the past? I have so many questions. What was it like for my father after he got out of the camps and made his way back into American society? How did he carry out his high school teacher's admonition in the camps to be two hundred percent American?

And what was it like for my mother in the camps? She says even less than my father about that time. I can at least picture my father as a young boy, a young man. Whenever I think of her younger self, she vanishes a moment later. It's as if she never existed before I knew her. Who am I to challenge her silence?

I know there are connections from my parents' past to mine, to my childhood and who I've become. Our stories can't be separated really. We are mirrors for each other.

Like a *bricoleur*—a handyman—I must make do with the tools I have left: a few anecdotes from my aunts, some stray remarks from my parents, history books, a few works of literature by Japanese Americans, my own guesses and intuitions. In the end I can't vouch for the truth of my version of the past. All I can say is it's mine. It's all I have.

The writer Garrett Hongo says that those of us who come from marginalized cultures are often bequeathed fragments, brief bits of the past, and nothing more. There are few unbroken threads, no fully developed tales or histories. There are too many secrets and occlusions, too many reasons to forget the past. And there are forces which do not want us to remember, do not want us to take those fragments and complete them, to restore them to some fuller life. In the mainstream culture, in the popular media, in our educational systems, the stories and histories of people of color are deemed irrelevant at best; for the most part they do not exist; they've been wiped away.

When Hongo said this, I realized that I had always thought my situation was personal, a result of my parents' silence and my own paltry imagination. As a writer, I lacked the powers of storytelling, the ability to enter and re-create the past. I let myself be defeated even before I started writing. And in that way, our story would disappear.

I did not think about how strongly the culture may not want it to reappear.

I am not a storyteller who grew up among storytellers, dramatic and detailed retellings of the past. I am not the son of those who believed in and practiced talk-story. I never heard exploits of what happened during the war or before the war in L.A., in Seattle, nor did my family members ever admonish me, "Never, never forget." The gulf I write against is not just my parents' silence, but the political and historical and cultural silence induced by the camps, a generational wound and amnesia buried in so many of the bodies and psyches of Japanese America. That condition was not created simply by my parents or their generation. America did not want to hear their tale, and told them in so many ways it was unimportant, shameful, something to be forgotten. In entering my parents' lives and the lives of their families, I enter more deeply my own life, the silences inside me and inside

America. The secrets of my family, the secrets of this country, the secrets of race in our history, are all intertwined, and there are powerful forces arrayed against remembering and telling, unraveling the truths that have shaped our lives. In my writing, I am trying to make central what is marginal, to re-create and reveal what others say should not be spoken of.

Imagination is intervention, an act of defiance. It alters belief.

A Nisei Daughter

"This is a race war . . . The white man's civilization has come into conflict with Japanese barbarism . . . I say it is of vital importance that we get rid of every Japanese, whether in Hawaii or on the mainland . . . Damn them. Let's get rid of them now."

MISSISSIPPI CONGRESSMAN
JOHN RANKIN, 1942

"You say with the few words and the silences: No stories. No past . . . I'll tell you what I suppose from your silences and few words, and you can tell me that I'm mistaken. You'll just have to speak up with the real stories if I've got you wrong."

—MAXINE HONG KINGSTON,
CHINA MEN

1.

By the early autumn the landscape had already impressed itself upon us. We could see the rows of barracks, their dust-brown sides, and just beyond the fences, a small river, with black and white stones, like a Go board, where the water ran clear and cold, with a surprising swiftness. Beyond the river lay grassy fields the color of wheat, and foothills, like loaves, and then the mountains, blue in the early light, gray at daylight, and purple on into evening. Trucks wound into camp, bringing with them clouds of dust, and everywhere you saw children scampering, their feet drawing up tiny puffs, and little whirlwinds creating their own swirls in the gaps between the barracks. The children called out to the soldiers in the towers and ran away, giggling. Inside the barracks you brushed away the dust from the table, swept it from the floors, hauled the blankets out and beat them in the open air. You caulked the seams of the rickety boards and the knotholes with scraps and cloth and even wads of clay, and the dust still seeped through, settling in the fine hairs of your nostrils as you slept, silting down on the overcooked, soggy rice, made soggier by syrup and peaches, an indigestible mess. Late in the afternoon, the air seemed golden, thicker, reflecting off the clouds of particles that hovered around us like fog. The days were growing shorter and endless, and it was hard to remember how we had gotten there or where we had come from.

It was said somewhere beyond the fences were beet fields and farms, a town with a bar and a church and houses with gardens and even a movie theater. We knew it could have been worse, that far beyond the mountains there was fighting, unimaginable heaps of corpses, trainloads of the injured, cities in rubble, but all we could see were streaks of heat lightning in the hills or the dark rumor of storm clouds high up in the mountains. There were rumors, too, that some of the men would be called on to fight, but there were so many rumors then, we'd lived so long with rumors, that nothing and everything seemed true, and what seemed most real was the gossip about the crack-up of the marriage in Block 13, the pregnancy of the young Oshima girl, the fights that took place behind the barracks, the card games that went on into the night.

Then the rains came, and the trucks, entering the camp, ground their gears in the thick mud, and unloaded their cargo of rice sacks and boxes of cans, and left them sitting in the mud, as the workers rushed to bring them inside. To the north the grove of poplars spilled yellow soggy leaves, each day the branches barer, stark against the horizon, melding with the wires of the fences. You could see the stray leaves in the current of the river, floating their shadows over the stones. The rains increased. People tried wearing geta, which helped, but the mud became so thick and deep, it was useless, it was like moving through a swamp, the pools like tiny lakes.

There were problems with sanitation, though everyone was thankful the stench of summer was gone. There was the fear of cholera, of how the war was going, of never leaving. There was boredom, more palpable and heavier than fear. It surrounded us like the mud, it annulled our dreams. The first of us died, a pair of old Issei, a man and a woman. A baby was born, then another, and another. The young men grew restless, the old men lost. The women saw their children growing stranger, further away. Up in the rifle towers, the guards longed for another duty. One morning the camp awoke, covered in this immense white blanket which stretched to the mountains. The children romped through the small drifts as in a magical playground, made fluted angels in the icy down.

• • •

MOTHER, is this what the camps were like?

I see you at ten, entering the gates of the Minidoka internment camp, staring at the empty wooden barracks and dusty grounds, the mountains in the distance marking the edges of that Idaho valley. You are wearing a sailor's dress; there's a ribbon in your hair. Your face still shows the soft curves of a child. Your mother's face looks worn and gray; your father shouts at the children to keep moving.

Your oldest sister, Sachi, pushes you along. Is this our home? you think. You brush Sachi's hand away, edge toward Miwako, who's closer to your age. You skip and mark your footprints in the dust. You feel anxious, but aren't quite sure why. Of course, it's this strange place, but there's something more, a look in your parents' eyes, a certain drained expression, and the muttering of the young people, those your sister Sachi's age, who complain of the surroundings in ways your parents do not. You wish you still had the dolls from your old house, your old bedroom. You wonder what has happened to them, what the little girl whose father bought them in the garage sale will do with them. You tell yourself you are too old for dolls now anyway. Will you go to school here? Who will your fellow students be? Your friend Keiko Nakashima was on the train with her family, but many others are strangers.

As you climb the steps and peer into the dusty, cramped room where your family is to live, the wind whistles in little streams of dust. Cobwebs in the corner, a couple of barren cots pushed against the wall. You turn to your mother. "I don't like this place, Okaa-san. Is this what Japan is like?" Your mother says nothing, sits on the edge of the cot, staring blankly ahead. *"Shō ga nai,"* she mutters. *"Shō ga nai."*

YOUR FATHER WAS NOT A LEADER in the community. Otherwise, he would have been taken earlier like some of the Issei men, sent to a special detention camp, grilled by the FBI. Still, he lost the produce store he owned in the heart of Seattle, and his business before the war had been booming, about to expand.

He came from Kochi on Shikoku, not the mainland island of Honshu. In the pictures he is a thin, balding man, with wire-rim glasses; he looks almost Hispanic, and a bit dapper, though only a hint. He wore a suit each day to work, rising early to hustle down to the farmer's market and pick out the best lots of produce. Apples and peaches, asparagus, lettuce, beans, watermelon and cantaloupe, corn, squash—he brought home bags full at the end of the day, his arms brimming with the bounty of America, the place he had come to as a young boy, back in 1908.

He was a quiet man, though not shy; there was about him a formal reserve. Some of this perhaps was due to his being Japanese, some perhaps that he had been educated and came from a family of teachers. Certainly, he told his children that they must study hard, they must keep the family tradition. There was a sternness in his voice when he did this, like that of a schoolmaster. This was about the only time he spoke to them. Nights, he would sit in his chair, smoking his pipe, reading the Japanese-language papers. From time to time, he'd take a sip of sake or beer, sometimes *shō chū*. He had this nervous habit of constantly fingering his waxed mustache. Your one distinct memory is of him tripping over you in the living room. Perhaps he had been drinking too much, perhaps he didn't see you. You were only six at the time.

Your mother in the pictures is delicate, frail, already old. Her life is circumscribed like the other Issei women's, she lives only in the island of the Japanese community. She knows no English, cannot barter or haggle like her husband with *hakujin* farmers (though mostly his suppliers are other Issei). She meets every other week with her *ikebana* club. The women sip tea, gossip, giggle, and you drink this in. You're the littlest child, the one your mother drags along, the prettiest of the sisters, so special and yet so foreign. You don't know much Japanese, it's your older sisters who translate for your parents the school documents, items about Japan in the newspapers, the internment orders posted up all over the neighborhood. You are Okaa-san's favorite, you think. But she doesn't spoil you. There's too much for her to do, cleaning and cooking for a family of five children, trying to sort out the needs of such different personalities.

In camp, though, the family slowly begins to unravel. There's the constant dust, blowing in through the cracks of the barracks. And of course, in autumn, winter, and spring, the mud. There is the food which your mother refuses to eat, growing thinner and thinner. At dinner in the mess, your father tries to force her to eat.

"You are spoiled," he says. "You will spoil the children."

She says nothing. From time to time she will nibble a bit of rice, broth if they serve soup. Early on the tins of pickles and eel she brought from Seattle are gone. When your father admonishes her, she looks through him as if he were a ghost. But it is she who is turning into a ghost, vanishing before your eyes.

Your father and some of the other men have concocted a homemade brewery. Rice wine, apricot brandy. The other men sit on the steps and drink together. Your father prefers to drink alone. Evenings, he sits, as he always has done, in the corner, drinking. In place of a cushioned seat, his chair now is wooden, pulled together from scraps. Still, something is different. Perhaps it's that he does not go out in the morning and return at night, but lodges instead in that chair all day. Perhaps it is that he no longer delivers sermons to the children on the values of education. They are always running off anyway, to some other part of the camp. Sachi, the oldest, is going to leave soon to work as a teacher in Chicago. Yukimi, the second oldest, has signed on to go with a busload of other Nisei to help out with the beet harvest. Soon Tad will answer Yes-Yes to the loyalty oath, and become eligible for the draft.

At first, your father begins to criticize your mother about her housekeeping. The floors are always dirty, his shirts dredge up dust from the furniture.

"Kitanai yo," he shouts.

She acts as if she hasn't heard him. She just goes on sweeping. What else can he expect her to do?

"Dame da yo!" Who does she think she is? She's just a carpenter's daughter, she had no prospects in Japan. She was lucky that he brought her to America. She has gotten too soft, things have been too good for her. Does she think she's too good? That she can't eat the food like the rest of the people? Is she some princess?

You hear their voices behind the blanket partition. You are reading a book about a girl who wants to be a dancer, a ballerina. You begin whispering the words to yourself, as if you could drown out your father's shouts. Why doesn't your mother say anything? you wonder. I will never be like that.

Then you hear your mother say, "Is this the life you promised me?" Only you can't be sure this is what she has said. Your Japanese is not very good.

But what you hear next you don't need a translator for. There is the muffled sound of weeping, a door slams. Silence.

No, there is never silence here, in the cramped barracks where you can hear at night the arguments in the other units, the Igawa baby bawling, and sometimes from the Murakamis a muffled moan that frightens you, as if someone were being beaten or someone was in pain. And then there is your mother's coughing, which goes on and on through the night, even worse than the sound of her weeping just now, because the coughing never stops.

Your mother pulls back the curtain.

"Are you here? I thought you went with Miwako and Yoshiko."

"They wouldn't take me," you say. "They said I was a nuisance."

"I'll speak with them when they get back."

"Mama, why does Papa speak to you like that? Did he hit you?"

"Oh, don't worry about that—*shimpai nai*—it's nothing."

There's a cricket underneath the barracks that keeps chirping and chirping. You hear Mrs. Igawa singing a lullaby to her baby, *sakura, sakura . . .*

"Your father is a proud man," she says. "You must understand that."

But you don't understand. You don't. But you can't tell her what you don't understand. You can't ask questions about that.

"Come on, I will take you to the movies. And then I will talk to your sisters."

"But Papa?"

"Oh, he'll be back. There's nowhere else for him to go."

MOTHER, when I was growing up, you were obsessed with cleanliness. The biggest fight we ever had was over an ink stain my typewriter had left on the kitchen floor. One summer during college when I was commuting to the city, Father picked me up at the train station. Immediately he began ranting about how upset you were at all of us children, our slovenliness. "You kids act like you think she's a maid. She says the whole house is a mess. You never clean up, and your mother and I are sick and tired of it. You hear me? Sick and tired . . ." At the dinner table, as his harangue went on, I finally burst out in tears and shouted, "We are a family, it's not supposed to be like this." I ran to my room. Later, at your insistence, Father came in and tried to apologize.

Years later, I understood that something more than simply a messy house must have set you and Father off, some tension in your life I didn't know about, but that still doesn't explain the focus of your tension. I know that cleanliness constitutes an important quality in Japanese culture; I know a dominant aesthetic in that culture stresses sparse, empty space, a lack of clutter. I also know that it must have been traumatic for your family to leave their home in Seattle, to find themselves in makeshift barracks, where dust and wind streamed through the walls and the streets outside were unpaved, churning to mud in fall, winter, and spring. Did Grandmother obsessively clean her portion of the barracks? Is there some repetition here of history? Or is your obsession one of the quirks of your personality? How am I to know if my imaginings are true or simply wild, errant guesses?

IN CAMP, you miss Seattle. You miss your house, the blue Hudson your father would drive to work, the long drives your family would take to the mountains or further up the sound. You miss the trips you would take with Miwako and Yo to the beach, riding the bus all the way across town, clutching your ten cents, which would pay your fare and allow you to buy a few penny candies, some gum, a sucker, an ice-cream cone, a treat for you to savor on the ride home. You miss your father striding home in his new suit, cut crisp and clean, and his arms full of fruit. You miss the Shirley Temple movies, the swashbuckling of Errol Flynn. Everyone still celebrates Obon or Oshogatsu in the camp, and the men in camp still pound rice to make *mochi*. Your mother and older sisters do their best to prepare the traditional New Year's meal, which must be cooked beforehand, because there must be no cooking on New Year's Day. But no one in camp really has the food to make a proper Oshogatsu meal. There's no fresh fish, no shrimp; the pickles are makeshift from whatever vegetables are at hand. It's difficult to get large supplies of *shōyu*. Everything is just a little off, the food just doesn't taste quite right, no matter how hard your mother and sisters work. Still, it's so much better than the awful stuff they serve you at the mess hall. You understand why your mother refuses to eat. You can't stand the food either. But you eat it anyway. You're too young to go hungry.

Thank God, everyone still celebrates Christmas. On an icy December's night, down in the assembly center, Santa Claus appears.

You're given an orange, not the doll you wanted, not the bicycle you hoped against hope for. The toys are for the younger children. You are growing older. You need to understand, says your mother. It's unfair, you think. Last Christmas, Miwako got a doll. And Yo had a bike back in Seattle. So what if Yo had to leave the bike behind. Why can't you have a bike?

Still, you don't complain a lot. You can sense your father would be angry. And your mother is already at another table, gossiping with Mrs. Omori. Yo says that Yukimi has a crush on Mrs. Omori's son, John. He is handsome, but he's very short, shorter than Yukimi, who's tall for a Japanese girl. Mr. Ueda is Santa Claus. You can tell it's him behind the scraggly cotton beard. He's too skinny to be a Santa, but who ever heard of a fat Japanese? Only sumo wrestlers are fat, and you've seen sumo matches only once back in Seattle.

That night Yo tries to explain to you about the birth of Christ, but you don't quite understand. What does it mean that his mother was a virgin? It doesn't make sense. Yo is becoming a Christian, she's taking classes from Mr. Fukuyama on Sundays, but she hasn't told your parents. They are Buddhist. You know they would disapprove.

As you fall asleep, you think: Maybe tomorrow Santa will bring me a bike. Even as you drift off, you know it's just a dream.

"POLITICS," says your father, "I don't want anything to do with politics. The nail that sticks up is the one that gets hammered down."

"But we can't ignore this," says Sachi. "We already stick out. That's why we're here."

"We have to make a choice," says your brother, Tad, the third oldest and the only boy.

"Jaaaa, I don't know," says your mother. *"Mêndokusai, ne."*

"We are Americans, we should do what Americans do," says Tad.

"What does the JACL say to do?" asks Sachi.

"What other choice do we have?" asks Yukimi.

"But then Tadao will have to go into the Army, *deshō?*" says your mother.

You are sitting on your bed. There's a spider crawling up the wall. You smash it with your shoe, then try to wipe it away on the floor. You don't understand what they're talking about. You'd be bored, but there's some tension in the air, something troubling, that won't go away in the tones of their voices, this grown-up talk.

"Ma, that's a long way off," says Tad.

"And against Japan?"

"They probably won't send me to Japan."

"That's not true," says Sachi. "I heard rumors that some of the Nisei are going to be used as translators."

"Well, if that's where they send me, that's where I'll go," says Tad. "We've got to prove ourselves, show everyone we are good Americans."

"We're all good Americans," says Sachi.

"But you are our only son," says your mother.

You turn back to your book. It's a story about a young girl who gets lost in a forest and finds a magical castle. You know you should be working on your math for tomorrow's class, but nobody's paying any attention to you. Why are they going on like this? Suddenly, in the forest, the beast springs forth. You wish you had some candy. Chocolate. That would be nice. Why is it always so cold in here? Why can't the wind stop slicing through the cracks?

"I can't answer no, Mama," says Tad.

"Why not? Tanaka-san's boy did."

"And they sent him to the camp at Tule Lake. I hear he might even be deported. Is that where you want?"

"I don't know. You would be safe there."

"I'd be disgraced. We'd be disgraced."

"A lot of people say Bob Tanaka and the others did the right thing," Yukimi interrupts. "They say the JACL are *inu*. They spy on the Issei, on everyone, and report on us to the camp authorities."

"*Inu? Dōshite?*"

"You don't understand, Mama," says Sachi. "They even say the JACL are helping the *hakujin* steal our food."

"*Bakarashī.*"

"Maybe. But what can you expect? They've got us all penned up here, like cattle. Everyone's angry, everyone's frustrated. They don't give us much choice."

"I understand why Bob Tanaka said no," says Tad. "But that's something I can't do. I'm an American citizen. I've got to fight for my country . . . Papa?"

"What does it say? What are the questions?"

Sachi reads. "Twenty-seven: Are you willing to serve in the Armed Forces of the United States on combat duty, wherever ordered? Twenty-eight: Will you swear unqualified allegiance to the United States of America and faithfully defend the United States from any or all attack by foreign or domestic forces, and forswear any form of allegiance or obedience to the Japanese emperor, or any other foreign government, power, or organization? You answer either yes or no."

Your mother asks what the questions mean. She doesn't understand them. Sachi tries to explain.

"Kedo, if we foe-sa-waa *tenō sama*, what will happen to us? We are not citizens. You know that. We wanted to be, but . . ."

"It's the only choice we have, Mama," says Tad. "Otherwise, you might be shipped out of camp, or even back to Japan."

"What do you think Papa?" asks your mother.

"*Shō ga nai.* Sign it."

"And Tadao?"

"There is nothing we can do," your father repeats.

"Thanks, Pop."

"You must make sure you will return to your mother and me."

"I will, Pop. Of course I will."

That night, when your mother says good night to you, you wish she would sing a lullaby like she did when you were little. But she won't. She doesn't sing these days. Her throat, she says. It hurts too much. She sits on your cot, her small weight crackling the straw mattress. For a long while she doesn't say anything. The light juts through at the corners of the blanket that divides the room and sets off the section you share with your sisters Miwako and Yoshiko. They are still up.

"Why do I have to go to bed so early, Mama?"

"Because you are the youngest. You need to grow."

"Do you think I'm short?"

"Short? No. You will grow."

"I don't think so."

"If you sleep, you will grow."

"Mama, why don't you sing me lullabies anymore?"

"Mah, you are too old for that. Besides my throat. *Itai.* You know that."

You can hear Miwako and Yo giggling beyond the curtain. It seems so unfair.

"What were you talking about, Mama?"

"Tonight? Oh, just adult things."

"What things?"

"It's too complicated for you to understand. Even I don't understand."

You want her to explain. You know she won't. After she leaves, you wait in the dark, trying to stay awake until Miwako and Yo come to bed. You don't want to fall asleep alone. You suddenly remember you haven't done your math homework. You'll need to get up early tomorrow. A blade of straw scratches your back. You shift your weight. You fall asleep.

Years later, you will not remember this night, these voices. You will not remember the name of the book you were reading or your fifth-grade teacher. You will not remember the train ride to the camp or the doll that you held as you entered its gates. You will not remember the sobs that pierced through the barracks that first night and, night after night, kept coming back. You will not remember how the coyotes howled in the dark outside the fences, frightening you, entering your dreams. You will not speak the names of Esther Suzuki or Keiko Nakashima, your best friends, or recall the tensions between your father and mother. You will not remember the No-No Boys, they were too old for you to think about. You will not remember the number of your barrack or what you were given on your eleventh birthday. You will not remember the lullabies your mother sang to you or the stories of Momotaro, the peach boy, or the Moon Princess. You will not remember your Japanese or your favorite dress. You will learn easily and quickly that to survive you must forget.

YOUR FAMILY was luckier than a lot of other families. In some, the loyalty oath cracked family ties right down the middle. Supporters of the JACL on one side, the No-Nos on the other. In families with children who'd been sent back to Japan to be educated, the young Kibei were especially bitter. They didn't fit in with the American-born Nisei, who often eyed the Kibei with suspicion. They were alien, tainted, even to other Japanese Americans. Some of the American-born Nisei were also bitter about their treatment. The camp bureaucracy, the FBI, the tensions that came with the overcrowded and ramshackle quarters did not help any.

The quarrels between your father and mother got worse, and then, as your mother's health began to decline, they became more infrequent. The fight had gone out of her, even your father could see that. For a long while, there was this uneasy and silent tension between them. But then your mother's coughing worsened. Once, you woke in the middle of the night to find your father sitting beside her on the bed, handing her a cup of tea, trying to ease her distress. His face looked infinitely older than hers, though she was the one who was sick, who was sinking. There was something resigned, almost placid in her expression, despite the hacks that wracked her slim body, causing her to jerk up from the bed, like the last gasp of fish thrown up on the dock. Helplessness was written all over your father's face, like a man drowning. He didn't know what to do. He just held the cup of tea, the steam rising from his hands. In a terrifying moment, he began to weep, at first a few small choking sounds, and then larger and larger sobs, more wracking than any cough emanating from your mother's frail chest. *"Daijōbu yo,"* your mother kept repeating, like a mantra.

The next morning he set up a small altar in the corner of their cubicle. He had never been a religious man, but he began getting up each morning and sitting himself before the tiny brass Buddha and the wooden bowl with one or two slivers of fruit. He lit a small mound of incense, made of grasses he had gathered, a few dried wildflowers. He knelt down, bowed his head, closed his eyes, and began to chant. It was a strange droning sound, the words almost unintelligible to you. It made you want to giggle, the sounds seemed so silly.

He did this more often when Tad left for the Army. Your mother did not get better. Sachi was going to leave for Chicago. It was as if, despite his chanting, his fervent prayers, his world was being stripped, piece by piece. Perhaps he feared that soon there would be nothing left. He even began to drink less and less. His hair was thinning; strands of it caught in his brush or on his pillow. He suddenly seemed old, though not as old as your mother, who now appeared almost ancient, a figure from a ghost play in Kabuki. You spent more and more of your time away from your family's barracks, wandering the camp.

One afternoon you went with Yo to Mr. Fukuyama's class for Christians. He talked about something called the Sermon on the

Mount, and a miracle springing from a basket of fish and loaves of bread which multiplied mysteriously to feed a crowd. "Blessed are the meek, for they shall inherit the earth . . ." Mr. Fukuyama recited. He talked of how it was easier for a rich man to pass through the eye of a needle than to enter heaven, how the poor were blessed. "Jesus came to forgive us, to wash away our sins . . ." Mr. Fukuyama never said much about what sins were. He seemed to assume that you knew. You wondered whether you were poor or not. What did it mean to be blessed? Would you gain riches? But a rich man could not enter heaven. Mr. Fukuyama said Jesus was the son of God. Who was God? What did it mean to be his son?

Mostly, though, the stories seemed very boring, and you wondered why Yo was so interested in all this.

"I believe in it," was all she said.

But one afternoon Yo and Sachi got into an argument.

"Have you told Mama and Papa about this?"

"Why should I? It's my own business."

"They are your parents. And they are Buddhist."

"This is America. I am free to believe whatever I want. And I believe in Christ. Besides, why should Mama and Papa care?"

"They would if they knew."

"Are you going to tell them?"

"No, they have enough to worry about as it is," said Sachi. "But it's my job to keep track of you all."

"No one said it's your job," answered Yo.

Things were never the same between Sachi and Yo. But then they had never been that close anyway. Sachi felt Yo didn't respect her. Yo felt Sachi was too bossy, she clung too much to Japanese things, she thought because she was the oldest everyone had to listen to her.

You sided with Yo. But that didn't mean you wanted to become a Christian. The whole issue seemed beside the point. There were rumors that they were going to close the camps down. Where would everyone go? Would you be going back to Seattle? Did this mean the war would end soon? You thought you wanted to leave camp, to live in a real house, like you did back in Seattle. But the thought of leaving scared you too. You were going to be in high school next year. What would it be like to go to high school outside the camp? Would it be any different? I don't know if you thought about what it would be like to go to school with *hakujin* again. Perhaps it's more a question I might ask than you. It's hard to tell. I've come up here against my ignorance. My imagination can only travel so far.

IT WAS ANOTHER year before you left the camp.

Tad did come home. He studied Japanese at Fort Snelling to become a translator, but by the time he was shipped out, the war was over. He became part of the occupying forces in Japan, translated for generals, traveled all over Japan, through the burnt-out rubble of cities, the black wreckage of the war. He handed out chocolates like the other GIs, drank sake in the bars near the base, and developed a taste for *uni.* Then he returned home to resume his life. He fulfilled his promise to your mother. She never received the telegram that Omori-san and Ueda-san received, the one delivered by a soldier in full military dress.

Your family never went back to Seattle after the war. Your father's business was gone, there was no reason to return. They moved to Chicago, tried to make a new start. Sachi was already teaching school there. Yukimi and Miwako enrolled at the Circle Campus, Yo went north to Minnesota. You finished high school in Hyde Park.

A couple of years after the camps, just after Tad returned, your mother died. From throat cancer, her voice getting hoarse and then blacker and blacker. She was rail thin at the end. In the funeral pictures, everyone looks properly somber. You are young, barely seventeen. Petite and beautiful, there's a haughtiness in your gaze, perhaps because of your long aquiline nose and sharp-chiseled cheeks. You and your sisters are dressed in black dresses with veils, elegant in your mourning. You are definitely the prettiest of the four sisters. Your brother, Tad, who wears his uniform, is equally handsome. Still, I'm struck by something about the frozen expression on all your faces in this picture, the obvious sorrow written there and the just as obvious will not to show a hint of emotional expression. Somehow I read your expression not as part of the occasion or even as some Japanese austerity, but as the outer rigor which you've formed in putting the experiences of the war behind you. Okaa-san has died, and you are now to go on shedding the past.

The whole day had been one long tortuous journey. Sachi insisted on arranging everything, from the flower arrangements to the place, priest, and length of the service; there was never a question of any Christian elements to placate Yo. On the drive to the Buddhist temple, your father said nothing, and when you asked him a question, he'd mumble yes or no, then look out the window, as if you weren't there. But it was really your father who wasn't there, lost somewhere in memories you couldn't start to fathom. In a way it didn't bother you; you and he rarely talked. For you, it always felt a bit awkward to be with him. Sachi, the oldest, could direct him, tell him about what would happen, how things were to proceed. You were just the youngest, someone barely to be noticed.

As you watched him emerge from the car at the temple, his bald pate looked almost fleshless, the skin pale and papery and spotted with age. When he glanced up, he was twenty years older. It was as if the breath had left his flesh, as if his blood were drained, as if he should be the one everyone would be staring at in the silk-lined coffin, laid out before the Buddha like an offering of flowers.

When it was your turn to view your mother's body, she seemed so much more at peace than your father, so much more alive. The wretched wails she let loose near the end, punctuated by lower, drawn-out moans, almost demonlike in their throttled hoarseness, and of course, the constant hacking, that was all over, all the seeds of pain that sprouted and spread from her throat to her lungs, from her throat to her face, had withered away, a cooling snow had descended, covering everything in its sharp and icy whiteness. You looked at her face, and wondered who she was, this pale peaceful creature. You looked at her face and knew you would never have anyone else to talk to, anyone with whom your thoughts would fly so freely from your mouth. You looked at her face and it was you lying there, your own ghostly visage, and you could rest there, calmly, coolly, sleeping forever, dreaming of nothing. There was silence all around you, encasing you in its sweetness.

And then Miwa placed her hand on your shoulder, urging you on.

A few years afterward, your father returned to Japan, remarried, sent back pictures of his garden and his new wife. A second life blooming out of the ashes of the first.

Later came the Sansei, when the internment was long gone, barely a memory. We had no inkling really of what split apart, what fractured up in the high mountain plains of Idaho. That we lived in some small diaspora, a minor moment in a century of migrations. We thought ourselves safe, and we were. Where our parents had been during those years possessed no bearing, no relationship to history.

I don't know what you would say of this story, Mother, but I can guess. Any number of sentences come to mind: *The camps are over. Also overly dramatic. Mostly we were bored. Men played* hana, *poker. The women cleaned, sewed. My father was never a drunk, never hit my mother. Our unit wasn't divided that way, my mother never tucked me in at night. She was too busy. That wasn't the way Sachi and Yo started fighting. Religion had nothing to do with it. It was so long ago. I know, I know. It's your job, your way, but why can't you see how far we've come, how useless that all is. What is the purpose of your making up lies.*

But I am, again, being unfair to you. Perhaps you would say little. Perhaps you would just let me go on.

When I showed you the final draft of *Turning Japanese*, you said to me, "I called up all the children to see if I was really that bad a mother. But it doesn't matter whether my feelings are hurt or not. I may not agree with you, but this is the way you see things. This is your book. You once said to me, after all is said and done, you're still my son. And I'm still your mother. This is what I can give to you."

Father said pretty much the same thing.

I know there are writers who would die for such clarity from their parents.

Who am I to ask for more?

2.

I AM SIX OR SEVEN. My mother is slicing potatoes and carrots on a cutting board in the kitchen. When she is finished, she goes to the stove, slides them into the great pot where huge pieces of chuck roast are stewing. The steam rises, dissipates in her face. She plunks the cutting board in the sink, goes back to the stove, unscrews a bottle of bay leaves, drops one in the bubbling broth.

Her face is angular, striking. She has the long nose of an aristocrat, of Utamaro's beauties. I take after my father, my face is wider, rounder. I barely escape being a fat boy.

Although she's just above five feet, I don't think of her as short. This isn't just my child's perspective. Whenever she argues with my father, she seems to engulf him, driving forward with an energy he can never match. He always ends up backing off, something he never does with us kids. In that way she appears larger than him, more powerful.

As I watch my mother set the table, I can sense she's upset. She's been talking on the phone with Aunt Yo, with my Aunt Miwako who lives with us, with Aunt Sachi. There's some argument, and I think it involves Aunt Sachi, but I don't understand what it's about. Still the strength of the tension in her conversations on the phone disturbs me. It makes her seem vulnerable in a visceral way I'm not used to. It's her vulnerability here I'll remember, not the substance of the argument with her sisters.

When my father comes home, her voice acquires a querulous, frustrated tone. Tears fill her eyes, and yet, there's something within her that doesn't break, I can sense this. The tears she can't help. Her resolve is another matter.

For some reason she is angry at my Aunt Miwako too. "Miwako just doesn't know what Sachi's like. She never sees anyone's faults. She's always making excuses for her."

I watch my father attempt awkwardly to comfort my mother. She's still too frustrated. I'm glad my aunt Miwa's still at work. Miwa is my favorite aunt; she lives in the room at the end of the hall. On weekends, my sister Susan and I run to her room and wake her up to play with us. She's the one who teaches us how to count to ten in Japanese, who plays *jan-ken-poi*, the Japanese version of scissors-rock-paper, with us, who treats me to movies, the zoo, who buys me candy. I think she's beautiful and slim like a model, and take as proof her sophisticated choice of perfume: Chanel No. 5.

Despite my love for my Aunt Miwako, I naturally side with my mother. But I don't really understand what the problem is, and even in retrospect can only guess.

Though my mother's angry mainly at my Aunt Sachi, I sense she's frustrated with all her sisters. Their father is coming to visit, back from Japan. He's not bringing his new wife, so that's not the problem. It's where he's going to stay, what's going to happen when he's here. There are issues of priority and control. Aunt Sachi, according to custom, should have priority. But who among them gives much credence to Japanese customs? Certainly not my mother, the youngest, the least traditional. She's married a go-getter, someone who's going to make it, who's assimilating and taking up the ways of *hakujin* as fast as he can imbibe them, who's not looking back. My Aunt Sachi, on the other hand, studies flower arranging, Japanese art, teaches at a school for Japanese culture, speaks Japanese and is the main source of communication with their father.

"I told Sachi he could stay with us, if that's what she wants," says my mother.

"It will be okay, honey. Really, it will. He can stay with her."

"But she won't say that. She wants me to ask her to have my father stay with her."

"What's wrong with that?"

"Oh, Tom, don't you see? She wants me to be obligated to her." Pause. "We could put him up, but we really can't. We don't have room. And Sachi doesn't have any kids."

"So why don't you tell her that?"

"Tell her what? You just can't talk to Sachi," my mother says to my father. "But I have to, because she won't talk to Yo."

My father nods. He knows there's nothing they can do about that. He also knows he can't stop my mother until she wants to stop, but he can't help trying to calm her down.

The reason Aunt Sachi does not speak to Aunt Yo goes a long way back. The most obvious cause is Aunt Sachi's belief that Yo's husband, my Uncle Dick, was entirely unsuitable. Dick's mother had operated a hotel, which, to Sachi's more Japanese values, was almost the equivalent of running a brothel. Dick, moreover, had not attended college, while Yo had received not only a BA but her nursing degree. When Uncle Dick and Aunt Yo started going out together, my Aunt

Sachi felt it her duty as the oldest to forbid them to marry. "If you marry him, I'll never speak to you again."

Over the years Aunt Sachi has almost literally kept her word, and though my Aunt Yo has made moves to engage a reconciliation, and though Uncle Dick died twenty years ago, Sachi remains adamant in her silent shunning. Recently, when my sister got married, Sachi complained to my mother that she's always seated at weddings away from the rest of the family. This time she wanted it to be different.

"But, Sachi, I can't sit you with Yo. It makes people uncomfortable."

"That's okay," said Sachi. "I just won't talk to her."

When my mother told me this, she shook her head and smiled, "I come from a crazy family."

This last sentence is one of the few telling things my mother has ever said about her family. Beyond my Aunt Sachi's grudge, I don't really understand what my mother sees as her family's craziness. When I asked her, she wouldn't elaborate. A few months ago, when I inquired about the argument she had with her sisters when her father came back from Japan to visit, she said she didn't remember.

"Ask Sachi," she said. "Maybe she remembers."

It's as if, for my mother, the past is a closed book. Or a lost book. Or perhaps it's something she's tossed away, she has no use for it.

My mother's silence about the past has always been greater than my father's. She makes him look like a tribal griot. While my father has let me have a copy of a diary he wrote during their first months of their marriage, and has allowed me to read his old short stories and poems, my mother threw away her letters to my father. I found out because I asked her if she had anything like my father's suitcase of writings. "Why would you want to read my letters?" she asked.

Once, a few years ago, as we were walking together along Michigan Avenue, Christmas shopping, I asked her how she and my father met. "This isn't the time to go into that," she replied, and quickly turned into Marshall Field's. I didn't persist. I knew it was useless. I had to ask my father.

3.

WHEN I WAS IN SIXTH GRADE, my mother joined a record club. For a few months, she received Toscanini recordings of the Beethoven symphonies, Schubert string quartets, Mahler. Van Cliburn hunched over the piano, concentrated as a surgeon. There was some lighter, more popular fare. Frank Sinatra was the one I recall best, the story of a man's life, laid out in the lovers he'd known, from the small-town girls to the women of champagne, chauffeurs, and limousines. I was still at an age when Frank Sinatra seemed cosmopolitan and cool.

I remember her playing the Sinatra record, but not the classical ones. I asked to take them years later when I came home from graduate school and found them in the basement. I played them a bit more than my mother, but now they reside in the dampness of my basement, victims of the CD age and to some extent my waning interest in high European culture.

Why had my mother bought those recordings of Beethoven's symphonies? How much was she motivated by a love of the music itself? How much by an image of culture and class? I find the fact of her buying these records touching, eliciting a sentimental ache I don't normally associate with her. In those records, that music, my mother perceived a depth of sensibility, of appreciation, that was somehow beyond her. Of course, she never took up the study of classical music with a scholarly or artistic seriousness that would lift her appreciation beyond mere aspiration. She must have sensed, even before she tried, that such appreciation was not to be for her. She did not have the time, the talent, the background. She was already living through a cross-cultural experience. Why create an artificial one?

That my mother's reach should have exceeded her grasp—that is what I focus on. As I picture her at the kitchen table, filling out the record club forms, I'm reminded of the romantic dreams of Madame Bovary, another housewife seeking a finer sensibility beyond her realm. But Emma Bovary persisted with this longing, succumbed to it, fought for it, until she had wreaked suffering and tragedy on those about her and on herself. She was blinded by this longing, she lacked common sense.

My mother does not lack common sense. She is not one to be carried away.

I, on the other hand, have often let myself be carried away, have embraced my longings with a ferocity that is belied by my composed and quiet demeanor. I am the passion my mother kept at bay, someone who has known unchecked obsession. In this I see myself as very much her child, a descendant of her desires. Whether in school or in sexuality or in my writing, I have refused to abate my aspirations. I have constantly had to learn the lesson over and over that my mother already knew—there are limits, the world will knock you back, sometimes declination and modesty are all we can afford, you just can't change the world.

MY MOTHER'S TASTES are more refined than the Sears, Roebuck, solidly middle-class tastes of our relatives. Her house is immaculately white, the rooms uncluttered, spacious, and filled with light. A few Japanese prints mix with reproductions of Monet, Andrew Wyeth, watercolors of some Carolina shore. She plays golf and tennis, her clothes casual, sporty, Ralph Lauren and Calvin Klein. She tapes tennis matches and golf tournaments, replays them on the huge sixty-inch screen in the living room, the faces of the players large as beach balls, their grimaces as they smash a backhand or blow a putt more intimate than a lover's embrace.

In casual conversations, there's not much about her that would mark her as distinctly Japanese American. She'd talk about her passions of golf and tennis, about children, her husband and his work, news items from CNN. Tan and in great shape for her age, still beautiful, she'd strike you as no different from thousands of other housewives in the North Shore suburbs, their children grown, their husbands moving into retirement, quietly comfortable in their life.

This past year my parents have been trying to sell their house in Vernon Hills, a suburb of Chicago. They plan to move South. The anxiety of getting the house ready for sale has begun to consume my mother. A few months ago, when I visited, she and I were in the basement, sorting through boxes of old yearbooks, issues of my high school paper, various academic and athletic citations.

This basement is cavernous, with a twelve foot ceiling designed to accommodate a driving net. There are several bags of golf clubs, a laundry basket of golf balls. Cookbooks, including a couple we've given her, line the metal shelves.

"I won't need these," she says. She seldom cooks now that there's only the two of them. When they eat at home, it's usually a simple pasta or salad.

"Sometimes I wonder how I did it. Raised you all. I couldn't do that again."

"Can I take this yearbook of dad's?" I ask.

"Sure. You'll probably make better use of it than us."

I pull out a box of photos and photo albums.

"I want to keep that," she says. "You can have your school photos, though."

"God, I looked so goofy in fifth grade. I really did need braces."

"You can take some of these throw rugs, if you want."

"What about this lamp?"

"Sure. . . . You'd think that with all the moves we've made"—every seven years she and my father have moved to a new house, it seems to give my mother a task to devote her energies to—"we'd have gotten rid of more stuff."

"You should see our basement. I've got the notes from half of my college classes. Susie thinks I'm nuts, but she's just as bad. We're both pack rats."

I pull out a packet of photos.

"This must be when John was still wearing the brace."

Just over a decade ago, my brother was involved in a terrible car accident. A friend was driving, and the car flipped over. My brother lost his spleen, cracked his vertebrae, and went into cardiac arrest during the operation afterward. For a year he had to wear this horrible halo cast, which was literally screwed into his head. He spent that whole year living with my parents. My brother says that's one of the reasons he's more forgiving and protective of my parents than I am. When he read *Turning Japanese,* and called me about his reactions, he kept saying it was my book to write, but he also kept contending I was a bit too hard on my parents.

My mother looks at the photo of my brother.

"You should have seen us cleaning out those holes where the screws went in. It was a mess. We had to do that every night." She smiles. "Dad and I would be yelling at each other about whether we were doing it right. I'd tell him he was doing it wrong and he'd say the same thing to me. And John just put up with both of us."

She opens another carton and peers inside. I'm aware that she's never said anything about where I was during that year. I never came home, never saw my brother. That was the year I was deeply into therapy, trying to make sense of why I felt so utterly abandoned and alienated, finding inside myself this tremendous rage at my parents, my childhood. I also didn't know how to handle my brother's accident. In the presence of illness or grave accidents, I shy away. I suddenly feel awkward and useless, shameful about my inability to respond in any useful or meaningful way. I become paralyzed. I'm sure my mother must have wondered why I stayed away that year. But she never remarked upon it either. Now, it's simply in the past, though I suspect it remains part of her evaluations of me.

As I thought about all of this in the basement with my mother, I suddenly realized how much my mother and I are alike. I've always felt she knew how miserable I was when I was growing up, saw how much pain I was in, but couldn't or wouldn't say anything. Something in both of us sees but cannot speak, cannot act. Perhaps we're both too controlled.

"Look at this. I've got this head like a beach ball."

"You were so chubby."

I laugh, though something inside me is bothered by this. My mother takes the photo from my hand. It's me at two years old, hanging on to the rails of my playpen.

"You were such a good baby. We could keep you in there for hours with some toys, and you'd be perfectly happy."

My mother held the photo before her a few seconds more, then slipped it back in the packet, slid the packet back in the box, and closed it up.

The next box I opened contained a few record albums. Frank Sinatra, Vivaldi, and, for some reason, Webern. Why would she have ordered Webern?

"I thought I took all of these back with me when I was in grad school."

My mother looked up.

"Can I take these?" I asked.

"What are you going to do with them, David? No one plays records anymore."

"But . . ."

"Really. You've got enough to bring back to Minneapolis."

"What can I say, Mom? I'm a pack rat."

My mother looked at me and sighed. She took the Webern from my hand.

"Just throw it away, David. Really."

SEVERAL YEARS AGO, Susie and my mother were sitting in the kitchen early in the morning, looking at an old book of photos.

"Sooze, if I'd only had one child, David would have been fine. He was so bright, so athletic, so talented. He would have been enough."

When Susie told me my mother had said this, I was stunned. "But you know, she would never say that to me. She would only say it to you."

It's difficult to let in what my mother said to Susie. In a way, more difficult than anything critical she's ever said about me. I want things more one-sided than they are.

A lot of parents do not compliment their children directly, and I know direct praise runs counter to Japanese cultural practice. Yet now that I have children, I find it easy to praise them, to talk directly about how I feel about them. Sometimes perhaps I overdo it. My daughter Samantha has ordered a moratorium on the phrase "I'm proud of you."

My mother and I have lived through different histories. In the end I can only guess about the effect of the past upon her. I think there are other constraints upon her, questions of culture and history I do not feel. I know I am not Japanese, do not bear within me parental figures from the Meiji era, with their old-country customs and ethics.

I also know, in a way she does not, that I am American. Part of me believes no one can take that away, and so I can speak louder than those who have come before me, I can challenge those who would ostracize me in a direct way my mother cannot imagine.

What grips my mother is what cannot be spoken. Perhaps that is why she severs herself from the past, why that severing keeps occurring over and over in the present.

All-American Boy

"Why are Asians doing so exceptionally well in school? They must be doing something right. Let's bottle it."

—Mike Wallace,
CBS: "60 Minutes"

"The goal pursued is the spread of a hegemonic dis-ease. Don't be us, this self-explanatory motto warns. Just be 'like' and bear the chameleon's fate, never infecting us but only yourself, spending your days muting, putting on/taking off glasses, trying to please all and always at odds with myself who is no self at all. Yet, being accused of 'ignoring one's own culture' and 'looking whiter than Snow White herself' also means taking a trip to the promised land of White Alienation."

—Trinh T. Minh-ha,
The Language of Nativism

1.

I AM WAITING, standing at the corner of the schoolyard, waiting for the boy there to become a man.

He bites his nails, his body slouches as if he were carrying heavy luggage. He is round, rotund, with the face of a fat boy. Perhaps he is eating a hot dog, marveling at the taste of mustard. He loves fossils, baseball, the names of the planets. He'll never be taken prisoner of war. He dies so gallantly, so dramatically, like John Wayne's buddy at Iwo Jima. He believes in the flag, the anthem of the Marines.

Every Sunday he goes to church, there are parables, and terrible stories of a sad, sad death. The boy doesn't really understand these parables and stories. He loves throwing noodles from the Sunday school luncheon out of the window in the Reverend Nakano's study. He and the others are never caught doing this. Amid the holy books, drafts of sermons, and the old hymnals, they giggle uproariously. He isn't terrified of God or sin or the reverend. It's his father who terrifies him, who teaches him sums and letters and quizzes him daily, who will not let him go out to play until he has done his lessons, many lessons, many more than any other boy he knows. When the two of them sit at his father's desk and go over his sums, there are only the answers, the terrifying truth, the mistakes at hand. Learning is hard, it takes work, the world takes work, you must buckle down, that is what his father says. The boy doesn't think of running to his mother. That's out of the question. He's not a mama's boy, though Michael Ogata calls him that. His mother is beautiful, the woman at the stove, stirring a bubbling vat. His mother is absent somehow at night, a voice in the dark, whispering, chastising.

At night there are horses rippling beside his bed, great herds of buffalo glide through his room, robbers in masks. His Davy Crockett rifle hangs on the door, his cowboy hat and six-guns guard the foot of his bed. Cattle stampede in the gully between his bed and his sister's. He hears murmurs, perhaps raised voices, his parents arguing down the hall, then only the muffled TV, Shane stepping into the dusty street. Suddenly, his younger sister begins to taunt, *You can't hurt me, you can't hurt me.*

Who can explain where this chant began? Or why the brother then hit his sister? Or how the sister's cries brought forth their father, who then hit his son to silence the cries, the chaos that had erupted in his house?

I think there was a song for us that none of us could sing, a hymn or dirge or lullaby that traveled many years and miles to arrive, so faint no one ever heard it, not even my mother and father, though it contained their voices; it ranged across the years in the dark, swampy regions of Arkansas, in the cold, high mountain plains of Idaho, in the smoky rooms where they waited and waited for the war to end, so much safer than others all around the world, perhaps they grew to believe it was for their own protection.

It is another night, after the night of the spanking. His father sits on the edge of the bed. He is telling us the story of Popeye and the three monkeys, how the three monkeys threw coconuts and conked Popeye on the head. *Katonk! Katonk!* The boy and his sister giggle with laughter. They never want to go to bed.

I hear my father's voice now in the stories I tell my daughter, the lullabies I sing to my son.

I don't hear the Japanese ones, I will have to learn them. No, I will never learn them, they are too far past, I am too lazy, too distant a son.

I see my parents once, twice a year now. I sometimes live my life *as if I've almost forgotten them. And yet, they cleave through this story, like the smell of smoke. I write my life as if they were present each moment, every hour of the day.*

God, said a poet, is a furnace that keeps talking with his mouth of teeth, his mouth filled with feasts, smells of gasoline and airplanes, train rides, long journeys, and human ash, a clear, cold river bottomed with dark round stones. God loves us like fire, he destroys us like fire, he consumes us all.

God, I would say, is my parents, their aging flesh and love, what I cannot see, what feels so distant and palpable, I keep trying to hold it back.

God, I would say, is my wife, who sleeps beside me each night, who listens to this song. Is the journey through which we would destroy and lose and still find at the end a boldness, a common tune: each other.

How did that boy disappear? When did he become a man?

CHICAGO IN THE FIFTIES. The great years of Ernie Banks, slapping line-drive homers into the bleachers at Wrigley Field, his lean, whiplike arms and ever-ready smile. Years of the brief ascent of the White Sox, who climb to the World Series, win the first game, which my father takes me to see, and then lose four straight to the Dodgers, Larry Sherry and his untouchable sinker. Years of Mayor Daley, when the city was still "safe" and, as in Mussolini's Italy, "things worked." The city of broad shoulders and clean winds off the clear surf of Lake Michigan, city of the stockyards and the El and the Magnificent Mile, of quiet ethnic neighborhoods where people know their place and the garbage is cleared like clockwork. Picnics at Wilson Beach or Foster Avenue Beach. School trips to the Museum of Natural History with its mysterious mummies in the basement, sealed from air and natural light. Trips to the great lions that guarded the art museum, confrontations with Seurat, the abstractions of modernism; trips to the planetarium, where the planets and stars reeled above us and I whispered to my maiden aunt Miwako so many names of planets and constellations she marveled at my memory. The train ride at Lincoln Park Zoo and the great cages of gorillas and tigers. Corned-beef hash and brownies at the cafeteria of Marshall Field's. Just a few years before the suburbs drained the city's whites and wealth (and our family too).

Their small diaspora of the war and the internment over, my family lived in an apartment on Broadway, about a mile from Wrigley Field, one block off of Lake Shore Drive, with its luxury high-rises. These towers loomed above the traffic with views of the lake we could only imagine. In their lobbies gleamed gold chandeliers, a doorman. The traffic streamed by, glinting in sunlight.

The building we lived in was an ugly brown three-story structure. Out back was a dirt courtyard, an alley entryway of shadows and cinder. The building was owned by my Uncle Lou's family, the Hirakawas; his wife, Aunt Ruby, was my father's sister. With the exception of one Jewish family, we were all *Nihonjin* (Japanese)—the Hirakawas, the Ogatas, the Fukuyamas, and the Uyemuras.

Uyemura was our family name until I was seven, when my father shortened it. "For better bylines," he said. He worked at INS, the International News Service. Everyone was always mispronouncing the "Uye." "You-ee stir-ee bowl-ee up," Michael Ogata used to say. He was the oldest among us, the best athlete, rivaled only by Jimmy Paris, who was Chinese and whose parents ran Paris' Hand Laundry just down Broadway. "Ooey, ooey"—rhyming with "gooey"—the others would chant. Whites would sometimes pronounce it "Oi-yea," which always reminded me of the phrase "Hear ye, hear ye . . ." called out by clerks of the court on television.

Everyone spoke English except for a few choice phrases and the names of food. Among themselves, the Nisei spoke English. Those who spoke Japanese spoke it to their parents, the Issei, and there weren't many Issei around. My mother's mother died shortly after the war; my father's mother died when I was four. Later, both my grandfathers returned to Japan and remarried. Usually, it was the older Nisei, the eldest children, who spoke the best Japanese; neither of my parents were as skilled in Japanese as Aunt Ruth or Auntie Sachi. Would my parents have spoken Japanese to us if they were fluent? Probably not. What purpose would it have served? And those Japanese Americans who settled in the Midwest probably had less of a desire to return to the past or nurture their cultural roots than those who went back to the West Coast after the internment camps.

Surrounded by relatives and other Japanese Americans, going to the Japanese American Congregationalist Church, marching as a bugler in the Nisei Drum and Bugle Corps, which practiced at the Uptown Buddhist Church, I lived in our little ethnic enclave cozily unconscious of race. Whenever the name of a new person came up in conversations, one of my relatives would always ask, *"Nihonjin* or *hakujin?"* ("Japanese or white?"), though even this simple bifurcation slipped hazily by me, because of my lack of Japanese. I sensed what these words meant, but I was never quite sure. Perhaps I just simply wasn't attentive enough.

Years later, I would be embarrassed when, in my first book of poems, I wrote the word for Japanese pickle as *"utskemono"* rather than *"tsukemono"* and some critic took this as a mark of my ignorance and distance from my ethnic background. Which, of course, it was.

AT THE AGE OF FIVE, in every picture of me, I've got a pair of six-guns cinched about my waist. Or else I'm pointing them at the camera, my black cowboy hat pushed back, my mouth snarling with a bravado and toughness I evinced only as a pose or when alone, walking down the dark steps of our apartment building out to the street. At each step I'd wave to the fans at the rodeo, shouting, "Howdy, folks," the way I imagined Roy Rogers stepping into the arena and mounting Trigger, the Wonder Horse. Before I went on to collect baseball cards, I collected cowboy cards, with the heroes from various television series, together with a slice of chewing gum for a nickel. *Have Gun Will Travel, Sugarfoot, Maverick, The Gene Autrey Show, The Lone Ranger, Cheyenne, The Rebel,* classic American icons of the fifties.

In one of my poems, I picture myself riding in the back of our Bel-Air, shooting at the glass, bouncing up and down in gunfight delirium, wearing the black cowboy hat and cold, cocked steely gaze of Paladin, who'd leave his calling card, "Have Gun, Will Travel," everywhere he went. When a Japanese Canadian playwright, Rick Shiomi, read the poem, he remarked, "Do you remember what happened at the beginning of that show? This Chinese guy with a pigtail would come running into the hotel lobby shouting, 'Teragram for Mista Paradin, teragram for Mista Paradin'?"

I don't remember this Chinese messenger at all, whose name, Rick informs me, was Hey Boy. All I see is Richard Boone striding down the stairs, the epitome of cowboy cool, his pencil-thin mustache and tight glinting gaze.

ONE AFTERNOON, in second grade, I return home from school, toss a note on the kitchen table before my mother, and run to my room. I know I'm to wait there until my father comes home. My teacher, Mrs. Berman, has kept me after school. I have been talking in class, have been disrespectful. I can't quite recall the specifics of my crime. Perhaps in the spelling bee I yelled too loudly and blurted the answer out of turn. Or perhaps it was during the filmstrip which talked about the whites and the red man, when I bellowed, "What about the pink men?" Or perhaps it's when Dolores Garcia is sent to the corner in the back, and I'm sent there too, for talking, and I twitter, "Good, I get to see my girlfriend," and jump into her lap.

Though I've forgotten what has prompted the note from Mrs. Berman, I do remember waiting for my father to come home, the endless, torturous waiting. Through the screen I hear the shouts of Michael Ogata and Jimmy Hirakawa, my cousins Marianne and Sharon. I slip onto my saddle chair and ride a bit through the range, but my horse won't quite come alive today. I fiddle with my six-guns. I feel this sinking in the pit of my stomach, a whole set of butterflies and the fervent wish that today were yesterday or the day before. If only the note from Mrs. Berman did not exist, if only I were anywhere but here waiting for my father . . .

The afternoon shadows lengthen in the room.

In the corner, unnoticed, is my Zorro whip. Zorro, who rides through the night when the full moon is bright; Zorro, the black-clad, masked horseman, whose sword leaves a dark and slashing *Z* wherever he goes, who escapes through the shadowy trees, whipping his horse to a gallop, rearing at the crest of a hill, saluting the night. It is this whip which will become the instrument of my punishment. I will remember it in my father's hand more vividly than any of my misdeeds.

I know there's an unfairness in my obsession with this whipping. I have a far greater recollection of punishments I received as a child than of whatever I did to drum them forth. The memory of my punishment memories takes on a force, a disproportionate weight, as if to prevent the surfacing of positive memories. The moments of happiness I do recall make me feel uneasy, they're too discomfiting.

Perhaps it's not the events of the past which shaped my character, but the way my memory shapes my life, the unsettling way it keeps returning me to my body.

I AM STANDING in the sunken courtyard which leads to the basement, the washing machines and the furnace of our apartment building. It's late afternoon. I'm five years old. There's no one about. In the dark under the porch are the rusted garbage cans, large industrial canisters, where Jimmy Hirakawa once saw a rat scurrying. I'm wearing corduroy pants, a T-shirt, a cowboy hat, and Keds.

I look up at the windows above me. Is anyone looking?

Slowly, deliberately, I begin to pull down my pants, exposing myself, hoping for what, frightened of what, thrilled with what, who knows, but the feeling that returns now in memory seems so familiar, echoed often in other experiences as I grow older. No one leans out the window and shouts, no one sees me; the crime, the secret goes undetected.

Two years later, I'm in the bushes, near the berry tree, in the vacant lot next door we call simply the Empty. Michael Ogata, the oldest kid in the group, is shooing out the younger kids; only he and Jimmy Paris and a fourth-grade girl are allowed to look. Flies buzz, zapping about in the heat; a cabbage white flutters by my face. I feel their gaze behind me; I'm riveted, confused by their attention, by what I've agreed to do, and again, this time under the watchful gaze of others, I pull down my pants and expose my buttocks. Why are they watching like this? Why am I doing this?

It is over in a few seconds. I walk out of the bushes, back into the sunlight.

PERHAPS IT WAS ALWAYS TOO LATE. Perhaps it was never my parents or the world around me. Perhaps there was something in my nature which accelerated me in the direction I was going without my knowing it.

There's a fleshiness to my photos as a child, I have the face of indolence, indulgence. I was always too eager to raise my hand, to shout out the answer. It's a face I've never lost, really, unpenetrated by experience, by weathering or scars. It's the face of a child who's never known poverty, knows he will never know it. A face capable of ingenuousness and shame.

Every day during those years my father was planning the future, his and mine. For several years he worked two jobs, one at INS as a reporter, one at the camera store owned by the Ogatas. Every afternoon, when I was in second grade, before I could go out to play, I had to work two pages in a fifth-grade math book. He wanted me always to be several years ahead, out in front of the pack. There's some tremendous drive churning inside him. Perhaps fear too. Fear he will not be able to keep rising toward the future, the promises he's made to himself, his wife and children. (When they were first married, he offered my mother a choice—money or his time. She chose money.) He is not yet thirty, older than I sometimes think I'll ever be.

I wanted what all little boys wanted. To be a hero. To ride horses and hit home runs and kill the enemy and never die.

BY THE TIME I was in first grade, both my grandfathers had moved back to Japan. By the time we left the city in third grade, I didn't think about them much. I was hardly aware they were alive. I can't remember when either of them died.

I do remember going to Buddhist ceremonies to commemorate my father's parents. We'd meet my Aunt Ruby and Uncle Lou and my cousins at the apartment of a Buddhist priest on the far North Side. In the living room there was a black shrine with gleaming brass bowls, sticks of incense, flowers, and bowls of fruit. Dressed in a suit, the priest would greet us all, go back down the hall, and return in his flowing black Buddhist robes. He directed us to the two rows of folding chairs, then he knelt in front of the altar, and lit a stick of incense. He picked up his prayer beads, rolled them around in his hands, and began to chant.

At first, the droning voice seems strange, half foghorn, half human. The syllables are nonsense, like no language at all. Na-na-na-na, na-na-na-na. A four-beat rhythm, as monotonous as the ocean, incessant as waves. Our parents bow their heads, their faces quiet and steady. A guttural sound, like someone gargling deep inside his throat.

My cousin Marianne is the first to break. I hear it. The priest drones on. Now it's in me. A small giggle. I feel it coming, gurgling up in my throat too. I can't help it. I hear my sister Susan begin to giggle. The priest drones on. Then my cousins Sharon and Debby. My brother John. I keep waiting for my father or mother to say something. Finally my mother says, "Shhh." But it's too late. The priest drones on. All of us kids are now in fits of laughter. My mother gives up. The priest drones on, never looking back, never stopping, never acknowledging the uproarious Sansei children behind him, his eyes closed tight, his mind centered on the prayers of Buddha, colorless and deep.

On the altar, Tatsue and Jinnosuke, my grandparents, stare out from the pictures at their daughter and son and their families, the uncontrollable grandchildren who find some unbridled mirth in these ceremonies for the dead. This is what they have bequeathed to the future, another strain of American song.

And so it goes, by now all of us kids are rolling on the floor, clutching our stomachs, laughing so hard, our sides ache, laughing so hard, we're out of breath.

THE SUMMER AFTER THIRD GRADE, we move out of the city and into our own house. Each week that spring before, we make the drive to Morton Grove, taking Lake Shore Drive, stopping at the McDonald's near Loyola. The house seems to signify the flush of luxury, though it's only a standard cookie-cutter bi-level. The boys in the neighborhood play softball in the street, talk to me of exploring our house when the workers are gone. My father stands before the house in its last stages and feels a thrill of accomplishment. He's made it to the middle class, the All-American dream—a house in the suburbs. He's working for the American Medical Association in their Communications Division. In his lectures to me about schoolwork, he'll tell me how he and his boss, Joe Stetler, stay long after everyone has gone, how Mr. Stetler teaches him what he needs to move up the corporate ladder. My father takes up golf, and we all go with him to the driving range at night, watching his drives lope upward into the lights. Soon, he'll trade in his Bel-Air for a Buick Le Sabre, a machine smelling of new money, with its black vinyl interior and solid wide frame.

Oddly, our block in Morton Grove is mainly blue-collar—Herbie Thompson's father drives a truck for Brach's candy, Terry Steinberg's father sells plastic slip coverings, the Walters' father is a mechanic. The Hoshizakis, Bob and Doug, live on the next block and their father is an engineer. They're the only Japanese Americans in the neighborhood.

In school, I'm a member of the elite in class. I get good grades, but more importantly, I'm the third-best athlete, behind Greg Jacubik and Gary Hancher. When we play softball or football, I tip the scales; whichever side I'm on usually wins. In basketball, Gary and I vie for the top slot. Back around my house, I'm a Little League All-Star, the quarterback whenever we play football.

Aside from my continuing check marks for unruly behavior at school, everything seems fine. Certainly, the issues of race don't trouble me. My sense of how my experience compared with other Japanese Americans wasn't a question I ever asked. I never talked about such things with the Hoshizaki boys; all we ever talked about was sports, when today's ball game was going to begin, if we were playing marbles or football.

In fifth grade, though, there's another Japanese American boy in my class, David Nakayama. Extremely short, with bottle-bottom glasses, and a crew cut, he's not like me at all physically. I'm one of the larger boys, at times running to husky, but also tall and a good athlete. David Nakayama is not a good athlete. He earns good grades, but gets into trouble frequently. I may make wisecracks in class, I may speak out of turn, but David Nakayama's behavior is truly bizarre.

He proclaims, for instance, that the area in front of his desk is his sovereign nation.

"You must have a pass if you are to cross here," he shouts. The pass must be issued by him. It must possess his official stamp.

Inadvertently, Tony Desalvo crosses David Nakayama's desk to reach the pencil sharpener. David springs up from his desk, shakes his fist at Tony, and shouts, "I declare war. You are now my enemy."

Tony laughs, sharpens his pencil, and goes back to his seat. At his desk, David madly scribbles a declaration of war.

Most of us think David Nakayama is crazy and avoid going by his desk. But Steven Cartwell is different. He can't resist goading David Nakayama. At least once a day, he rises from his desk and deliberately walks toward David's desk.

"Don't you dare, Steven Cartwell," David barks out.

"I'm going to trespass," Steven taunts, "I'm going to cross into your country without a pass."

David eyes him like a hawk, like a gunner waiting for the target to get in range.

"I don't have a pa—asss, I don't have a pa—ass," Steven sings out. Now he's crossing right in front of David Nakayama. David cannot believe it. His face scrunches up, livid with rage.

"Steven Cartwell, you are a traitorous spy." David raises his fist, brandishing a pencil—sometimes it's a compass—and starts to chase after Steven, yelling, "I declare war," at the top of his lungs. They run around and around the room, chasing each other like Sylvester and Tweetie Pie, until Miss Phillips finally gets hold of both of them and sits them in the corner. On those times when David draws blood, she sends him to the principal's office.

From time to time David shows up at our desks offering a news-letter which spews spirited attacks against the scurrilous Steven

Cartwell. There are articles about his spy activities, about how he's an agent for a foreign government, betraying secrets, conducting clandestine fifth-column activities. There are pictures of him with devil's horns on his head. There are headlines, of course, declaring war on Steven Cartwell, blasting his sneak attacks.

I tend to steer clear of David Nakayama and Steven Cartwell. To me, they are spazzes; neither of them is good at sports. When we play baseball or football at recess, neither of them takes part. No one would pick them for their team even if they tried to play.

By junior high, David Nakayama became less of a wildly eccentric figure and more a figure of mild ridicule. He was someone people picked on or laughed at from time to time, but wasn't quite noticeable enough to be the constant brunt of bad attention. The other boys called him "Nak-nak" (pronounced "knock-knock"). I don't think the girls noticed him at all. Occasionally, he still put out his newsletter, but he had ceased backing it up with his grade school antics.

He was most conspicuous in gym class, where his short stature and slightly plump body marshaled him to the margins. Indeed, his lack of physical prowess seemed almost astonishing. The shortness of his long jump was improbable to us, a joke. The rest of us could have jumped that far on one leg.

Of course, I continued to avoid any association with David Nakayama like the plague. He and I weren't even in the same league. I don't think anyone took particular notice that we were both Japanese American, but if I'd been confronted with this connection, I would have spilled forth a list of our differences—from his glasses and crew-cut hair to his tiny, unathletic body to his nondescript clothes to the stories of his wild exploits in grade school and his obsessions with secret pacts and trespasses which continued to propel his self-published newsletter. If, by junior high, I wasn't exactly in with the "in crowd," I still had hope of being invited to its parties.

And then, one day in the locker room, Mike Wrangel starts to yell at David Nakayama.

"You moron, you can't even catch a ball."

David says nothing. He's naked, still dripping from the showers. He's putting on his T-shirt.

"Look at his underpants. They're all brown."

I look across the bench to where Wrangel and David are standing. I don't want to say anything. Wrangel has just transferred to our school last month. He smokes, wears a leather jacket, sports sideburns; he's flunked once, which means he's a year older than the rest of us. Not someone to be messed with.

"God, you're a spazz," Wrangel continues.

David tries to turn toward his locker, away from Wrangel. He gropes for his thick glasses. His body is that of a little kid really, and Wrangel towers over him. In my mind, I suddenly see the image of a huge polar bear descending on a penguin, a strange mixture of terror and absurdity. I hesitate. It's not my fight. Why should I do anything? Maybe Wrangel's going to stop. No, he's not. I can't stand it any longer.

"Leave him alone, Wrangel."

"What's it to you?"

"Just leave him alone."

Wrangel strides down the bench to me.

"What are you going to make of it?"

"Nothing. Just leave him alone." I try to laugh it off. "He's not worth the bother."

Wrangel looks at me for a moment. We're about the same size. I could probably take him on the wrestling mats, but in a street fight, no way. My stomach gurgles. My skin takes on a malarial heat, tingling all over, my arms feel leaden and limp.

"Oh, so he's one of your buddies," he sneers.

"No way, man. . . . Just let him go."

The bell rings. Wrangel takes a look at me, at David Nakayama, then turns and walks away.

Neither David Nakayama nor I look at each other as we dress in silence. We're still in two separate worlds.

IN EIGHTH GRADE, I was captain of the intramural basketball champions. Every year, the champion team played a team of all-stars from the other teams. The odds were generally in favor of the all-stars. But that didn't faze me. I knew we were going to win.

It wasn't just that I was the leading scorer in intramurals. I studied the game, checking strategy and plays in the sports books from the library. I read through Bob Cousy's biography, his book on playing in the NBA finals against the Lakers, books with titles like *Full Court Press* and *All-Star Forward*. I understood the chemistry needed to make a winner, how each player fit like a cog in a machine, from the rebounding role player to the playmaker to the defensive specialist to the scorer.

The night before the big game I sat outside the school with Steve Fine, the second leading scorer on our team, waiting for the bus. Fine was quiet, intelligent, and better-looking than I. He had this small hint of a pompadour that seemed to curl just right and which I envied. His jump shot was smooth and accurate. He said he hoped he played well in the game, because on Saturday everyone would be talking about it at Marla Friedman's boy-girl party. I nodded; I felt the same way. Our breaths came out in clouds in the chilly evening air. In my mind I ran through the last few pages of *Full Court Press*, the description of the nail-biting title game, the gritty guard who made it all happen. Lost in reverie, I was jolted by Fine's voice.

"Hey, man. The bus." He looked at me and laughed. "You better be more awake tomorrow night."

The game was close throughout. But Rick Gordon, who was guarding me, constantly overplayed his hand, and I ripped past him for several layups. Although I usually looked for assists first, spotting Fine in the corner, the flow of the game was pulling me more and more to look for my shot. Every time it looked like the all-stars might pull away, someone would make a key basket, often me. In the fourth quarter huddle, I kept shouting to everyone about defense. "No zone. Just good man-to-man. Just stick to your man."

When the clock had wound down to the last seconds, the game was tied; the all-stars had the ball. I saw Allan Rosenbloom glance at Rick Gordon and I pounced into the passing lane, intercepted the pass, and before they knew it, in a long floating drive I remember to this day, I made the winning layup. I'd scored over half of my team's points.

I dressed for the party on Saturday night carefully, with the proper Levi's and paisley shirt and brown penny loafers, the style of dress that the kids from Skokie called "collegiate." Its opposite was "greaser," and if you were in neither of these categories, you were simply unworthy of mention. I spent several minutes before the mirror, patiently grooming my pompadour. I walked the three blocks to Marla Friedman's house, still warmed by the memory of my last-second basket, immune to the brisk November wind that buffeted about me. I recalled how Laura Bennett seemed startled at how good I was, better than Allan Rosenbloom or Rick Gordon or any of the other guys from Skokie, the ones she'd gone to grade school with. Laura Bennett, the prettiest girl in the class, whom I had a secret crush on and who, through the luck of the draw, was my science partner. I'd feel this soft caving inside me whenever I was near her, whenever I thought of her, and I kept envisioning some time when she would see I was not like the other guys, that what I felt for her was deeper, purer. Week after week I'd been helping her with her write-ups, wishing there was some way we could talk about something else. Here was my chance.

But when I got to the party, no one talked about the game.

At first, everybody talked about what records to play. There were arguments about the Beatles versus the Rolling Stones; everyone wanted to hear the new Beach Boy album Marla had just bought. We were in the basement rec room, and from time to time, Marla's mother would call down. It seemed clear she wasn't going to interrupt us. I kept waiting for someone to mention the game, but somehow the center of things always seemed to be whatever Rick Gordon or Jeff Lappins was talking about, even though Lappins hadn't even played in the game. Gordon was a year older than the rest of us, wore a leather jacket, and regaled everyone with tales of the fights he'd been in on with his older brothers. He pulled out his switchblade, flicked it open and showed it to everyone. Laura laughed and pretended to shy away from him, as if she were frightened. Lappins had hair just like the Beatles, and it was rumored several girls in the room had crushes on him. He talked about how fast the girls were from Crandall, a junior high just across town in Evanston.

"You can't believe what they're like. They even give hand jobs."

"That's disgusting," said Marla. Lappins laughed. It was just the response he was looking for. The other girls giggled.

Watching all this, I wanted to jump into the conversation, but there never seemed a spot to slide in. I made a show of looking at Marla's records, reading the album covers. I tried to talk to Fine about the game, but he didn't seem interested. And then, Marla came out of her utility room carrying an empty Coke bottle, and several girls started giggling. Riki Leavitt took the bottle and shouted, "It's time for Spin the Bottle."

What was that? I didn't know, but of course wasn't going to ask. Fortunately, Riki explained, then ordered everyone into a circle. Rick Gordon grabbed the bottle to spin first, and it landed on Riki. Everyone oohed. There was a rumor Riki and Gordon had a crush on each other.

I began to feel this flush of excitement. When was it going to land on me? I wanted it to happen and I didn't. What would I do? I'd never kissed a girl before. How was I supposed to do that?

Then, as the Searchers sang "Needles and Pins" on the stereo, Andi Levine spun the bottle, and it slowed to a halt, pointing at me. I scrambled across the center of the circle. She sat up, leaning forward slightly. I think she expected just a simple peck on the lips, like everyone else was giving. I don't know what I expected, but when I pressed my lips to hers, something seemed to pull me toward her, pressing my lips tighter, and I kept them there, thinking I should let go now, feeling I didn't want to let go, I couldn't. And then I heard people around us cheer, and this spurred me on, until she finally pulled herself away, as if trying to grab her breath. The calls erupted louder then, and my face reddened with the attention. Suddenly people were talking about me. So I did the same thing on the next spin. And the next.

Finally, the bottle I'd spun pointed to Laura Bennett. I turned to look at her dark face, her long dark hair, her almost Italian-looking eyes, her full mouth, all vaguely reminiscent of Sophia Loren, of someone several years older. But what I saw in her eyes was a mixture of mock horror and a real, though slight, repulsion, as she made a show of backing up and putting her hands up before her face, fluttering them there as if waving away a stream of gnats. She ran to the other side of the room and refused to kiss me. Everyone laughed.

The next Monday at school I was labeled "Lover Lips." I tried to wear this moniker as a mark of distinction, though I sensed that wasn't quite the case. All I knew was, the rules had changed.

2.

ON A SUNNY SEPTEMBER DAY IN 1959, my father showed up at my school, wearing a gray suit and a felt fedora. Although his black glasses will seem geeky in photos thirty years later, to me he looked tall and darkly serious, powerful and businesslike, out of place amid the blackboards, tiny desks, and my fellow-second graders. He explained to my teacher the reason he was taking me out of school: I was going to see all my heroes, Luis Aparicio, Nellie Fox, Minnie Minoso, Early Wynn, in the first game of the World Series. My father and I took the El to the South Side, shuttling noisily on a trip that seemed to take hours to the edge of the black sections of the city. At the game I loaded myself up with hot dogs, pop, and popcorn. I was a bit chubby, and my father laughed and chided me that I'd come to eat and not watch the game. In the first inning, Duke Snyder of the Dodgers dropped a pop-up even I could have fielded. Aparicio, Fox, Landis, and Minoso all came through, and Early Wynn mowed down the opposition like a reaper through a wheat field. The Sox won 11 to 0. Back at school the next day I regaled my friends with stories of the game, feeling proud and full of myself, as if I too had been out on the field.

As with many American boys, my best memories of my father center on sports. He took me to a fair number of Northwestern football games, the Bears and the Cubs at Wrigley Field, the All-Star game in '63. Though he traveled frequently on business, though he often worked late hours, he seemed to be there as much as any of the fathers in the neighborhood. He helped me carve my soapbox-derby car for Cub Scouts, started me off as a left-handed batter to be closer to first and present a problem to right-handed pitchers; he'd hit grounders to me in the big field near our house, shouting, "Two hands, two hands." He could talk sports before the rec room television with my uncles, played a mean game of poker, and became eventually a very decent golfer. You could tell by the way he carried himself he was a good athlete. While not of heroic proportions, like the father of my neighbor Herbie Thompson, who had once played for the Green Bay Packers, my father presented me with what I took as a healthy masculine figure, a fact which I considered of utmost importance while growing up. In my obsession with sports, I conformed pretty much with the lines of the culture, and I appreciated the fact that my father did too. I wanted desperately to be normal, and I think my father wanted the same for me. Why things did not turn out that way is still difficult to explain.

A FEW YEARS AGO, for a men's course, I gathered poems, essays, psychological texts about the fathers of my generation and us, the sons. In one study, only one percent of the men questioned said they felt they had a satisfactory relationship with their fathers.

My father's generation generally didn't ask such questions about their fathers. They were more stoic, less introspective, less inclined to inquire or complain.

What explains the distance of our fathers? Some trace it to the industrial revolution, the end of an agrarian economy in which sons worked alongside their fathers in the fields, the end of guilds in which sons learned a craft through the hands of their fathers. The work was passed down like an inheritance. Or perhaps, for the middle-class sons of my generation, it was the rise of the white-collar worker, a change that placed our fathers beyond our ken, in some remote realm where, invisible and absent, they became at once larger and smaller, more mystifying and less powerful, and yet, because more mystifying, even more powerful.

At home with the children, mothers of our generation ended up explaining the fathers to the sons. These tales were much less heroic than those Penelope told to Telemachus and much more ambiguous and confusing (in my case, my mother never tried to explain). The fathers came home silent, tired, angry, frustrated, home to a world of trikes and diapers, lawns and swimming lessons, crayon drawings, Barbies, Roy Rogers. And this world, so chaotic, so brimming with the energy of tiny babbling bodies, frightened and confused them. Yet perhaps there was no more confusing time than when it became apparent their daughters were becoming women—the accouterments appearing in the laundry, the medicine cabinet—and their sons men—the signs in the showers, stains marked by mothers on the sheets, or, in my case, magazines stolen from their fathers' closets (these magazines also a product of the times).

In eighth grade, on a gray rainy day in March, a few weeks after the party at Marla Friedman's house, I discovered my sexuality.

It's late afternoon. I am lying in bed. My room, on the second floor of our bi-level, is dark. My mother has gone to the store. I cross the hall to my parents' room. There's a dresser in Swedish modern, two mirrors at each end; a nightstand on each side of the bed. Everything is neat, uncluttered.

I slide open my parents' closet. The hangers all face one way, as do the shoes, lined precisely in a row. There's a gold quilted garment bag. I slip my hands inside—I don't know even now how I knew it was there, though my therapist, years later, remarked that news travels unconsciously, silently, in families—I pull it out. A *Playboy*. June 1964.

Quickly, I open to the foldout. I have seen *Playboy*s before, in my friend Terry Steinberg's basement and in the locker room once at school. Each time I felt fascinated, drawn to them, at the same time feeling their forbidden nature, the sense of trespassing on something I couldn't name. But this is the first time I have seen one alone. The woman inside, Donna, is a blonde, a UCLA coed; her breasts seem enormous, the areolas as large as my fist. Though only eighteen, she seems frightfully older. Overwhelming, imposing in her beauty.

I sit down on my parents' bed. My penis is hard. I keep staring. I pull down my pants and look at my penis, fascinated by how big it is. I look at the glossy picture. How she leans on the edge of a red folding screen, over which a red blanket is draped, so that her body seems to be emerging from the act of undressing. She doesn't stare at the camera, it's me she's staring at. The curves of her breasts, the dark brown of her nipples, float off the page, both attached to her body and detached, constituting a vision, a realm of their own. I make a game of pulling my foreskin tighter, trying to make my penis grow bigger. It too seems somehow detached, to take on a force of its own.

I look at the blue vein on the back of the shaft, the way it rises, can be seen through the skin. I feel this pleasure coursing through my body, a trembling I cannot control. A wave washes over me, another, a rending of my body from my consciousness, my consciousness from my surroundings, this instant from the continuum of time.

The moment I ejaculate I'm startled, overwhelmed, staring at what shoots out of me, seeing, sensing that this is what explains the morning sheets, wet, sticky, cold. At the same time I feel I've done something wrong, something which should be kept secret; I know somehow I'm trespassing. But whatever frightened or guilty feelings arise, there also arises an urge to feel this pleasure again, to look at the pictures again, to experience this explosion inside. I bend down and wipe up the milk-white pool on the floor. I repeat the ritual. My secret life has begun.

MY DISCOVERY OF SEXUALITY was, I suppose, no different from that of many American adolescents. But the fervor with which I subsequently went back to this discovery, the endless, compulsive repetition of that act, marked me as different, though at the time I had no way of knowing this. I simply put the magazine back in my parents' closet, and again and again, waited for a chance to steal back, to take another look. In between I contented myself with the darkness under my covers, each morning when I woke up, each night when I went to bed. Two, four, six times a day. In a way my father's *Playboy* was like a stash of alcohol an adolescent alcoholic has discovered, only I didn't need that stash. All I needed was to be alone, behind a closed door.

Only now does it occur to me to think of how my father perceived these *Playboy*s, why he bought them or what my mother thought. Did he too masturbate over them? Did my mother object to them and, if she did, did she voice this objection? How did he reconcile these pictures with his increasing participation during those years in our Episcopalian church?

All of these seem the expected questions an American son might ask in such a situation. But there is an added element here. My father was a Japanese American in a generation in which Japanese Americans almost always married inside their race. I remember reading a journal my father kept when he was twenty-four and living in Chicago, working at a country club. In the clubhouse kitchen one night, he and a few of the other Nisei boys are talking about women. The line that sticks out in my memory went like this: "Mas has gone out with white girls, and he says it wasn't that bad." I'm surprised at this remark that dating white girls wasn't significantly different, and at the same time, I wonder if he could have expressed what those differences were. His awareness of the color line was not the same as mine. From adolescence on, I felt that my inability to attract girls had something to do with my race. Yet I was only attracted to white girls, that was all there was around me.

I try to imagine my father staring at the foldout of Miss June, the UCLA coed, try to imagine what are the connections through which he yokes his sexuality to hers. He is sitting on the toilet, in a washroom of blue walls and blue tile and blue porcelain. I can see him there, a magazine on his lap, but when I try to imagine him staring at that image I feel distressed, that unbearable ache when we see the pain of a parent in a moment of vulnerability, yearning, shame. He puts down the magazine. She, the girl, the woman, is too far away. Beyond his world. Perhaps this explains why, in a few years, I find no more of these magazines in his closet; in a way, they are like my mother's longings for higher culture, for Mahler and Beethoven.

It's me, not my father, who keeps the images from *Playboy* in my briefcase, my closet, in my head. The images there, the beautiful white bodies, are not too far away for me to dream of, though they seem beyond my touching. By coming back to them again and again, perhaps I am completing a path of desire that my father started, driving further into the psyche of America, piercing beyond his sense of sexual possibility. In this pursuit, I will experience frustrations and denials he never approached, though, for a brief period, these images, these *Playboys*, were part of his life too.

ON MANY NIGHTS, listening to Mantovani-like strings on the FM radio, my father sits at the kitchen table and spreads his work papers. There he marks changes in the margins of news releases, articles for the in-house paper of the AMA, speeches for his boss, or writes out new copy, sometimes in long hand on a yellow legal pad, sometimes on an old Remington. His glasses propped at the edge of his nose, he keeps pushing them back. The house is quiet, we children are upstairs in the bath or in our beds. Soon, he'll be the only one awake.

The strongest image I have of him at this table has him licking his fingertips and turning the pages of typed material, reading and pondering, as I have come to do, even with this piece, years later. He lifts the mug of coffee, sips, continues to work. This image is, I see now, part of his legacy to me, an image of serenity, the calm that is the joy of writing. He never spoke of this calm, and certainly would not have described it as joyful—it was making a buck, putting bread on the table: that's how he'd frame it—but calm and joy are the feelings that arrive with this image. Whatever differences between us, whatever distances we have created, there is this: we both put sentences together.

But there's another image I have of my father at the kitchen table, one more ambiguous and unsettling.

It is spring, my freshman year in high school. I have written this scene before and always it is stiff, lifeless, two cardboard figures. My father and I are hunched beneath a cone of light. I stare at the pictures of spice bottles on the wallpaper, at the dishes in their rack, at the cupboards. I look at the Formica table, its flecks of blackness. I am tense, shifting in the vinyl chair, waiting for him to speak.

It must have been bewildering, disturbing, to him. I don't know what my mother said to him. Talk to David, it's your responsibility, she might have said. But would she have added: It's your magazines, it wouldn't have happened if you hadn't bought them?

No, to say that would have required an awareness, a consciousness of sexuality and her own feelings and rights, that my mother would not have possessed, especially in those years. Still, my father would have understood that she was blaming him somehow for her discovery that his *Playboy* had suddenly appeared in one of my desk drawers (she had surprised me by coming home early; I had no time to put back what I had stolen).

My father is stern, angry. He mentions my mother, mentions trust, mentions their privacy. "Your mother was very upset."

In other situations, when I have done something wrong, he grills me over and over, question after question—how could you, don't you ever think, what's gotten into you—questions that have no answers or any I can devise. But here he doesn't ask those questions. I see now this reticence came from something inside him, some unsureness, as if he too were somehow in court with me, brought before some nameless, faceless judge, some absent primal father.

Did his father speak to him of such matters? Or was the gulf between father and son made broader, oceanic, by the barriers of language and culture? I know that Japanese culture doesn't locate shame in the body and in sexuality the way that the puritanical strains of American culture do; in traditional Japanese culture families bathed together, men and women shared public baths. Are my father's difficulties here due more to his assimilated ways?

In the middle of the talk, he surprised me: "I suppose you're wondering why I can have these magazines and you can't."

I hadn't even thought to question this. He didn't realize this was a question his conscience was asking, not mine. He talked about how I would understand these things when I was older, I needed to wait until I was an adult. There are dangers.

"I don't want you burning yourself out too early."

He tells me I can't date until I'm seventeen. I'm devastated and perplexed. The chance of my getting a girl to go out with me seems impossibly remote. Now, even if I would be able to go out on a date, I couldn't. It seems so unfair. And what does he mean by the phrase "burning myself out"?

It all came across like a biblical parable: You cannot indulge, you must hold back, and this holding back includes not just these magazines, but anything else, holding hands, kissing, even going out on dates, all this must be forbidden for years. Or you'll burn yourself out. You'll burn yourself out.

At the end of our talk, he handed me a book from the AMA on reproduction, which showed crosscut diagrams of ovaries and testicles and talked about reproduction in the sort of clinical scientific language I'd heard in phys ed at school.

"If you have any questions about it . . ."

I was silent. I wasn't a fool. I didn't want the conversation to go on any longer than it already had. I kept my questions to myself.

THIS SCENE—my father lecturing me at the kitchen table after my mother's discoveries—was repeated a few more times during my adolescence. There was one more time I was discovered using the magazines in his closet and then I began to look for other sources. According to my father, my mother's discovery of these items in my closet was particularly troubling to her, though she said nothing of it to me.

One final irony: This time period, eighth grade, was the last during which I was ever to get in trouble at school for conduct. Through my grade school years, I was constantly being reprimanded for talking in school. Although I did well scholastically, I always seemed to be mouthing off, making wisecracks.

Were my actions in school a result of the strictness of my home life? My father had a second-generation immigrant's fierceness, and he still retained some of the severity of Japanese culture and schooling. I was not to be frivolous or misbehave like other kids; I was constantly admonished to "buckle down," and on my report cards my father regularly wrote—in his second-generation prizing of formal English—"I have talked to David and he has assured me his deportment will improve." In essence, what he meant was: "I have smacked David and told him that more of the same will be coming if he doesn't shape up." Somehow, as evidenced by the F in deportment I got in science for the first semester in eighth grade, these punishments never helped.

But at the discovery of my sexuality, all this changed. I stopped acting out in school, stopped misbehaving. And each night, in my sheets, each morning, in my sheets, I spilled some part of my desire, some part of my outrage, but this was always hidden, or in the few cases it was discovered, that knowledge was quickly buried. Everyone thought I had become good, had "buckled down," had "improved my deportment." I became, in the eyes of my parents, the model son and student they wanted.

OVER THE YEARS, I've begun to think about certain moments of closeness between my father and me, intimacies that seem to me now almost biological. A couple of these moments carry a certain mystery, a zone of memory beyond interpretation. It's hard to find a place for the images in the weave of narrative; they seem timeless, permanent, existing in their own aura.

The first is of my father emerging from the shower, the steam erupting as the glass door opens, and he steps forward, bulky, beefier, larger than his present weight, and to me, nine or ten, he is huge, overwhelming. His tortoiseshell glasses rest on the sill of the washroom, their lenses covered with steam, and he squints as he reaches for the towel and starts drying his arms, his stomach, and now the groin, the long, strange root flushed with wiry black hairs.

I realize now that part of the strangeness of seeing my father naked came from the fact that I was circumcised and my father was not; at the time it seemed only that his penis was different, foreign, larger. I don't know now why I was there in the washroom to see this, but I sense I felt comfortable in that washroom with the steam rising about him, more at peace than I ever felt with him clothed. It was a setting of intimacy, of fathers and sons.

The second image occurs six years later. The same washroom. I am staring at that windowsill, at the thick glass bricks, at the moths fluttering at the screen. My father is bending down, kneeling. I have an infection on my penis, a raw and red, moist swelling. He takes a cotton swab and smears it with ointment, tells me to pull my loose skin down. It hurts to do this. I don't want him to touch it, I know it will hurt even more, and he's impatient with me, it needs to be done.

Then he is wiping, gently, the ointment across the tip of the penis, trying carefully not to scrape the wound. And then it is over. I pull up my pants. The ordeal is done. For the next few nights this will happen, and then the infection will heal. It will be years before I recognize, in a poem, this gesture of love.

3.

MY FRESHMAN YEAR of high school at Niles West, the first student union dance. Faced with finding a niche in a new school, I feel ill at ease, unable to scry the social rhythms, to sense the beat. The students from my junior high in Skokie compose a small minority. As a Christian, I'm also a minority, since Niles West is mainly Jewish. Not knowing anybody except the guys from the football team, I wander the edge of the crowd circling the dance floor. The band's on a break; the Animals are playing on the turntable "We Gotta Get Out of This Place." I sidle toward the kids from Lincolnwood, the ones I sense are "cool," whose clothes and manner bespeak authority.

Perhaps I'm prompted, or offered some introduction, I couldn't have simply started all by myself, out of the blue. But after whatever preliminaries, I start to call out, "Hear ye, hear ye, you sinners, repent for the Lord is at hand, I tell you, the Lord is at hand." Then, in the rotund and oracular tones of a Southern Baptist preacher, I launch into a mock sermon, a tirade against sin and degradation. I rant about the cities of Sodom and Gomorrah, about the sulfuric brimstone and high-banked fires of hell, about the sins of lust and greed and envy, about coveting thy neighbor's wife, about blasphemy against God and Christ, about the wonders of the sweet arms of Jesus and his healing gaze, about how the sinners about me are doomed unless they fall to their knees and accept the Lord Jesus into their hearts.

"And Jesus preached on the mountain and in the hills of Galilee, preached by the shores where the fishermen dipped their nets. . . ."

A crowd starts to gather about me. The girls giggle nervously, the boys begin to shout words of encouragement. "Go, preacher, go." I ask for an "Amen," and they give me an "Amen," and I ask for a "Praise the Lord," and they shout back, "Praise the Lord." I'm aware of the irony in doing this bit before a group of Jewish kids, but at least they're paying attention to me, at least the girls are laughing.

"And I ask you, you sinners . . ."

"I'm no sinner, Reverend," calls out Bob Hernstein, kicking in a line. He's an end on the football team, one of the cool kids. He goes out with Gail Golman, one of the prettiest girls in the class.

"Oh, son, I can see you're a sinner, I can see the fire of lust burning in your eyes and in your loins, I can see you have sinnin' in your heart, and in your heart I hear the demons singing, singing around the campfires of hell, and do you know what they are singing?"

"What, Reverend? 'Camptown Races'?" Hernstein tries to joke. I can see he's a little uncomfortable.

"No, son, they are singing of lust, the sins of the flesh, all that you have dreamed of in your dirty, evil little mind . . ." Here one of the freshman guys jabs Hernstein in the arm.

". . . they know you are off to the races of degradation, the races of damnation, the races where brimstone burns, flesh sizzles, and there is no redemption and there is no savior and there is no water of truth to slake your thirst, but only fire, fire, burning your tongue, burning the hair from your head, the flesh from your bones, and still the fire will not abate. No, no, don't walk away, son, don't turn your head. Now is your chance, your chance to hear the word of God, the hymns of the lord, to change your evil ways, baby, and just as the Animals have sung, we've got to get out of this place, you, you have to get out of this place and rise up and get out of detention, stop playing hooky, and go, go with the Lord unto Galilee and cleanse your soul . . ."

I finish my sermon to applause and laughter. The band starts up its set, "Little Deuce Coupe," and the crowd melts away from me, though several times during the night someone herds up a group of people and asks me to perform my sermon, and I oblige. All that I'm missing is a tin cup to pass around for an offering, all I need is a crowd.

GRADUALLY, I get a name for myself as a loud, obnoxious person. It's not quite the persona I want, though I don't know what that would be. But at least it's not like the stereotype of the quiet, studious Asian student. I refused to be seen as part of the same group as Alvin Chong, with his white shirts and pocket pencil holder, or David Nakayama, who, by high school, seemed to have lost all traces of his former Tojo-Mussolini, little-dictator, I-declare-war persona and settled into an honor student wallflower role.

Perhaps what I desired was to expose my sense of difference, rather than hide it. Only today do I see how similar my sermonizing preacher was to the wild-eyed antics of David Nakayama. Was there something in common fueling our fury, were we trying to work through the same things? Or were our problems mainly individual, unaffected in any major way by race?

I don't know. All I know is I couldn't have asked any of these questions at the time.

All through my growing up, there was a seemingly natural assumption that the way I looked, my Japanese American background, was incidental to who I was. My parents taught me I'd be judged by other qualities—my behavior and grades in school, my athletic abilities, the type of clothes I wore, the type of house we lived in, what kind of car my father drove.

When we moved to the suburbs, the kids in the neighborhood saw the distinctions among Catholic, Jewish, and Protestant, much more than the differences between Asians and whites. Most of the Catholics in the neighborhood went to parochial schools, which were the source of a certain envy because of their Catholic youth sports leagues.

We Asians, on the other hand, were too few to be remarked upon in detail, even by ourselves. In many ways, it was easy to keep up our semblance of sameness. The basic philosophy, though never stated, was: "Act as if you are like everyone else, and you will *be* like everyone else." Yes, my parents felt a certain kinship with the Hoshizakis, on the next block, but I explained this more by the fact that my father and their father played golf together and that our parents played bridge together than that they were all Nisei.

In short, it's difficult to underestimate how much as a teenager I wanted to fit in, how deeply I assumed a basically white middle-class identity. When a white friend proclaimed, "I think of you just like a white person," I'd take it as a compliment, a sign I'd made it.

The problem was this: From the onset of my sexuality, I stumbled into experience after experience which pointed to my difference. At some level of consciousness, I was aware of racial differences in standards of beauty, that my sexual desires were crossing racial lines. Yet I had no one to talk with about this, nor any language to describe it, even to myself. Since I was so desperate to deny my racial identity, I never sought to break out of this zone of silence, to become more conscious of how race or ethnicity affected my life and my desires.

Instead, I pressed harder to prove my uniqueness, my difference from other Asian Americans. I wanted to star in football and basketball, wanted to make it in the glamour sports, not in fencing or golf, where the few Asian American athletes played. Rather than dress like a science geek nerd, I was one of the first jocks to sport bell-bottoms, trying deftly to stride the line between a manly All-American athleticism and the incipient sixties Aquarian sensibility (my father did put the kibosh on moccasins—"No son of mine is going to look like a hippie"—he'd worked too hard becoming part of Middle America to have me throw it all away). I ran for student council, class president, and though I was always defeated, I refused to sink back into the anonymity that characterized the handful of Asian Americans at my school. As in my pursuit of athletics, where I only managed to make the varsity basketball team as a third stringer, my reach always exceeded my grasp. Of course, I would go on to the Ivy League, and then an Ivy League law school, and by Ivy League, I meant Harvard, Yale, or Princeton.

From the start, there was something overblown in my ego and my attraction to status, to placing myself ahead of the pack, a striving and an overstriving that was bound for a fall. Perhaps this is what my mother meant in her frequent comment to me during adolescence: "David, you think too much of yourself." Perhaps she wanted to protect me from the hubris that seemed inexorably tied to my own upwardly mobile strivings.

LOOKING BACK, I can see how off-putting my overly zealous ambition and opinion of myself must have been to others. Freshman year, I bragged to people that I was going to hit .750 next year in Pony League, told everyone I was going to make the A team in basketball. "No way," said Bob Hernstein and the group of guys from Lincolnwood. I was just blowing smoke.

Of course, I accomplished neither of these two goals, but neither Hernstein's chastising nor my failures stopped me. In English, I let my teacher promptly know that although this was a regular class, I was definitely advancing to the honors track next year. I needed all honors if I was going to get into Yale or Harvard. After all, I was already in honors math, science, and social studies, and everyone knew English honors was the largest and easiest to get into. Secretly I could hardly believe that I wasn't already there.

"Honors?" said my teacher, Mrs. Campbell, peering over her cat's-eye glasses, which rested below a helmet head of hair. She had a vaguely military demeanor, and her sack dress hung loosely on her bony body. "Well, we'll see about that."

I didn't know then how soon this would become her battle cry. I got an inkling a few days later when she asked me to diagram a sentence on the board. She marched up to my sentence and promptly slashed a huge check next to "clearly," which I had labeled as an adjective.

"Honors?" she asked, raising her eyebrows in mock astonishment. The class laughed. I slunk back to my seat, red-faced, in mute fury, as she explained to the whole class that I had pretensions to honors English and we would all see whether I was really cut out for this promotion.

And so it went, whenever I missed a character's motivation, whenever I blew a question on a grammar quiz, whenever I misspelled a word on a paper, she'd hold up the paper, waving its red mark, and intone, "Honors?" The class responded with its expected laugh track.

I grew more and more sullen in class, tightening my demeanor to a silent grudge. In the years since, this has often been my way with authority figures, a position where I never challenge them in any open and large risk-taking way, but simply stew in resentment, letting my pouts and lack of verbal comment speak for themselves. Mrs. Campbell took my demeanor as an added challenge. She was going to break me, that was all there was to it.

She informed me if I ever hoped to get into honors English I should be doing extra-credit reading, and she assigned me James's *Portrait of a Lady*. I wasn't a prodigy in English, otherwise I would have been in honors in the first place, but even if I had been, James was hardly a suitable choice for a freshman in high school. With its sweeping English lawns and its clash between New World innocence and Old World decadence, with James's famed circumlocution and his prolix, august prose, the book baffled me. I kept plowing through it, reading words without sense. Halfway through the text, I realized it was divided into two volumes. I had a whole other volume to go. I promptly quit reading.

To make up for this, I substituted Joyce's *Portrait of the Artist as a Young Man* from my father's small selection of college books. This seemed to satisfy Mrs. Campbell, who remarked about Joyce's use of stream of consciousness and epiphanies. I had no idea what she was talking about. Unknown to her, the aesthetic yearnings of young Dedalus weren't what drew me to this classic. Stephen's intonings about the "smithy of his soul" and his chantings about forming the "uncreated conscience of his race" meant nothing to me. No, I was captivated by something baser—his visits to the prostitute, which I read over and over. (In this the courts were right; Joyce stirred at least *my* prurient interests.) And where the priest inflamed Stephen's con-science, picturing in his sermon the demon fires of hell, the endless, endless burning there, I quickly sped over the passage and hoped in-stead the young Irishman would soon return to the wayward streets of Dublin and the unnamed darling who called him a little rascal and in whose lips and body he found a "pressure, darker than the swoon of sin, softer than sound or odour."

I thought I was putting one over on Mrs. Campbell, that my outside reading would placate her. For a brief while, it worked. But I soon made one of my occasional mistakes, she countered with her mocking "Honors," and I reverted to my basic pouting demeanor.

Finally, she became so disgusted that she sent home an interim failing notice, which said that although I was getting an academic A in the class, my attitude was one of sullen disrespect. When she showed me the notice, her face sported a look of gravity and triumph. "You've left me no choice," she said. I started a few words of protest, but she would have none of it. She was going to send it to my parents. I stood there for a moment and stared at her. I was outraged, and yet enervated by fear of how my father would respond. For a brief second something bubbled up inside me, some rage, some feeling akin to hate, but that was quickly stifled by my renewed knowledge of the power she held over me. I slunk out of the room, and for the next couple of days worried myself sick.

"What's the meaning of this?" my father bellowed when he read the notice. Oh God, I thought, now I'm really in for it. I started talking fast, it was my only way out, yet as I started my defense, I felt I was entering some new aspect of my character, some guile I had never exercised before, even though what I said was mainly the truth. I explained to him what was going on with Mrs. Campbell, how she had resented my ambitions for honors English, that I was already doing extra-credit work, and I pointed out that academically I was getting an A in the class. Mrs. Campbell had it in for me, I didn't know why. She just liked to pick on me.

"Okay," said my father, relenting. He too wanted me to get into honors, and so he simply told me that I should try to behave. He did not explode into one of those towering rages that he'd let loose over my failures in deportment during grade school. I felt in some small way I'd gotten the best of Mrs. Campbell.

Still, none of this taught me the lesson it could have. Had my ambitions and my ego been less, I might have suffered less disappointment, engendered less resentment from authority figures, and melded in a bit better. Instead, I was, from the very beginning, ripe for *ressentiment* and fantasy, for a furious and often useless fight against the realities around me. I was an upstart, and no one, really, likes an upstart, including perhaps the upstart himself.

DESPITE MY ESCAPE in the Campbell affair, there were, my father thought, things wrong with me. I was, as anyone could see, lazy. He had to get on me constantly about mowing the lawn, about properly driving the mower both horizontally and vertically, not just one way, about properly edging all the sidewalk, all along the bushes and the side of our house, even the corner hidden by bushes.

"But no one can even see there," I protested.

"That doesn't matter," he said. "A job's not worth doing unless it's worth doing right." (I did not possess either the temerity or the wit to reply, "You're right. It's just not worth doing.") Whether making a soapbox-derby car or gluing a model airplane, I didn't take my time. I wasn't neat enough. I didn't follow directions. I didn't understand how hard you have to work to get ahead in this world. "I knew a lot of guys like you at INS. They thought they could get by doing a half-baked job. Not like my old boss, Joe Stetler. Now there's a man who knew the meaning of work."

It wasn't just with school. When he went to my freshman football games, he could see clearly I was slacking. "You missed that tackle on the end around. He was right there in front of you, and you just flopped down. You're never going to make varsity like that. Look at that kid Becker, there's a kid who can tackle. Your coach told me he busted some guy's rib last game." Becker seemed like an animal to me; he had this power, this killer instinct, I couldn't hope to possess. It was mysterious to me, this power, how some had it and some didn't. I simply didn't, I had no guts or gumption. So I bowed my head and listened to my father's litanies.

The trouble with you, David, is you think the world owes you a living. The trouble with you is you don't hold your head up; your coach says so too. The trouble with you is you don't think about what you're doing. The trouble with you is you think you're so smart. The trouble with you is you think it's okay to get a B.

In all fairness to my father, much of what he had to say about me was true. All, that is, except for the grades. I never wanted to get a B. Ever. Every B seemed like a small death to me. That was why I wanted to get into honors English, that was why Mrs. Campbell's blockade looms so large in my memory—not because I see her as an obstacle in my own artistic *Bildungsroman*. No, I was mad at her because if I got a B in honors English, it was 4 points, the equivalent of an A in regular English; an A would be 5 points and boost me one notch higher in my class. Maniacal in my obsession, I pursued my grades the way Becker pounced on his hapless prey on the football field. What kept me back were other troubles, those I hid more effectively, ones my father never really felt comfortable speaking of. I wanted to be a good son, I wanted to listen to his admonitions with an open heart, I wanted to honor my hardworking, go-get-'em All-American father. But even as he lectured me, his voice fell on the same silent, sullen resentment as Mrs. Campbell's voice. I could not hear him. I was listening to other voices, emanating from deep inside my own wayward being.

IN CONTRAST to my extroverted-wise-guy act, a second self starts to appear: the loner, someone drifting away from the hubbub of the crowd, alluding vaguely to a wider world, attuned to a quieter, more meditative mode. I possessed neither the sophistication nor the reading to develop this into anything like a conscious sophomoric imitation of romanticism. I seemed instead to stumble into this second self partly because of an obsession with basketball. Whenever I wasn't alone studying, I spent hours alone on the courts practicing my jump shot. The fact that I'm short—five-nine—with a vertical leap of a rock and the speed of a sumo wrestler didn't deter me.

On weekends during the school year, days and nights during the summer, I pound the ball on the asphalt, practicing moves, juking and spinning, letting fly long jumpers from the corner, at the top of the key, counting off the seconds before the buzzer—*five, four, three, two* . . . —rippling the nets with the winning basket. I'm obsessive in my practicing as with my studying or my sexual fantasies, I don't let up. No one else spends the time I do on the court, no one practices like me. All I need is for the coach to give me a chance . . . I know I won't do this forever, I'll only be a kid once, and I don't need some scholarship to get me out of the ghetto; I'm far from that good. But I love the solitude of shooting and dribbling alone on the court. I enter some deeper part of myself, where my mind empties and fills with dreams, with the immediacy of the ball against my fingertips.

On trips with the basketball teams on Saturday mornings, the freshmen and sophomores watch the junior varsity play their game after ours is finished. I don't sit with everyone else in the stands, though. I take long walks through the fields at the edge of the various high schools we visit. The schools are in the far northwest of Chicago, suburbs just filling, converted farmland. One late winter morning, as I tramp out after the game, the sun shimmers off the loping landscape; there's a rural feeling to the area, rows of blond corn stubble bristling up in fields of snow, a stand of cottonwoods on a hill. Strings of smoke curl from the smokestacks of the high school. As I cross into the next field, I find a magazine in a ditch. What I see startles, scares me. The pictures are of boys and men naked together, cavorting and caressing in a cabin, on the sand, in the woods. There's some loneliness emanating from the photos that I respond to, some sense of sexuality I don't quite get.

I look at the photos for several moments, then toss them back in the ditch.

In my other hand, as always, I'm carrying a copy of *U.S. News & World Report,* which I always read on the bus. It's a badge of my seriousness. I don't really understand much of what I'm reading, analyses of the arms race, the first troop movements into Vietnam, the War on Poverty. I know I'm going to become a lawyer and do poverty law, defending those who are indigent and have no means to defend themselves. I know no one who is indigent, of course, nor anyone who's ever had even the least brush with the law. My images are formed from Perry Mason or Gregory Peck in *To Kill a Mockingbird.* As I head back toward the buses, I open the magazine to an article on Martin

Luther King, Jr. He seems to me noble and long-suffering, my image of a Negro, someone to be pitied and supported. I have no idea what segregation is like; my images of the South come only from movies. I walk into the gym reading the article. Bob Hernstein looks up.

"What's that?"

"*U.S. News & World Report.*"

"You read that?"

"Yeah. So what?"

"Boy, you *are* weird."

OFTEN AT EVENING, after basketball practice, at fifteen, sixteen, seventeen, I see myself hunched over my desk. I am supposed to be studying. Instead, as the harsh white fluorescent light bleeds up through the page in the newspaper, then through a page of notebook paper, I trace the lines of bodies modeling dresses from Saks, lingerie from Marshall Field's. Or, in a sad farce of desire, the images are Betty and Veronica from the *Archie* comic books. I brush in the sexual details, feel my body accelerating to the moment when the picture is complete, when I will absorb these lines—how impossible, how strange, these are merely lines—and find a pleasure, a solace, a compulsion I will cling to all my life. Whenever I am alone. I should be studying, I know, but this, this must come first. Then I will study some more. Then I will do this again. I cannot take time to play, I must study. Only these breaks I cannot help, I cannot hold back.

I am constantly scouring for new sources of fantasy. Certain books in the public library provide a few passages, which seem to be everywhere once I start to search. Once a month, in an office over Sun Drugs, I bicycle to see my orthodontist, who was, thankfully, saving me from the fate of buckteeth. One afternoon after my appointment, in a book carousel in the drugstore, I immediately spot a cover with a stripper wearing only a pink boa. With her heavy blue eye shadow and bouffant blond hair, she looks like Dusty Springfield, the rock singer, caressing the edge of a sparkling curtain.

Something starts coursing through me, a rush of adrenaline. Should I buy this? Can I? This is the real thing, not just a passage or two in Joyce or in the political novels at the library. I don't think of swiping it, something in me is still tied to an image of myself as a good boy, one who doesn't do such things. I don't think about the contradiction in my thinking. In an instant, I'm edging up to the counter, my head slightly bowed, offering the book up to the cashier. The old man stares for a moment at the book, then at me, then turns to the cash register and rings it up. I let out a breath. I'm going to be able to do it. I ride home with the book slipped beneath my jacket, breeze in, and rush past my mother in the kitchen.

"How was the orthodontist?"

"Oh, fine."

"Do you want some milk and cookies."

"No, I'm not hungry." What cool deception I am capable of, what cunning, like a master spy. I leap up the stairs to my room, lock the door, and stow the book in the briefcase in my closet, where I keep the drawings. Another treasure for my stash.

That night I pore through the book, reaching a passage where a man is tied to a chair, held prisoner by thugs. He begins talking to the woman who is to watch him, the talk sexual and slow, filled with the clichés of pornography, which aren't clichés to me because I want to believe them, because I'm sixteen and have no knowledge of the world. The man discovers the woman is getting aroused, that her compulsion is to hear a man talk about sex, and as she unties one arm to let him touch her, he knows he will be able not only to escape but to have her, over and over.

I hear someone, my father, hunkering up the stairs. My body tenses. Though the door's locked, I shove the book back in my desk and pretend to pore over my algebra. My father goes back downstairs.

I retrieve the book, stare again at the cover, the blond stripper in her boa.

Over and over through night after night, all through adolescence, I will repeat these actions. I will try to hide the wads of Kleenex by stuffing them deep in my garbage, by stealing quickly across the hall and flushing them down the toilet. At the end of the night I will say to myself I have studied all night. And will almost manage to believe that lie. I will stroke myself to sleep, and clutching a wad of Kleenex, doze off. When I wake in the morning, I will begin again.

MY PSYCHE at that time was becoming mired in contradiction. While I was constantly fantasizing about sex, I also carried a certain priggishness derived from Christianity—we went regularly to an Episcopalian church—and from the zone of silence about sex at home. I accepted the division of sluts and good girls, the concept of the virgin as the ideal. There was something conservative in my attention to rules, to doing the right thing. I believed in the general social order; I wanted to be a part of it; I wanted to believe it would accommodate me.

Years later, studying *Measure for Measure*, I sensed similar contradictions in the character of Angelo, a puritan who polices a city that's become a cesspool of sexual corruption, adrift in the dreams of Venus. Isabella, who is about to enter a nunnery, comes to him to plead for her brother, who has been sentenced to death for crimes of lust. In the turning point of the play, Angelo is, in an instant, stricken with his own lust for Isabella, and, as Ted Hughes puts it, Angelo's "brittle puritan mask is split—and another being emerges." From a driven enforcer of morals Angelo transforms into a sexual demon, a lust-crazed tyrant, someone whose desire is spurred in part by a need to defile Isabella's purity. Behind her mask of physical beauty he craves to see a demon to counter his own, and he is driven to create that demon in her, to destroy what he sees as her pretense of innocence.

Out of his own frigidity arises a boiling, deranged energy he cannot control, which mocks the very thing which before he had worshipped. In his mind there is no possible combination of lust and love, sexuality and purity, only the fatal turn from one pole to the other. Eventually, in his attempt to realize his lustful vision, Angelo instigates his own downfall.

In many ways, after several years, my story eventually resembles that of Angelo as a puritanical man of color, shaping the eruption of the demon through a desire that equates beauty with whiteness.

All along, my secret sexual life was played out against an outward high school life of apparent normality. In my parents' eyes, in the eyes of our relatives, I was getting A's in school, I was in honors and advanced-placement classes. I lettered in basketball, played football until my junior year, played baritone in the band, was in the chorus of *Guys and Dolls*. The fact that I didn't mention girls or dating would hardly have been great cause for alarm.

The area I lived in was about seventy-five percent Jewish, and this certainly affected my romantic prospects. Still, I didn't think my Jewish suburban surroundings incongruous for a Japanese American. To me, it seemed perfectly natural that nearly three-quarters of the students would be absent on Jewish holidays, that in junior high talk about bar mitzvahs and bas mitzvahs was de rigueur. I never thought much about the fact that I was never invited to one. I took it as another sign of my social marginality.

In high school, we studied the Holocaust and read Elie Wiesel and Anne Frank. My friend Jerry Horn talked about his parents' miraculous escape from the Nazis, their plane lifting off just as the SS guards drove up, shooting after them. Both of Jerry's parents spoke with an accent. To Jerry and me, they seemed a bit quaint and, at the same time, heroic, almost mythical. I knew more about their past than that of my parents. I knew more Yiddish than Japanese. My favorite book was Philip Roth's *Goodbye, Columbus*. I identified with Neil Klugman, the Newark Jew dazzled by Brenda Patimkin and her suburban Short Hills Jewish aura. I instinctively understood his status as an outsider in her world, his contempt for the materialism of her family and his attraction, all the same, to her status as a Radcliffe coed and a member of the country-club set. I imagined myself as Neil and Gail Mandel, Bob Hernstein's girlfriend, as Brenda, the two of us swimming naked late at night in the country-club pool or making love in the basement rec room with a refrigerator full of fruit, a cornucopia of plenty, humming beside us.

Of course, Neil was Jewish and I was not, and this created problems for me he didn't have. The Jewish girls in my school weren't allowed to go out with goyim, and if some of the girls tried and did pass off goyim like Tom Kristoff and Paul Sortal as Jews, they could hardly do that with me. I could have dated a non-Jew, and did indeed date a couple of non-Jewish girls, one from my church and one from school (my dad relaxed his age limit of seventeen to sixteen). But the goyim were so few at my school, and it was the Jewish girls who occupied my consciousness, my strivings. Most of the classes I was in were honors classes and were dominated by the Jewish students, as was the school paper, the yearbook, the drama department, indeed all aspects of the school save for sports, where a few goyim made their mark.

Each time a Jewish girl informed me she couldn't date me because I wasn't Jewish, I felt bewildered and forlorn. At times I also felt outraged, but I didn't quite know where to direct my rage. Were the unseen parents to blame or the girls who went along with their parents? I didn't see these rejections as racially based, but more as a group provincialism I couldn't understand. Sometimes, I suspected the girls were using religion as an excuse, but this hardly made me feel any better.

Perhaps the real reason for their rejections was my own peculiarity. I tended to do things like call a girl up and try to impress her by talking about the threat of nuclear war or civil rights. "A mere slip of a finger might end civilization as we know it . . ." "What this means in terms of the Constitution or the Fourteenth Amendment . . ." Though this elicited such remarks as Julie Kreiter's "Gosh, you are deep," it hardly made them feel I'd be a fun date. How much of my approach was ingenious self-destruction, how much simply nervousness, and how much my own irrepressible nature, I'm still not certain.

IT'S DIFFICULT for me to know how to view that young man, so troubled, so lacking in perspective or a sense of history. In the *18th Brumaire*, Marx wrote that history occurs first as tragedy and then repeats itself as farce. To move from the Japanese American internment camps to the sexuality of one Japanese American boy in a suburb of Chicago—even I can look at this as a movement from tragedy to farce. A large-scale, community-wide anguish and humiliation is replaced by an adolescent's discomfort and awkwardness, not very different from any other American boy's coming to terms with sexuality, whatever his color. My grandparents worked to eke out a living against Alien Exclusion Laws, which forbade them to own land or become citizens, against openly hostile whites who saw them as competing for jobs and land that rightly belonged to "real" Americans; my parents grew up in the shadow of the internment camps and wartime hysteria and worked themselves toward an upper-middle-class life of a top executive; and their son writes poems of his Issei grandfather and the internment camps and how he couldn't get a date in high school on Saturday night.

A Nisei Father

"A viper is nonetheless a viper wherever the egg is hatched. A leopard's spots are the same and its disposition is the same wherever it is whelped. So a Japanese-American, born of Japanese parents, nurtured upon Japanese traditions, living in a transplanted Japanese atmosphere and thoroughly inoculated with Japanese thoughts, Japanese ideas and Japanese ideals, notwithstanding his nominal brand of accidental citizenship, almost inevitably and with the rarest of exceptions grows up to be a Japanese, not an American in his thoughts, in his ideas, and in his ideals, and himself is a potential and menacing, if not an actual, danger to our country unless properly supervised, controlled and, as it were, hamstrung."

—EDITORIAL,
LOS ANGELES TIMES, 1942

1.

HAVE THEY EVER CHANGED, those American carnivals? The merry-go-round and Ferris wheel, the spinning cars that whirl the world around in a blur, swirling colors and lights, the speed and power and nausea, the joy of adrenaline pumping and the hurtling that is America in this century. And then the barkers, in T-shirts, suspenders, and oiled mustaches, in straw hats, a cane in their hands, tapping the counter like judges rapping the court to order, and behind them all the stuffed and furry creatures of the imagination, teddy bears and tigers, penguins and doe-eyed puppies, pigs and elephants, and the glittering trinkets, watch chains and cigarette boxes, cheap rings, necklaces, and bracelets, growing brighter in the lights and shouts of the barker, the come show your manhood and try your luck, the need for attention, the crowd's murmur or a girl's arm.

Of course, it's all hokum, but at thirteen, what do you know? If you're my father in 1939, you know you're tired of working in your father's nursery, you know the names and batting averages of all the Yankees, you know you're part of a gang of boys who call themselves the Jap Town Pirates, and you know you're all going down to the dock, because the carnival has come and for once in your life you've stashed in your pocket not just two bits but several dollars.

And so my father bolted down his *udon*, slurping the noodles, splashing the front of his T-shirt, so that his mother yelled at him, not for slurping, which the Japanese allow, but for making more wash for her. With four children and a shady, gambling husband, she was busy enough. Before she could say another word, my father fled from the house, perhaps telling her he was going to Mas Nagata's house, perhaps saying nothing. His words were becoming fewer and fewer, and more and more in English. His mother shook her head and said nothing. She knew it was already too late.

Evening in L.A., the light on the street was flat and golden, taking off the distance. Tiny stucco houses, neat lawns, each garlanded by small rows of bushes, tiny plots of flowers. At the corner, near the Packard, Mas was waiting, with Ted, Ichiro, and Kenji. They started off to the ocean, stopping only at Matsui's Drugs to get some gum.

When the sparkling Ferris wheel reared up above the dock, they quickened their pace, and by the time they reached the boardwalk, they were running. All of them wanted to go on the Ferris wheel first, and though my father was a bit nervous about the circling, he didn't get sick. Still he knew enough to beg off on the whirling cars. Instead, he tried his luck at the baseball toss, winning, after three tries, an ugly stuffed teddy bear, which the others mocked. Later, they ate popcorn, cotton candy, drank lemonade and snow cones, and listened to Ted demonstrate his symphony of belches. Then the lights began to go out, one by one along the midway, and the night suddenly became a few degrees cooler, the air quieter with the thinning crowd.

"Hey, why don't we hang out on the docks and watch the fishermen go out," said Ted.

"Are you crazy?" said Ichiro. "It's late enough already. My mother would kill me."

"So you're chicken?" Ted replied.

"Who you calling chicken?"

"You, that's who. Little mama's boy, you can't do anything without your mother."

"Bakayaro."

They were suddenly together, Ichiro and Ted, wrestling with each other, not really hitting, as if that were too scary, but trying to pull each other to the ground, both of them grunting and cursing, and you could hear the harsh rip of a shirt tearing. My father had taken judo classes, and managed to separate them only by throwing Ted over his hip, and Ted landed with a thud on the ground. He lay there gasping, the wind knocked out of him.

"I'm sorry, Ted," said my father. "Are you okay?"

At first, Ted was too dazed to answer, but as he caught his breath, he began calling my father an idiot, which only made my father feel more guilty. Ichiro and Mas stomped off, not wanting any more trouble. They'd had enough of Ted. Finally, my father placated Ted by saying that he'd stay out with him.

My father understood Ted the way the others didn't; he felt in some ways they were probably alike. They both had problems with their father, though Ted's was far worse. Mr. Ueda not only hit the kids, he sometimes hit his wife, and for days on end, he'd roar through the house on sake binges, disappearing only when he got the urge to gamble. Often, Ted's mother would bring the whole family and sit them on the curb outside the house where their father was gambling and one by one send the children in to call on their father. It never worked. Finally Ted got too old for that; he began staying out late at night too, just like his father. Recently his father had taken to not just leaving for the night but traveling north, using the excuse that he could find work in the logging camps. He never sent money back.

Later, to the hum of the engines and the slap of the nets, the fishing boats pushed from the dock and chugged off to sea. Gulls hovered above them in the first glints of light. My father and Ted stared at the foamy wake and talked about their parents.

"Was your mother a picture bride?" asked Ted, still chewing his gum from the night before.

"No. My father went back to Japan to find a wife. It was all arranged, but they knew each other. They're from the same town."

"Yeah. Well, my mother was a picture bride. She didn't know what she was getting into. And you know it's not because my father's ugly. Jeez, half the problem is he's more beautiful than her. He thinks he ought to be with some aristocrat or movie star, some geisha."

"Your mother's not bad."

"No? She's so scrawny and tired, she can't fight my father back. *Shō ga nai*, the good Japanese wife."

"It'll get better. We've all got it tough. Wait till high school. Things will be different then."

"Oh yeah? How?"

My father looks down at the iridescent swirls left by the gas engines, and the rocking motion of the tide slapping against the docks. He's tired, and though his body refuses to give in to sleep, he's feeling the waning of nervous energy that comes with watching for the dawn, staying up all night for the first time. It's as if he expected something miraculous to happen, some revelation about what it's like to be grown up.

Or perhaps he just thought that the mystery of the fishermen, whom he'd only seen coming in later in the day, bearing on their decks the flapping, silvery flesh of the sea, well, that the fishermen must start the day more mysteriously, setting into the darkness with some ancient ritual, some secret technique, to loosen from the arms of the sea all she could give. Instead, he had just seen the men, quiet and groggy, their cigarettes glowing in the blue light, puttering about their boats, gathering the nets, tinkering with their engines, their matter-of-fact faces reflecting another matter-of-fact day, a day of work.

Just as he is about to tell Ted he has to get going home, my father sees a familiar figure striding down the dock. His body shivers.

IF MY FATHER'S ARM HURT from being yanked from the docks to their Packard, it was nothing to what he felt once my grandfather got him home. Of course, my father knew he shouldn't have stayed out all night, knew he should have told my grandmother where he was going, and he couldn't help but wonder how my grandfather had found out where he was, and each yank on his arm raised not only the level of fear but also the level of suspicion that it must have been either Mas or Ichiro who gave him away, and whoever it was he was going to get them back. But as my grandfather threw him through the gate into the yard and the boy tripped and sprawled on the grass, Mas and Ichiro were far from my father's thoughts. All he wanted to be was anyplace but where he was, staring into my grandfather's enraged face.

There was such a fury in what happened next, such a bursting forth of frustrations that lay deeper than a son who stayed out all night. My father kept scrambling and scrambling around the yard, hoping not so much to escape as to soften the blows; it was almost impersonal, the way the two-by-four came down again and again on my father's buttocks and back, and though most of the blows glanced off, some hit their mark solid, a dull, wooden sound, as if striking a sack of wheat, but the cries of the boy kept letting on that this was flesh, this was pain, this was fear. Whether his father was drunk or not, my father could never tell, just as he could never tell the story of this night without a slight smile, years later, as if it were all settled in the past, the wounds healed, justice served, the lesson necessary and completed long ago.

1944. My father, at eighteen, has just left the Jerome, Arkansas, camp and is on a train bound for Chicago. As the train leaves the cotton fields of the South, the ridges and hills begin to disappear. The trees change from cottonwood to oak and maple, and the land flattens to miles of corn and wheat; the summer heat loosens its steaming grip, coming into the autumn of the North. My father peers through the window with astonishment and anxiety. Despite his newfound freedom, the camps have been a womb, the faces around him familiar, no threat of difference. He thinks of how far he's traveled from the sun-flattened streets of L.A., how far away he is from the Uyemura nursery, the Watanabe market, Morita's Chop Suey, the streets where dancers and kimonos and drums would parade on holidays.

The train will stop first in Chicago, the home of Al Capone, the Purple Gang, the Valentine's Day Massacre. But it is not the gangsters my father is worried about. Even when he turns from the window, he has only to look around him: What are those white faces thinking? Are they wondering why he is out of the camps? Has their son or brother or father been killed by the Japs? Were they right now trying to hold back a murderous rage or preparing to begin shouting, "He's a Jap, he's a spy, he's one of those that killed my cousin." The old man in a porkpie hat across the way, smoking a cigar, appears intent on his paper. Or is he? And that young mother, in back of him, peeling an orange for her son, is her husband somewhere on an atoll in the Pacific? Is she saying something to the boy about the Japanese? When he passes her on the way to the dining car, she doesn't look up. Is that a sign of hatred or indifference?

In the dining car, he sits alone at a table; the colored waiter is polite, though all my father orders is coffee. My father lights a cigarette, lets out a drag. He's being paranoid, he says to himself. After all, he's just as American as anyone else. They have other things to worry about, there's a war going on. He looks at his face in the glass, the fields of stubbled cornstalks shuttling by in the dark. His face looks lonelier than I have ever seen it. The train rolls on.

Two hundred miles away, in the barracks in Jerome, his mother stares up at the ceiling, as his father snores beside her. She is waiting for sleep to descend, her dreams to begin. The moon spills on the floorboards, mice scurry in the shadows. She closes her eyes and begins speaking to Buddha, to the gods of dharma. Her breath makes little clouds in the dark. She says a prayer for her American son.

• • •

IN THE MONTHS after he left camp, my father lived in Darien, Connecticut, working as a handyman in a house where his sister Ruth also worked. He mowed the lawn, painted, bought groceries, trimmed the shrubbery and planted the garden, mended broken shutters or leaky faucets, cleaned. It took him a while to adjust to his new surroundings. The smell of the Atlantic seemed stronger than the Pacific. The scent from Long Island Sound blew across the rose bushes, the long, meticulous lawn that sloped imperceptibly toward the sea and stopped at a stone wall.

I picture him there in summer, the heat drawing globes of sweat from his brow as he pushed the mower back and forth. There was no longer a reason to mutter curses at my grandfather, who had made him mow lawns for the family business in Beverly Hills and Hollywood. My grandparents were still in camp, and my father and Ruth and Ken were free, gone to seek their way in the world. Ruth was commuting to NYU; Ken was at Miami of Ohio.

As for my father, he didn't know what he wanted to do. All he knew was he wasn't going to mow lawns for the rest of his life. You could bet on that.

He paused for a second, wiping his brow. His muscles were taut and strong, his skin a dark brown, his face a bit cocky, like a young prizefighter. He looked back at the house, with its gables and balconies, the waist-high windows where gauze curtains fluttered. The architecture seemed to him French, though he didn't know why. His boss, Mr. Mackey, and his wife were eating breakfast on the veranda. She wore sunglasses, a white sunbonnet. Mr. Mackey was reading *The Wall Street Journal*. He was an heir to a pineapple and sugar plantation in Hawaii. Every morning he'd read the paper to find out how much money he'd made. Or lost. Usually, though, he won. The Japanese Americans in Hawaii hadn't been put into camps, they could work in the fields, and even when the Nisei boys began to enter the service, there were still their wives, mothers, and fathers, as well as the Filipinos and Chinese. It was safer, though, here in Connecticut. And Mrs. Mackey preferred the mainland, the nightlife of New York. She never wanted to be stuck back in the islands again, she once told Ruth. "You can't believe how provincial it is out there."

My father often wondered if Hawaii was the reason Mr. Mackey hired Ruth, and then Ken, and then, when Ken left, himself. Perhaps Mackey was used to Japanese American servants, he knew their worth, their hardworking ways. Not everyone was willing to hire a young Japanese American. After all, there was a war on, and American boys were getting killed by Japs out in the Pacific.

So far, though, things had been smooth. There was always work for my father, the Mackey's estate was so huge. But mowing the lawn, how he hated mowing the lawn. As he pushed the mower nearer and nearer the seawall, he could feel the calluses start to burn on his hands, the wood begin to scrape a bit against his palms. He wondered whether he could take off his shirt. Would the Mackeys mind? He looked back up at the veranda. They had gone. Only a pitcher of orange juice and a bottle of vodka remained.

He took off his shirt. Brushed back his hair and gripped the mower again.

As I watch this young servant boy, my father, I'm suddenly struck by how his body reminds me of William Holden's when he takes off his shirt to do some chores for Kim Novak's mother in *Picnic*. It is a body that would make a woman whistle if women whistled. A body like William Holden's. No wonder my mother fell for him.

"DID YOU SEE what the Yanks did yesterday?" my father says.

It's early morning. Ruth and my father are in the kitchen. She's squeezing oranges, twisting the rinds. The kitchen is spotless and large as a living room. The sea out the window is blue slate, picking up the first glimmers of light.

"How did DiMaggio do?"

"Don't you know anything? DiMaggio's in Europe, fighting the Jerries."

"Of course I know. I just like to get your goat."

Ruth is glad he's here. They get along better than she and Ken, who's too dreamy, too delicate, a bit of a prig. Ken's always been that way, even when they were little. He was a mama's boy. She takes after her father, Ruth supposes, though she's not like either of them, really. She's too American, too outspoken, too boyish. Ken's going to be an artist, he's known that since he was ten. She doesn't know what she wants to be. And Tom, all Tom wants to do is have a good time.

"I'm thinking of going to Florida next month."

"What? And quit this job?"

"It's not as if I plan to mow lawns all my life."

"Well, what are you going to live on?"

"I don't know. I'll find something."

"Why Florida? You don't know anyone there."

"I'll write Mark Hohri. He'll go with me. He just got out of camp a couple of months ago and he's living in Kalamazoo."

"Like the song?"

"Like the song."

"I don't like it."

"What? The song?"

"No, your going to Florida. You don't have a plan, you don't know if you'll have a job. At least here you have a roof, three square meals, and some pay at the end of the week. And besides, Mom and Dad are going to get out of camp sometime. Who do you think is going to take care of them?"

"They can take care of themselves. They always have."

"That was before. Dad doesn't have a business now. And they're getting old. It's going to be tough for them to start all over."

"Well, who knows when they'll get out? I'll deal with that when it happens. I want to go to Florida, and you or anyone else can't tell me what to do."

"*Baka.*"

"What?"

"Nothing. Why don't you just get out to the garage and start painting? It's going to rain this afternoon."

"*Monku, monku, monku,*" chants my father as he goes out the door.

Ruth pours the juice in the pitcher, puts it in the refrigerator. She's got to hurry if she's going to make the train and get to her class on Shakespeare in the city. She worries about Tom. He's so young, and he thinks he knows it all. She needs to reread the last act of *Henry V* on the train. She thinks of Falstaff, his portly pursuit of drink, laughter, and other pleasures, of the profligacy of the young Hal. Oh well, she thinks, perhaps Tom will grow up sometime.

WHEN THEY WERE YOUNGER, Ruth and Tom would play catch in the front yard in the L.A. twilight, the ball spinning through the odors of eucalyptus and the dancing moths, barely lit by the porch light. Ken would be inside with their mother. In an old chair on the porch, their father sat playing his *biwa*, his voice quavering, singing out the tales of the Heike, feudal battles and tragedies centuries old. The smell of his cigar hung in the air. Day and night he'd be there, often when he should have been working at his lawn service, manicuring the lawns and gardens of movie stars, doctors, and lawyers.

Their mother, though, had given up complaining, just as she'd learned long ago there was nothing she could do about his games of *hana* and poker down in Little Tokyo or the smell of sake on his breath as he stumbled into their room and climbed into bed, still wearing his clothes. Instead, their mother had forced him to buy a greenhouse, which she ran with a Filipino worker and Ruth and Ken. Tom she left to her husband. Tom was coarser than Ken and couldn't speak Japanese nearly as well as Ruth. Tom lacked the meticulousness needed to care for the roses and delicate orchids of the greenhouse. He was better off mowing lawns, though she knew he hated the work and often complained to her husband. Still, it was better that her husband and Tom fought, rather than her husband and Ken. Tom could take it, he wouldn't ever cave in. Ken, on the other hand, might have been crushed by her husband. Ruth should have been a boy, she used to think, and Ken the girl, but by the time they had bought the greenhouse in the late thirties, she'd resigned herself to her children's characters as well as her husband's. As for my Aunt Ruby, she was just the baby of the family. She came too late to figure heavily in their internal dynamics.

My father didn't understand all this, didn't see this arranged division of the family. Ruth did. She accepted it matter-of-factly. It was more about the boys than her. What she cared about was getting away from the family, from the Japanese community. All the Japanese boys were shorter than she was and afraid of her intelligence, everyone gossiped too much, no one around them was interested in higher intellectual things. Even if the war and the camps had never come, she would have eventually gone away.

With my father it was different. He liked hanging out with the other Nisei boys, playing ball, chewing bubble gum, going to the beach. In camp, it was even better. He got more time to hang out with his friends. At dinnertime, they'd run from mess hall to mess hall gobbling up extra meals. They'd filch cigarettes and smoke them at the far side of the camp, near the *benjo*. He ended up class president of his high school class. Why would he want to leave all that?

So even though he was out of the camps, and away from any parental supervision, he felt adrift in Connecticut, working for the Mackeys. It wasn't like there were lots of people he could socialize with. There was a black maid, but she kept to herself. Ruth was about the only person he really talked to and she was his sister. At least she got to go into the city to NYU.

No, he thought. Ruth doesn't understand. She's got her own things to do. I have nothing. I'm going to write to Mark Hohri and his brother and Bill Omori, and see if we can't all go down to Florida. We can play poker anytime we want and lie out on the beach. Maybe we can go down to the Keys or even to Cuba. I'm not staying here.

FLASH FORWARD five decades. We're driving to the Disneyland Hyatt in Anaheim, where my father's fiftieth high school reunion is being held. I keep trying to steer my father's talk to the camps, but he seems to want to talk about his life after the camps. My mother, who didn't really want to come to the reunion, is asleep in the backseat, resting from our eighteen holes at a course in Malibu. Finally, I relent with my leading questions, and let my father talk about what he wants.

"Ruth and Ken got out of the camps first, and they were living in Darien, Connecticut. So when I got out of Heart Mountain . . ."

"Heart Mountain? I thought you were in Jerome."

"But they closed Jerome before the war ended, and people from Jerome were sent to all the other camps."

I suddenly realize how little time my father actually spent in the Jerome camp, whose existence for me has come to take on mythical proportions.

"Ruth was commuting to NYU and working for this rich family. She was a cook's helper and babysitter, Ken worked the yard and did chores, and then when Ken left, I worked there. I was corresponding with Mark Hohri, and I told him I was going to go down to Florida. And Mark said, 'Don't go down to Florida, you're crazy, you can't get anywhere without a college degree." You see, I wasn't very ambitious then. I didn't know whether I really wanted to go to college."

"So when did you get ambitious?"

"I guess after I got married, and you were born, and I thought: By golly, I'd better get my ass moving."

"There was this point about six months before Samantha was born," I tell him, "and I was talking to Susie and I was lying on the kitchen floor, and all I could hear in my brain was this chant: *Money, money, money, you've got to make more money.* I felt like I was lying there on this rack. That's why I got an MFA."

My father laughs, a moment of mutual recognition about fatherhood and what it means. There's also the irony of a son who's always protested his antimaterialism against parental pressures now lying on the floor and chanting about money.

Afterward I'm struck by how much my father's decision to go to college was due to happenstance, how little his younger self resembled the hard-driven go-getter of my childhood. Somehow his drive was tied to my birth, what I represented.

Of course, Samantha's birth represented similar things for me. Once she appeared, there was no question then about who was the child. It was actually quite freeing, there were all sorts of neuroses I suddenly let go, there wasn't time for them. I had to grow up.

All this makes my father seem less alien to me. I feel I understand a bit better who he was, what he's become.

MARK HOHRI, it turned out, was going to college in Kalamazoo, Michigan, where he'd ended up mainly by chance. He wanted to see the town that spawned "I've got a gal from Kalamazoo." He was going to college there, and he was rooming with a professor, a Mr. Bigelow. "Why don't you join me?" he wrote my father.

So, in August 1944, my father again travels across the country on a train. As he passes through Ohio, he recalls his trip out of the camps. He laughs at how nervous he was then, how frightened of the world.

Still, as the train nears Detroit, he feels his anxiety begin to rise.

He checks the letter again in his pocket. "Dear Mr. Uyemura: My family and I are looking forward to . . ." Good, it's still there; what would he do if he lost it? There couldn't be many Bigelows in Kalamazoo, he could look in the phone book. Or are there? Is it a common name? What nationality is it? The professor never said. But that didn't matter, what mattered was that he was good enough, kind enough, to offer my father a room in his house.

The Bigelows were wonderful. They took my father into their family, almost like a son, and my father never forgot their kindness. "They showed me the meaning of work," he would say. That house, Professor Bigelow, his wife and his daughters, were like nothing my father had come into contact with. In Kalamazoo, there was no old man, half plastered with sake, whining and strumming on the steps, no curses of *bakayaro*, no admonitions to get the *mimiaka*—the ear wax—out of your ears, no nights spent wondering where in town and in what bar his father might be, no panic when the bills came due, no empty refrigerator, no squabbles about money late into the night. In Kalamazoo, the house was filled with the smell of fresh baked bread, chocolate-chip cookies, pies, a roast on Sundays, with mashed potatoes and gravy. The only music came from the radio, strains of Mozart, Chopin, and Beethoven that my father found difficult and not altogether pleasing. But he also sensed, in those harmonious strings, a counterpoint to his parents, a culture they had no inkling of.

It dazzled and provoked him, that house of the Bigelows. It made him feel small and insecure and wonderfully high on the sensation that he was there, in the house of a man who lectured on Napoleon, on the French communes, the guillotine and revolution, on Voltaire and the Age of Enlightenment, a man who spoke not only French but Latin as well. My father felt grateful for the chance to wash the dishes, even to mow the lawn, to somehow pay this man back for the indescribable gift he had given him.

Of all the chores, he loved most raking the leaves, gathering them in great, multicolored piles, then lighting them in the backyard, the smoke spiraling with a freshness, a coolness, that was more than the contrast between the leaping flames and the crackling October air. It was a moment when everything seemed possible, the past forgettable, and the roars of the college stadium, the shouts and cheerleaders, the banners waving, echoed a promise that clung like the smell of smoke to his sweater, long after that autumn had passed.

Professor Bigelow understood that my father came from a different world. The professor had traveled to Europe, had always been conscious that the globe was larger than this small Michigan town. After all, the drive to know the larger world, to reach beyond the small Indiana town where he had been born, was part of what had made him so eager to know history, so eager to teach it to others. It wasn't just that old bromide about learning from history. The sense of the variety, the possibilities that history offered, captivated him. He was not intrigued enough, however, to leave the Midwest, to actually live elsewhere; there was nothing of the nomad or expatriate in him. But from his spectator's vantage, two hundred years away, he loved viewing vast tumultuous dramas, Napoleon's trek through the snows of Russia, Moscow smoldering, pouring its existence out in the smoky winter sky, or the point during the French Revolution when people began firing pistols at the clocks, killing off the old era. And he imparted this passion to his students and my father.

The professor knew little about Japan or Japanese culture, and he knew almost nothing about the camp from which my father had come, but that didn't seem to matter to my father. He never expected anyone to understand and so was never disappointed. Instead, he worked as hard as he could in the professor's class, both to show his gratitude and to show the professor he wouldn't think of taking advantage of their relationship at home. In certain ways Professor Bigelow was even tougher on my father than on the other students. Often he'd turn to my father when his questions were met with silence; my father came to expect this and prided himself on his answers. My father got his A and earned the professor's respect.

At dinner, the professor was less gruff, less demanding, though still retaining a certain stiffness in his manner. He wore a tie, and though he didn't require the four other students in his house to do so, the tie told them: you are adults here, you are expected to act like adults, no boardinghouse reach, elbows off the table, no shouting, or roughhousing (cursing, of course, was out of the question). Yet he also took a genuine interest in the boys, asking them about their studies in a way that was not too parental. He kidded them if he'd seen them walking with a girl, and told awful jokes—"What's red and white and black all over?" "Why did the chicken cross the road?" "Knock, knock. . . ." The boys and the family were permitted to groan, and my father found something else of this man's character he wanted to imitate.

Another teacher that year was Miss Benedict, an English professor. In her early thirties, with stunning red hair and sharp dresses, with a sensibility cut on the hard edge of modern poetry, she managed to impart a romantic air without turning poetry into slush, or losing either intellect or irony. Perhaps because she was a poet, a true poet, and more of the Louise Bogan school than of Edna St. Vincent Millay, Miss Benedict inspired my father in a way Professor Bigelow could not. (Then again, perhaps, it was because she was extremely pretty.) She took my father through his first Shakespeare. On a weekly quiz the students had to identify passages and analyze their part in the play. This required they read the plays several times, something most found nearly impossible to do. For my father, the plays were another hurdle, a doorway gleaned when Professor Bigelow went over his schedule and said, "Yes, you ought to take Shakespeare. A man can't consider himself educated if he doesn't know Shakespeare."

Late at night, in his room, as the winter wind whipped the panes, plastering them with frost, when the rest of the house was in bed, my father peered into a dim cone of light, marking the page with a red pencil (the marks are still there in the volume of Shakespeare I take to college years later). The ghost appears, rising from the depths of the stage, clanging its armor, and Hamlet scurries down the ramparts, maddened by a vision. This father of revenge, this chiding ghost: Does my father connect him at all with his father? Probably not, though perhaps he feels a certain ambivalence; after all, the play is partially about the loyalty to fathers, the son's inability to free himself from the father's grip, from the father's obsessions. My father puts the book down, goes to the window, looks down on the streetlight at the corner, the smooth pelt of snow layering the lawn. Nothing like this in L.A. Nor in Jerome. He returns to his task, trying to lose himself in the cadences and complexities of Elizabethan English, in the abstractions that muddle through his brain. He must memorize it by morning, he must know it by heart. "List, list, O, list!" the ghost intones. And Hamlet looks up, seized by wonder.

THE LETTERS from my father's parents that year described the making of a ghost town. Many of the Nisei who were old enough had left the camp; those that remained were mainly the old or the small children. Of course, the Issei who remained wanted to return to the past, to the way of life they had left before the war. But that was just a dream. Most Issei had had to sell their goods at a hard loss; most would never return to their businesses after the war, they had sunk too far, there was too little time left for one more great push to break the surface. Already in camp, some of the men took to drink, took on a distance in their eyes that said they might never come back.

My grandfather's letters would have been in the most rudimentary Japanese, so that my father could read them, perhaps using as few *kanji* as possible and relying on *hiragana*, the phonetic alphabet. Even then my father had trouble with them. Often he had to read between the lines. It did seem clear that his parents were not going to return to the West Coast. His father was too bitter, saw no evidence that the racial hatred would lessen after the war. No, said his father, let's go elsewhere, let's make a new start. Perhaps they would go out East where Ruth was. Or perhaps to Chicago, the place in the Midwest where the most Japanese were staying. There was, of course, no mention of going to Kalamazoo, and my father was thankful for that. He was just beginning to build a life here, what would he do if his aging Issei parents showed up, not a cent to their name, barely speaking English, knowing no one else but him? What kind of job could he find for his father? His mother? And how would he introduce them to the Bigelows? It wasn't exactly that he was ashamed of his parents, but that they didn't fit in here. He barely felt he fit in (though perhaps he was too frightened to admit this).

In the letters his father would mention various people, some of whom my father knew well, some of whom he didn't. "You remember Sone-san's girl, Kai-chan. Well, she's gone off to Chicago to become a dental assistant, and her brother, Michio, is going to college in Indiana. Nakamura-san's son, Tosh, the one that went into the Army, he's been wounded, but he's all right. In a way he and his family are lucky. He'll be coming home now. He won't be killed. I keep thinking about the poor Ogawa family. First they lost Frank, then Bill has just gone into the Army, though both his father and mother tried to keep him from going. I don't understand it myself. The mother is particularly bitter. She didn't want Frank to go. How can they do this to us, she asks, and points to the fences, how can they do this to our family, our sons? And I have no answer. Frank's wife, Sono, is planning to leave next week. She's got a teaching job in Chicago. It seems so many of us are going there. What kind of city do you think it will be for us to live in? Is it dangerous? . . ."

·   ·   ·

IN 1945, spring arrived with a quickness that felt part of rush toward victory, peace, and promise. All along the campus, buds exploded overnight, the leaves slipped out in the first warm breezes as if they'd always been there, hidden only by an illusion. There were tulips and azaleas in the Bigelows' garden, and my father, coming down the stairs one morning, suddenly realized that he'd lost that hunch that quivered over his back each time he stepped out of the house in winter. He'd stayed the distance, he was entering the seasons, becoming a Northerner. Whistling "Don't sit under the apple tree," he leapt down the stairs and headed for town.

He is a man with a purpose this day, he's going to buy his first book. He fingers the two dollar bills in his pocket, rubbing them as if for luck, feeling pleased with himself for the willpower it took to save up this money, going for a whole month without malts or Cokes. He doesn't know what he's going to buy, he wants it to be a surprise, a present to himself.

The bookstore is across from the movie theater, next to the drugstore. On the white lines of the marquee, my father sees Bill Owens changing the sign to "They Died with Their Boots On." I've got to see that one, my father thinks, who loves Errol Flynn's effortless style, the smoothness that moves as if whizzing bullets, slashing swords, charging horses, and kisses from beautiful women were no more difficult than turning the pages of a book. At the bookstore, my father saunters past the cashier, the section on history, the popular paperbacks, and finds himself staring up at the section marked "Literature." Shakespeare and Donne, Carlyle and Dickens, Austen, the Brontës, Homer and Sophocles. He glances past them, seeking something modern, less classic, more unusual. He picks up Hemingway's *The Sun Also Rises,* but the opening paragraph, gossip about boxing, fails to intrigue him. His eyes move a few books to the right, and he spies the Modern Library edition of *Dubliners.* Why he picks this book is hard to say; perhaps he's heard about *Ulysses,* the scandal it created. Perhaps Miss Benedict has talked about Joyce as the new genius of English prose, perhaps he has read a story, "Eveline" or "Araby," in an anthology and been captured by the spare, epiphanic stories. Surely the story "Araby" would have appealed to him, all about the young boy who waits anxiously for his guardian uncle to come home and then pleads to go to the bazaar, who finds, when he arrives, an irrepressible disappointment, a tawdriness which belies his dreams, and he sinks down in realization of his own fatuous innocence. For my father was an innocent then (and, in many ways, remains so).

But I am losing my story.

And what I am losing is how much this first book meant to my father, how long he hesitated before he finally brought it to the counter, how, when he laid down the money, he fought a certain feeling that perhaps no book was worth so much money, especially one he had not been assigned. What I am losing is how, when he finally had the book back in his hands, a smile broke out on his face and would not let go, and he had to fight off the urge to tell the clerk, a gaunt bald man in suspenders and horn-rimmed glasses, that this, this was the first book he had bought in his life. What I am losing is how, as he stepped out in the street, he noticed that a wind had come up, the sky had darkened, and halfway home, a storm burst out, so that he ran, cursing, tucking the book under his shirt, the half mile home, worrying what the drilling drops were doing to the pages of his book.

Up in his room, taking the book from under his shirt, he finds a water stain and hopes desperately it will disappear when dry. It doesn't. It is still there thirty-five years later when, telling me this story, he gives me the book.

PERHAPS the Bigelow my father was closest to was the youngest daughter, Ann. She was six when he arrived, ten when he left, and her youth made her less frightening, less forbidding than the other members of the family. With so little knowledge of the world, how could she realize the distance between her world and his? Perhaps because he was still unsure of the friends he made in class, my father paid more attention to her than the other students in the house. He was totally willing to get down on his knees and deal with her at a child's level, erasing the distance between them. He'd growl like an animal, chase her around the yard, chanting lines about the big bad lion, or the wolf that howls at night, waiting for Little Red Riding Hood. He made little clicks and whistles, a popping noise by swiping his index finger across the inner cheek of his mouth, the buzzing and whooing that comes when you blow into your cupped hands. It was like a magical orchestra, all the instruments in his body. At first it captivated her most just to see him make these sounds. She'd try to imitate and fail and that would just increase her wonder at his skills. He taught her how he made the sounds, and they would do duets together, sitting on the front steps. "Turkey in the Straw," "Buffalo Gals," "Won't You Come Home, Bill Bailey," "Harvest Moon"—they developed a whole repertoire.

Later they went on to games—hopscotch, jacks, catch, stickball, chutes and ladders, war, go fish; he even taught her scissors-paper-rock in the Japanese style, where, instead of one-two-three, you count "jan-ken-poi." Sometimes, running with her on the lawn, she'd jump up on him or in his lap, and throw her arms around him, in a show of physical affection that pleased and yet disconcerted him. After all, he had never been taught or allowed to act like that; physical touching was simply not done by the Japanese he knew. There was always this physical distance, which implied and reinforced a certain psychic distance, a sense that a person was allowed their privacy, their solitude, their island self.

And, perhaps, he was aware that, were she ten years older, she would hardly be acting this way with him. After all, the white girls in his classes, though polite, and sometimes even friendly, never gave him the sense that they were interested in him as anything more than an acquaintance or casual friend. With their neatly curled blond and brown hair, their plaid skirts, bobby socks, and saddle shoes, they strode in a world beyond him, on the arm of one of the frat boys, out of Johnston Hall, down fraternity row. They would go to the prom, to homecoming, to sock hops, wear corsages, fraternity pins, engagement rings, and all this he only knew of from magazines or books, the locker-room gossip. Of course, this distance, this unspoken segregation, engendered a certain bitterness on his part, but the bitterness frightened him, seemed an unwillingness to be thankful for all the chances he'd received, a gaping hole of anger that might pull him down. He couldn't afford to go near it; it needed to be kept at bay, far from consciousness.

Only now, spurred on by Miss Benedict, he was writing poems. They required of him to think about what he thought and felt, what others thought and felt, and this brought him close to feelings that were much too raw. It didn't help that he had a slight crush on Miss Benedict, and didn't know what to do about it. She had the advantage of being more mature, more cultured, than the girls in his class, whom he sometimes thought of as shallow and silly. He respected Miss Benedict's knowledge and skills. She had published poems in *The New Republic* and *The Nation,* the *Michigan Quarterly.* She'd even published a book of poems.

But he couldn't exactly write poems to her; to use her as his dark-haired lady of the sonnets would expose too much. Instead, in his newfound sense of being an American, he took up the themes of Whitman and Sandburg, the teeming mixture of races and tribes, the rough-hewn, tumbling spirit of the prairies, the electric charge of the cities, the hog-butchering fatness and freedom of America. He wanted his poems to be modern, to possess the energy of big-band jazz and

M-G-M movies, and in one of them, he pictured the various faces in a theater staring up at the screen, each reflecting the light in their own way, white, black, yellow, and brown. He wrote of the clink of glasses in lonely bars, the swooping rise of the saxophones, eight to the bar. All of this perhaps came out more clearly in his vision of the poems than in their actual execution, which seemed too tight and self-conscious, too influenced by the sound games of e. e. cummings, but my father sensed a freedom, an energy in this writing he had never felt before. It gave him a feeling of omnipotence, a sensitivity to the world that others lacked; he succumbed to that inarticulate yearning which drives an adolescent to poetry. Perhaps, just perhaps, he might become an American writer.

What did all this, though, have to do with Ann, the youngest Bigelow daughter? In a poem he wrote, after the war ended, in his senior year, my father for once articulated the sense of distance he felt from the world in which he was living, the house of the Bigelows.

It is a late-spring morning, the midwestern sky spilling a blue with depths to rival any ocean; my father sits on the lawn, near the campus library, watching the couples walk past, groups of girls giggling, their books clutched to their chests. A butterfly dances over dandelions marking the lawn. My father presses his paper over his copy of *Moby Dick*, thinking of how he played in the yard yesterday with Ann, wearing a blindfold, his outstretched arms grabbing the empty air in front of him, searching for his prey. At last, giving up, he pulled up the blindfold, shouting, "You win," and she came running to his arms, giggling, telling him to stop it, he'd given up too easily. The lines of description arrive slowly, my father struggles for the words. The feelings are too jumbled, too complex. Then the thought arrives with the line, the image, the doubt that asks, how long will it be before you hesitate to put "your tiny white hand in the brown skin of my hand?"

Twenty-five years later, I am in graduate school, writing my own poems. In the basement of his house in Northbrook, in an old briefcase, I find this poem. An irrevocable gift.

I HAVE A FRIEND whose father is a *hakujin* American and whose mother is Japanese. She says when you grow up in two cultures, you aren't split in half. Instead there are two distinct beings inside of you. If you're separated from one of the cultures, that being dies, at least for a time. It has no light to bathe in, no air, no soil. It can, like certain miraculous plants and seeds, come back to life, but the longer it dwells in that state of nonbeing, the harder it is to revive.

During that first year in college, my father lived with the two beings inside him, each struggling for existence, each with a voice, a vision of its own. There was the self that dressed each day in a V-neck and button-down, whites socks and oxfords, that carried Shakespeare, Voltaire, *Principles of Economics, Biology*, in the crook of his arm, that sang "Long Ago and Far Away," under his breath. This self was beginning to study for confirmation at Professor Bigelow's Episcopalian church, was learning the names of the disciples, the gospels of Matthew and Mark, Luke and John. In the late spring, as the aroma of alfalfa crept up from the fields, and tiny green flecks of insects hopped on and pecked his lamp, this self could be heard reciting the Nicene Creed: ". . . and I believe in one holy Apostolic Church . . . in the resurrection of the dead . . . who died on the cross, was buried, and on the third day he rose again . . ." This self was writing for the school newspaper, articles on the Campus Carnival, the baseball team, a guest lecturer on the future of Europe after the war. This self was becoming addicted to Mrs. Bigelow's bran muffins and chocolate chip cookies, the smell of fresh-brewed coffee in the morning, was coming to at least know the names of the composers whose music Mr. Bigelow listened to on his phonograph. This self joined with the guys in the house when everyone went out to play softball or shoot baskets. This self was flourishing, growing in strength, finding each detail learned, each belief accepted, each conversation, caught a feeling of newness and hope, promises he had never known existed.

And the other self? Well, this was the self that once sang songs with the Issei in camp, in that quavering vibrato where the notes possess no Western definition and reliability, where over and over lovers are saying goodbye, someone is remembering their parents, their lover, weeping over the distance between them, where the hands in clapping sway from side to side with each clap. This self watched Mrs. Miyamoto do the *Buyō,* the classical dance, before the barracks, watched her dip back and forth in the dust, using her kerchief as a prop, first to show coyness, then to show interest, then to pull tight, one end clenched in her teeth, in a gesture that was both erotic and comic, causing laughter and delight to come cackling from the crowd. This was the self whose taste buds were formed from *shōyu* and *miso,* from steamed rice, from rolls of *norimaki,* from *tsukemono,* the puckery sweet pickles, a jar of which could disappear in the course of the meal were it not for the swift hand of his mother, slapping at the wrists of her children. This was the self that knew the names of everyone in his barracks, the Ogawas, Sones, Nishimuras, and Oshimas, who watched the bonfires spring up from the oil drums at night as the older people talked about Japan, about politics, about the issues of loyalty he barely understood, about traitors in their midst, spies for the government. This was the self for whom a birth, a death in the community was known by everyone. There was nowhere to keep a secret, no spaces for privacy. This was the self that went to Japanese school in L.A. and addressed the teacher as *"sensei,"* that struggled to learn the eighteen strokes of the *kanji* for *"kan"* (simplicity), that earned a brown belt by defeating Jimmy Honda, using a throw so simple, so pure, it took his opponent off guard and left him sprawling like a worm on the canvas mat. This self found comfort and closeness in his mother, who had little contact with anyone outside the Japanese community, and retained her Japaneseness in a way her husband could not. Because of his mother's quiet, gentle personality, my father sensed this Japaneseness not as a challenge or a criticism, but as a place he could find a stability, an ease, a conversation he could never have with his father.

But that was over now. He was becoming American.

All those years in Kalamazoo, my father's Japanese self seemed to be gasping for breath, its being gradually forgotten. This self believed in the quickness of spirits, the unspoken messages born of the silence that rests in the Japanese language, in the messages of gestures and hovering implications, in the visions that reside in dreams. This self, like his mother, was becoming a ghost.

2.

A FEW YEARS AGO, I gave a reading at the Japanese American Community Center in San Francisco. As I was browsing through their small library, I came upon some issues of the *Nisei Vue*, a magazine about Nisei which came out for several years after World War II. I remembered my father had been the editor of the magazine for a while. I thought again of his early literary ambitions, the stories I had found in a suitcase in the basement during my twenties, the pages where he talked about the great Nisei novel, the one that would etch the lives of his generation into the memory of America.

Propelled by the Nisei's release from the camps and the boom of the postwar years, the magazine exuded a freshness and optimism, a sense of wondrous things to come. There were Nisei entering all types of jobs, from lawyers to nurses to business. There were beauty pageants and dances, sports leagues with national tournaments, returning GIs with their war medals. Paging through one of the issues, I came upon an article on Nisei bobby-soxers in Hyde Park on the South Side of

Chicago. These teens were in love with swing, they bobbed their hair and wore saddle shoes and pleated skirts and giggled and gossiped and organized dances like any American teenagers of that time. They swooned over Frank Sinatra, the biceps of William Holden, Richard Widmark's steely-eyed gaze.

And there, in one of the pictures, was someone who looked remarkably like my mother. Another picture showed this look-alike teenager at a slumber party. It must be my mother, I thought. She and her family did live in Hyde Park just after the war. (Later, when I ask her about this photo, she says it probably is her, she vaguely remembers the article.) Her face was pert, cute, with an emerging beauty that I'm sure must have been somewhat intimidating despite her small stature. At the time of the photos, she was probably just about to enter Frances Shimer, a woman's junior college.

A year later, in a story my father once told me, she will go to a Nisei mixer, probably on the South Side. My father, just arrived from Western Michigan University in Kalamazoo and now taking English graduate courses at the University of Chicago, will see her across the room. He nudges his friend and says, "That's the girl I'm going to marry." As in a fairy tale, it happens in an instant.

Several months later, at nineteen, she will marry my father, who has recently been drafted, and move with him to Virginia, where he is stationed. He will never go back to graduate school. Instead, in the Army, he will learn, as he put it, "how many stupid people there are in the world," and that his skills as a writer can separate him from the crowd, allow him to move into more interesting jobs.

In the diary my father keeps during their first month of marriage, March 1951, there's a tenderness and innocence I find touching and yet incredibly remote from my sense of the world. After describing their hotel room on his wedding night, he says to his diary, "I cannot tell any more, but I know I will remember last night all the rest of my life."

Struck by my mother's diminutive size and her beauty, my father wonders in the diary about taking her away from her family, from the city they have lived in since the end of the war. When he talks to my mother about this, she replies, "You're my husband now, and I go where you go. My place is with you," and my father's prose swells with love and gratitude for his new bride. He elaborately describes each meal she prepares for him in their small one-room house on the Virginia base, and if the type of food is ordinary, though with a hint of their background—fried chicken, rice balls, peas, and Jell-O—my father's praise for it is not. Then there is a first fight, prompted by what my father later perceives as his own crabbiness and displeasure with having to wake up so early for maneuvers. He worries about the consequences of their fight all day, till he returns and finds her forgiving and loving as ever.

To me, this portrait of their married life seems something out of *McCall's*. Yet I have no doubt that in many ways my father's diary is a fairly accurate description. Certainly, compared to many, my parents have had a steady, successful marriage, with few troubles. When their children grew up, my parents made a fairly easy transition into a new life, where tennis and golf and Nautilus became the center of their lives, learning to play together in a way that many couples, victims of the empty-nest syndrome, cannot. Both my parents' marriage and their selves can be characterized by the word "resilient," and in that, they mirror the rise of their generation of Japanese Americans after the experience of the camps.

And yet, I do know that my mother, at some point, made adjustments. On certain occasions when my father seemed to be working too much or when he seemed unaware of tensions between relatives or within our family, my mother let me know in casual remarks that this was part of marriage. "After a certain point you give up on changing someone, you realize you can't change them. You just learn to live with it."

She said this without anger or bitterness; at the same time I could tell this wasn't some traditional belief, a cultural code set in stone to uphold male privilege. Instead, her tone conveyed a sense of practicality, a sense that such accommodation was part and parcel of love. Such accommodation wasn't being unromantic or easy, but realistic; it involved a recognition of your own limitations as well as your partner's.

This lesson and her marriage have been, perhaps, my most valuable legacies from her. Whatever else happened in my childhood, I knew my parents loved each other. There was a lesson there in their perseverance, in their steadfastness.

And yet, it's one of the paradoxes of my life that out of their happy marriage should come a son so troubled about the relationships between women and men, so ill at ease with his own sexuality.

TODAY, holding my son in my arms, feeding him his bottle, rocking him to sleep, I suddenly felt there was something less selfless in a father's love for his son than for his daughter. When the son marries, there is not the sense that some cord must be broken, something let go. The son has already broken away by virtue of his being a male and a rival; the father can love the son without becoming a rival to his son's lover (though if the son is gay, all this changes slightly).

Then I looked at my Nikko's almost balding head, his long eyelashes that people tell me women will love, his button nose and chubby cheeks. As his body relaxed into the rhythm of sleep, his arms falling at his sides, I marveled at how intensely I love him. I thought of how, in the future, the breakages of father and son, the almost inevitable cracking of bonds, might, perhaps must, take place. Fathers see in their sons a mirror of themselves; this is the selfish side of our love.

And what of a son's love for his father? Perhaps I feel that most when my father steps up to the tee, trying to settle himself, to aim his club. As he takes his backswing, at the very top he suddenly freezes, much too long; this hitch has hit him in old age, the sign that his muscles will not flow as smoothly or as powerfully as they once did, that his nerves have taken control. It tells of my father's growing fallibility and mortality, something I can barely stand to see, especially those times the hitch causes him to dub the ball only a few yards off the tee. This doesn't happen often yet, but each time it happens and I am there, I feel this deep and abiding sadness, this ache that wishes each of my father's shots to be picture perfect, to grant him this tiny bit of pleasure at this point in his life.

When the hitch first appeared, it was an embarrassment to my father and almost an affront to my mother. My father was ready to give up the game and he blamed my mother's critical eye in part for the decompensation of his swing. My mother said that for years she felt golf was my father's mistress, and she grew jealous of the time it took him away from her. Unlike with a mistress, there was simply no way for her to compete.

"I finally take up golf, like he wanted me to, and then this happens," she said. "And it's no fun anymore, for him or for me. I feel like I finally tried to do what he wanted, finally figured out a way to compete with this mistress, and then he gets this hitch and he can't perform."

The implications of this were not totally unapparent to my wife and me.

"It sounded so sexual," I said. "Do you think hypnotism might help?"

My wife often hypnotizes her oncology patients when they are suffering from the pains of chemotherapy or when she has to stick them with a needle. She's used it with others, including me, for dealing with psychological problems and tensions.

"I suppose so. It couldn't hurt."

The next day Susie went into my father's study with him. My mother paced downstairs in the kitchen. After the session, my father immediately went down to the basement, where he has built a driving net, and when he came back upstairs fifteen minutes later, he was overjoyed. My mother kept asking what Susie had done. She was amazed.

My father then had Susie make a tape that he could use to hypnotize himself when she was not there.

"You know," said Susie, "I suspect it's at least partly your mother that's causing the hitch. I'm sure she's part of the reason he keeps freezing up. So I told your father not to let anyone listen to the tape, that it was his alone."

"Did you tell him my mother couldn't listen to it?"

"I told him it was just for him." Pause. "And I told him that I thought it would be best for him not to golf with your mother for a while."

"Oh God," I said. I knew this would drive my mother insane.

The tape continued to work. My father's hitch disappeared, and my father was full of praises for Susie's hypnotic abilities. He told her that he had told an old Blue Cross/Blue Shield colleague about how hypnotism had helped his game. Later, the man came up to my father and asked him if his daughter-in-law had ever done any work with impotence.

Soon my mother became intensely curious about this tape. She would watch my father go into his study, lock the door, and listen to the tape, and something about this routine piqued her. She began to badger him about letting her listen to it.

"I just want to listen to it," she said. "Maybe it might help my game, did you ever think about that?"

He kept telling her that he didn't have time at that moment to let her listen to the tape or that he had left it in the car. He didn't feel he could tell what my wife had told him: *Don't let Terry listen to the tape. It's yours alone.*

"You told me I could listen to it yesterday," my mother would complain when he gave her one of his excuses.

"I'll let you listen to the tape. I will."

"I don't understand why you're making such a big thing about this."

"It's not a big thing. You're the one who's making a big thing about it."

Finally, he told her he would rewind the tape to let her listen to it. Instead, by mistake, he erased the tape.

"Freud would have a field day here," said my wife when she found out about this.

Gradually, my father's hitch came back. There was no more talk about hypnotism. He and my mother learned to live with his hitch and began to golf together again. One more adjustment to age.

I suppose, if this has been one of the testier episodes in their marriage, my father is indeed a lucky man.

Still, when I watch him swing, it is not my father's luck I think about, but mine, how he is poised on this precipice from which the body declines and never recovers. I am not on this precipice, and in this vanquishing of my rival, I feel a certain faint guilt, and beyond that an affection I have not let myself feel until now. My father pulls the club back, it freezes for what seems several seconds above his head, and I am no longer a child, I am no longer the one held in terror, no longer the one whom I pity. What I feel coursing through my body is a connection deeper than the years or memory and more basic than biology and duty, more mysterious than love. I am the son he has wanted me to be, standing beside him on the first tee, watching a moment later his ball soar off into the morning, landing softly on the dew-heavy grass, glistening almost as far as his failing sight can see.

The Descent

"His blood was in revolt. He wandered up and down the dark
slimy streets peering into the gloom of lanes and doorways,
listening eagerly for any sound. He moaned to himself like some
baffled prowling beast. He wanted to sin with another of his kind,
to force another being to sin with him and to exult with her in sin.
He felt some dark presence moving irresistibly upon him
from the darkness, a presence subtle and murmurous as a flood
filling him wholly with itself. Its murmur besieged his ears
like the murmur of some multitude in sleep;
its subtle streams penetrated his being . . ."

—JAMES JOYCE,
A PORTRAIT OF THE ARTIST AS A YOUNG MAN

1.

MY WIFE AND I know each other incredibly well, having been together for more than twenty years. Our habits are those of the long-married, though we spent eleven years together before we finally made that commitment. We get each other's jokes and references, the private vocabulary that comes from a potpourri of sources—Woody Allen films, Robert Lowell poems, Japanese phrases, medical slang, children's books. We share over two decades of memories, good and bad. We know each other's quirks and weaknesses, the ways our neuroses work. Our tastes are bourgeois, our politics far left. We adore our children, worry about our lack of discipline and organization, and are adamant about no pets. We laugh about how, before the children came and ordering out became de rigueur, we used to be good cooks. We love jokes that are cynical and sarcastic, that poke fun at sacred cows. Our life has a rhythm, a working ebb and flow, that we labor hard at and yet it strikes us as easy and lucky, something we don't quite deserve. Our early years went far beyond a normal turbulent twenties; we're grateful now for this serenity. We believe fiercely in our ordinary, everyday life.

At the center of that life, of course, are our children. Our son, Nikko, is a year old now, hell-bent on danger wherever he turns, pulling things from tables, picking up whatever's on the floor and putting it into his mouth, peeling the plastic safety guards from the wall plugs, hurtling himself into the bathtub. We call him Bam-Bam, for his physical prowess, the slapping motions he makes with his hands as he comes at you, like a defensive end on a rampage. Samantha is five, lanky like her mother as a child. Physically, she's more tentative than her brother, more prone to give in to her fears. Perhaps that's because her imagination is so vivid. She doesn't brood but she can be obsessive. She's at an age when large metaphysical questions come up with a disarming and informal manner.

"How many stars are there?"

"More than you can count, honey. They go on and on."

"But what if there was a God who never slept? I know there might not be a God, but if there were, wouldn't a God who never slept be able to count all the stars?"

I try to tell her about the concept of infinity and then stop, realizing the infinite is where God, the spiritual, enters. Samantha goes on to talk about a second god who always sleeps, and as I mention the Indian god Vishnu, I'm struck by what she's tapped into, what I have left out.

The next night, at bedtime, she asks me if I believe in angels. We talk about souls, spirits, what lives on after you die. Other nights she asks why we are born as children rather than fully grown, why each baby must have a father and mother. She's not asking about sex, I think, but more abstract, philosophical questions. Five-year-olds are metaphysicians, in touch with the mystery in the basics, the wonder in the givens of our existence.

In 1994, we bought a new house on a street near the river. Our backyard is thick with trees, bird-thronged. Samantha's room is shaped by the roof, with curves and nooks and crannies, a secret passageway into the attic. Nikko's is flooded by the afternoon sunlight, with waist-high windows. Unlike our previous house, built in 1902 with a crumbling infrastructure and a boiler ancient and rusty as a hulk stranded on the dunes, the new house was built in 1940 with impeccable craftsmanship, the bricks hauled in from Virginia, the doors three inches thick, the ceilings without a crack. For years Susie and I said to ourselves we were downwardly mobile yuppies. We would always live a rung below our parents. Now that she's in practice and I've made something of a way in the world as a writer, this is not the case. I have a house with fireplaces, a tile roof, built-in bookshelves. Mornings we wake with both children sprawled between us, one of their hands pressing our face or our back. I know I've never known such happiness, that these are the best years.

Whatever sadness and terror attended our beginnings, I remain a very lucky fellow.

Susie, understandably, is not very keen on my telling the story of our beginnings. It dredges up too many memories, cuts open the wounds we've healed. At the same time she knows memory and the body are my writerly obsessions, that my persistent questioning of the past is part of who I am, part of why she is with me, how we mesh together. In the end, it's the life we live now that anchors us and helps us to abide what my writing brings back.

2.

GRINNELL COLLEGE, 1970. I was going to be free there, to create a new self, and that first day, after my parents left, I walked barefoot to the campus student union, wearing bell-bottom jeans, a macramé belt, and a tie-dyed T-shirt, feeling a seemingly endless sense of possibility. Everyone I saw wore similar clothes, the faint smell of marijuana drifted here and there, Crosby, Stills and Nash singing about the Marrakesh Express. In high school, I'd shuttled back and forth between various groups—the honors classes, the jocks, band—and my dress had moved from a studied collegiate to a midwestern version of British rock star foppery. I didn't fit in anywhere. But at Grinnell I found a place where being smart wasn't a drawback, where intellectual acumen, measured to a great extent by grades, was part of being cool, and where I finally knew what I was—a hippie. I'd picked Grinnell as my safety school—after Harvard, Yale, Princeton, and Stanford—simply because a couple of honors students at my high school had gone there. Though I didn't get into any of my first four choices, I liked the small, cozy feel of Grinnell, the friendliness and intimacy achieved in part by its size, 1,200, and by its isolation, plopped down in the middle of Iowa's vast sea of cornfields. I was excited about the fact that there were virtually no social rules—i.e., sexual activity was rampant and unchaperoned—and few academic requirements. Retaining some of my high school conservative temperament, I didn't do drugs, and in this I was something of a pseudo hippie. The thrill of being around such widespread drug use was, for a while, enough for me.

The sexual mating dance in the first days of a college year are intense. The photo book of incoming freshmen was called the "herd book." But the sexual revolution then in the air did not descend upon me. Most of the freshman girls, certainly the most attractive ones, went off with upperclassmen, guys with long hair and beards who were from the East, who knew Miles Davis and Bach, who could quote Wordsworth's worst line: "A six inch darling of pygmy size." There was definitely a sense, as in high school, that some people were cooler than others, though I felt confused about how this coolness was achieved, which is often the case if you are not cool. Gradually, I came to embrace again my high school image of myself as a loser.

After several weekends of being alone, I joined forces with some of the other freshman guys in the dorm who had no girlfriends. No one dated in those days, you'd just show up at someone's room, do some things during the evening, return to her room or your room, talk, and then if the conversation extended past midnight, you'd probably end up sleeping together. This never happened to us. We didn't even know how to start such conversations. Instead, Rick Nash, Al Bloom, and I would talk about how we were losers, how we were never going to get a woman, how we were going to remain alone all our lives. It was no use. We might as well not even try. We were destined to failure. In a fit of group despair, we'd sometimes just lie in the hall and literally howl and kick our feet. There was a comic-book quality to our angst, as if we were acting out a sitcom version of college students in a state of desperate sexual deprivation. I sought solace in masturbation, with a compulsiveness only slightly less than in high school.

Sophomore year, I grew more introspective about my state of celibacy, pursuing a self-imposed solitude as if it were a drug. I took long walks in the cornfields at the edge of the campus; I studied alone in out-of-the-way places on campus; I masturbated. Weekends, in sophomoric imitation of a poetic monk, I sat in my room, a single candle lit in the dark, and listened to Laura Nyro, lyrics about New York streets at midnight, junkies in Harlem, sea captain lovers who brought roses and boots from Russia, running away in the morning, past empty sidewalks and stray pigeons. I was a boy from the suburbs, tracts of bi-levels, a high school for overachievers. The urban images soothed me, gave me a language for my overly self-conscious and adolescent embrace of loneliness.

I read e. e. cummings that year, and went to sleep listening to my roommate make love to his girlfriend in the room next door. Her moans moved through the grate above the door, a steady rhythm that kept my mind alive with the possibilities of what was happening just six inches away, beyond the wall. My roommate, John, spoke of the elites and the plebes, and never let on whether I was a plebe or not. John had read all of Faulkner; while other students eked out our five-page papers for our freshman seminar, he wrote twenty-page papers on the division of the Apollonian and the Dionysian in the shield of Achilles. He fell into a rage when he got one A−. John was Jewish and from Niles East, a high school a few miles from mine. He'd been salutatorian, president of his class, had slept with his high school girl-friends, smoked dope and still maintained his grades and intellect. In comparison, I was a boob. I saw myself as a bit slow, like Lenny in *Of Mice and Men*.

All this, though, changed very quickly junior year.

IT'S ONE OF THOSE DAYS you remember, perhaps like the first time my father saw my mother. Unlike my father's experience, though, no thoughts of marriage suddenly surface on the steaming late August day I first meet Susie. My thoughts are more carnal and immediate.

Just after they've driven up to the door, Susie's father lifts her bags out of a blue Ford station wagon and hands them to me. He's a bulky, balding man with deep-sunken eyes and black-rimmed glasses. His hair and clothes are rumpled, in slight disarray, like a professor on a camping trip. He keeps pushing his glasses back up his nose after handing over each bag.

I've already noticed his daughter. Her face is classically pretty, without wild, distinguishing marks. With her long brown hair, she looks like Ali MacGraw in *Love Story*. Her lips, though, are slimmer than the movie star's and lack the ability to pucker into a pout. While MacGraw's face carries the hint of an Ivy League coed snootiness, Susie's face is more open, easier.

The prettiest girl in the dorm, I think to myself. Already I've helped with the bags of several other coeds, and am keeping my own mental list. I'm the student adviser on the floor, and I work the incoming freshman women in the guise of my official capacity.

This is not to say I am experienced in seduction. I've only lost my virginity last summer to a casual friend. She was a year older, not particularly attractive, with a slight mustache on her upper lip. It was done after a long night of talking, as if there was nothing else for us to do. I wanted to leave immediately afterward. We made it two other times that summer. It did not get better.

But already I sense something with the incoming women, a new assurance in my bearing, a new responsiveness on their part. I'm two years older. They are away from home for the first time. But it's more than that. I'm finally beginning to entertain the idea that I might be attractive to the opposite sex. After all, near the end of my sophomore year, I had had brief flirtations with two upper-class women. These never came to anything, in part because they sensed in me some vague desperation, a too ready eagerness and vulnerability. But this taught me something about holding back a bit, learning to play things in a cooler, calculating mode.

As Susie's father leaves with the bags, he says to her, "Seems like a very mature young man." (Susie and I will laugh about this years after. "It just shows you can't trust first impressions," she'll say.)

Later, she sits in her room with her friend from high school who has driven up with her. Friendly and sincere, in my best student-adviserly demeanor, I inform her if there's anything she needs or if she has any questions, my room is just across the hall.

After years of joking about how she wasn't really attracted to me when we first met, Susie told me last year that after I left, she looked at her girlfriend and in an instant of recognition concerning me they both smiled. It was a sign they both thought I was cute. Upon hearing this, I felt confused. Even though we've been together for twenty years, some part of me still finds this mutual smile difficult to believe. It doesn't fit with my conception of myself as an Asian, a Japanese American. As a rule, white women are not supposed to find such men attractive.

At twenty, that August in Iowa, I am beginning to surmise that I might be an exception to that rule. But the rule is still there, a constant backdrop, lurking in my subconscious, though unspoken. If I think of myself as at all attractive, it's in spite of my Asian features, not because of them. Mainly, I want the racial issues covered over, to vanish from sight.

After I leave Susie and her father, I go back to my room and put on James Taylor's *Sweet Baby James.* I've fashioned my own look after his album-cover photo, and, like Taylor, I wear a work shirt, jeans, and my hair long and parted in the middle. I stare at the album and wish I possessed Taylor's high cheekbones, the jut of his jaw, the intensity of his dark brown eyes.

What I do not think about is the shape of our eyes—that's too open a racial comparison. I come up short compared to James Taylor as an individual, not as a member of a race. It's me whose face is too round and too fleshy, me whose nose is too small. After all, his looks, his romantic air are something no one else at the college possesses either.

Across the courtyard I hear the same album playing, a different cut. I stare at the yellow India print hung on the wall, the posters of Crosby, Stills and Nash, Peter Max, James Taylor. Taylor's big hit is "Fire and Rain," a song about the mysteries of suicide and heroin addiction, hints of a life on the edge, a sensibility I want to comprehend and am too restrained to approach. I've imbibed a certain amount of my father's puritanism, his homemade mixture of All-American ideals and Christian rectitude. I have a conception of myself as exceptional, pure, a loner, yes, but one who does not waste himself, who does not let go, who studies more than anyone else in the dorm. Gunning for law school, I'm a poli-sci major and an English major, though the latter's just for fun. After all, what's important isn't any particular subject but my grade point average.

The late-afternoon sun spotlights the used stuffed chair, jammed into the tiny corner of a six-foot-wide dorm room. It's here Susie and I will make love for the first time, though I can't yet imagine it. I'm merely filled with a sense of anticipation, things will be different this year.

A few minutes later, I go to the window, peer down. Another car has arrived. I wait to see if the new student is female, as pretty as the one before.

• • •

A COUPLE OF WEEKS LATER, Susie's high school boyfriend drives up to the college one day in a pickup. Over six feet and lean, with hair flowing down to his shoulders, Paul looks hipper than me, or so I think. He's just been to Alaska, has driven thousands of miles to ask her to come back with him to homestead.

"It will be a bit lonely," he says, "but after you've shot your first bear . . ."

Susie can't laugh at this absurdity, she's too terrified. She doesn't know what to do. She doesn't want to go to Alaska to shoot bears, my God. She decides to speak with me, her student adviser. She doesn't know I'm less experienced in relationships than she, even if she is still a virgin. As we take a walk out to the football field, I talk to her in the calming tones of a big brother, telling her things will work out, to just say what she wants. I don't know this is impossible for her, to say what she wants, to reject someone. She doesn't know this either, though she senses in herself an inability to refuse, to say no to those who ask things of her. All she knows is she is terrified. She wants the boyfriend to go away.

On the walk back, I drape my arm on her shoulder. It has begun.

Years later at dinner parties, we talk about this night. It becomes a familiar anecdote, a humorous source of contention.

"You were interested in me. I know you were."

"I was not." Pause. "He likes to think that. He thought everyone was interested in him."

"They were," I say.

"Yes, but not me." And then she laughs and goes on with the story.

AFTER TWO WEEKS, five or six of the freshman girls have developed crushes on me. News like this travels quickly in a dorm, and when I hear about it, I am both exhilarated and troubled. It engenders in me a fit of schizophrenic moral quandaries, which I quickly manage to evade. I have responsibilities, I shouldn't take advantage of my situation, I should be acting as their student adviser. I just want to be their friend. In my ponderings, I'm a bit officious and take myself too seriously. After all I'm twenty years old.

I am attracted to only two of these freshmen, and really only to Susie, but the irony of suddenly being at the center of female attention is a delight that I keep wanting to deny even as I revel in it. One woman waits outside my Yeats class to watch me pass. Others try to sit with me at lunch or dinner, though, caught in my faux romanticism, I often go off to the corner of the dining hall to sit alone, a copy of Yeats's *Collected Poems* open before me. When I am talking with one of the freshman women in my room, another goes outside to see if my lights are still on. One woman tells me of a dream where I stand on a balcony and all the freshman women on the floor are calling to me and I jump into a pool of water and disappear.

One night Susie comes to me and tries to insist that she wants to be just friends. She's not like the other girls, she's not interested in me. Much to her consternation, I reply that she is the one I am really interested in. (Years later, she'll tell me that when I said this, she said to herself, "Damn, I just blew it.")

The next night, I go to *On the Waterfront*, with my roommate from last year, John, whose girlfriend is in France. We sit between Susie and another girl who's interested in me.

Now we all sit in a row, watching Brando pick up the tiny glove that Eva Marie Saint has left behind, slipping its delicate leather onto his prizefighter's knuckles, watching him later stagger across the threshold of the shipping yard, his jaw busted, gut kicked in, knees buckling beneath him. I'm as conscious of the women around me as of what's happening on the screen.

"That was strange," observes John afterward as we walk back to the dorm. "I kept feeling all these weird vibes going back and forth. Are you going to do anything about it?"

"I don't know. I'm supposed to be their student adviser."

"All last year you complained about being alone, and now you don't want to do anything? You're crazy. Listen, I'm going to talk to her."

"To who?"

"To the one you're interested in, stupid."

Later, while I'm upstairs studying, John ends up sitting with Susie in the dorm lounge. It's near midnight. She's wearing her nightgown. He starts the conversation by saying that David is awkward with girls. He hasn't had a girlfriend, and he's too shy to say anything.

"Do you know you're attractive?" John asks. "What would you say if I told you I find you attractive?"

Susie says nothing. She wonders why he is saying these things, for whom is he speaking? "He was a real jerk," she'll say years later.

That night I knock on her door. A faint answer. I enter, stand over her in the dark as she begins to awaken.

"Do you want to come to my room?"

She's neither surprised nor disturbed at my presence or my question. Instead, she gets up and follows me quietly, without hurry, as if she were sleepwalking, as if her movements are inevitable, part of a dream.

THE COLLEGE is like a small village, with its gossip and scandals, its elites and those who pass through unnoticed. Some professors are like gods, others fools. One professor is having an affair with a student, another has recently attempted suicide, a third will come out of the closet and leave next year for Colombia to run a gay bar there. Drugs are everywhere, marijuana, mushrooms, Kool-Aid acid on a sunny May day during a mock Olympics. John McLaughlin, Quicksilver Messenger Service, play concerts in the gym. It's there, at Susie's urging, I finally break down, smoke my first joint and find out, making love afterward, why it's so compelling. The school band, we say, is Luther Allison. The dances don't mean what they did for me my first two years. I'm finally with someone.

Her father has traveled as a public health official to China, India, Malaysia, Switzerland, the Soviet Union. He brings home his tastes for curries, peanut sauce, couscous, stuffed grape leaves. She has been to Europe; in a café on the Mediterranean, she has watched a dubbed version of *The Rifleman*, Chuck Connors' voice half an octave higher.

"In Paris, I was so proud of my French. I ordered shrimp for the whole family. But when the dinner arrived, it turned out I'd ordered calf brains. That's what happens when you learn French from someone with a Cobb County accent."

"My family hardly ever traveled. About the only place we'd go was to my aunt's, who lived in Connecticut."

Though we're roughly of the same class, there's something daunting about her. When she was seven, the prince of Togo visited her house. In her living room, there's a statue of a smallpox god, a tapestry from Nigeria. Her church, which was Unitarian, joined with Martin Luther King's church in civil rights marches. The youth group was wild, constantly worried her mother. The adults swapped mates, the kids did drugs and drank gallons of Ripple.

"My friend Linda and I were the only virgins. We were known as the Gruesome Twosome."

At first we seem like any new couple on campus. We study together, eat meals together, go to movies and concerts together. We make love often, the Allman Brothers blaring on the stereo almost drowning out our pleasure. There's a fervency in our lovemaking that frightens her a bit, but we're in love for the first time in our lives, really in love.

We have no inklings about where this is going, it seems to unfold naturally; there's a rhythm, an ease, to our togetherness that surprises us. At night, in my small closet-sized dorm room, on the single bed, we sleep together, a chair beside the bed to rest my arm, which doesn't quite fit on the narrow bed. Joni Mitchell on the stereo, the blueness of night.

Susie opens up something in me. It's not the sex, or not just the sex. She's not really wild, that's not how she sees herself. She's simply a part of the times in a way I haven't been. She talks of watching the Allman Brothers shoot up before their concerts in Chandler Park in Atlanta, of bringing her friends down from bad trips. I enter her love affair with exotic food, she mine for poetry. I read to her Yeats, Roethke. She tells stories of the children she teaches at the college preschool. I play piano for her in the dark, late at night, when everyone is asleep.

Very early she picks up on my fanatic pursuit of grades, my endless study hours. An underachiever in high school, content with B's, she starts to develop a competitive edge with me, and though she never quite takes this competition seriously, the A's start coming, our intellects match. There's a merging of our sensibilities, an acerbic take on the world. We mock the students who come back from their London semester wearing leather pants and worshipping David Bowie, the disciples of the German professor with their poems about bombs in suitcases, their papers on *Death in Venice* and the desultory decadence of genius. "Oh, Tadzio, oh, Tadzio," we moan and break into giggles. I'm freer with her, more able to open up, sillier, less self-conscious. One evening listening to old 45s—"Silhouettes on the Shade," "Stop in the Name of Love"—we act out the lyrics, falling to the floor in oceanic laughter.

We decide to live together the next year, a comfortable arrangement. When I tell my parents about this—with the naive candor of youth I proclaim I will not be hypocritical and hide what Susie and I are doing—they say little. "I just don't want some father showing up at my door with a shotgun," says my father. When the time comes for me to pack for school and I ask for a set of sheets from the linen closet, my mother says, "Here are some single sheets. I don't want to feel like I'm encouraging you." Susie's parents, of course, know nothing of our arrangement.

I TOOK my first creative writing course at Grinnell, mainly because I was interested in writing songs; it was the era of Bob Dylan, James Taylor, Joni Mitchell, Neil Young, singer-songwriters whose lyrics were dissected in the pages of *Rolling Stone*, in student papers for indulgent professors. Gradually, though, I sensed my musical pitch and rhythm were hardly that of a genius, and as I started piling up A's in English, which, à la Mrs. Campbell, had been my worst subject in high school, I found myself becoming more and more interested in poetry. I copied out the lines from William Carlos Williams' "Asphodel," about how men die every day from lack of the news embedded in poems; I imbibed the intricate metaphysics of Wallace Stevens, his hymns to a world without deities or religion. I loved the celebration of loneliness and meditation in the short lyrics of James Wright, the jewel hidden in the cave in the air behind his body, "a cloister, a silence / closing around a blossom of fire." The words seemed to resonate with the first fervent inklings of an inner life that I'd discovered while practicing alone on the basketball courts or walking through the fields on high school road trips.

The summer before my senior year I wrote Susie long letters about Keats and Rilke's "Letters to a Young Poet." I was working at Blue Cross/Blue Shield in a job my father had arranged and taking the train with him into Chicago. Riding in our mutual silence, I was struck by what I perceived as the deadness of the routine, the hollow boredom of the commuters, and like many an adolescent, I so feared becoming one of them that I had no notion of why my father had made the choices he had, the forces he found himself battling, the duties he'd undertaken. I was constantly clashing with him about the Vietnam War, about my applying for a CO, about my atheism and refusal to go to church. My dress, my music, my politics, seemed to him a perpetual affront. His one consolation was that I was still going to law school.

But as I worked at his company, writing for its newsletter, penning various memos, my diligence proved less than that of a true Blue Shield scion. Instead, I was incessantly pulling out my poetry books from their hiding place in my desk and reading them whenever I could. One day, as I was poring over the passage in Keats's letters exploring "negative capability" when I should have been finishing an article on student summer employees, I heard my supervisor coming around the corner and quickly stashed the book back in my desk. Suddenly, it hit me: If I became a lawyer, if I followed my previous dream of a noble toiler at poverty law, if I buckled into my father's career plans, I'd have to hide my poetry books in my desk my whole life. I wanted to keep them *on top* of my desk. Amid what I had branded as the tedium of corporate life, constrained by profit and soulless conformity, I realized that what I hated most in life was to be bored, and I was, in that office, most definitely bored.

These were hardly unique desires or thoughts. What was a bit more unique, perhaps, was that deep down I knew my father wouldn't be able to change my mind or stop me. When he later said to me, "I wanted to be a writer once," implying I should assent to his wisdom concerning the world's ways and the barriers before me, that sealed it. There was no choice but to prove him wrong.

FOR SUSIE AND ME, the first couple of months of my senior year are like the year before. Eventually, though, something else begins to emerge: I start talking about an open relationship; either of us should be able to see other people. I urge this on her for weeks. She has no real desire to see other people, though she says she accepts the principle. After years of dreaming about having sex, I find, I feel, one person is not enough. There are too many opportunities. I start stepping onto a course of escalation that seems, at the time, a natural progression. Ours is the first generation to grow up with freely available contraception (AIDS is a decade away). There's a sense of moving out of the Dark Ages. I speak of the uselessness of jealousy, of how love doesn't mean you make a possession of the other person, something you own. I quote the songs and slogans of the times, the rhetoric of "free" love, William Blake and his mythical figure, the jealous Nobodaddy: "And priests with black gowns were making their rounds / And binding with briars my joys and desires." I low Stephen Sulls sings that, if you can't be with the one you love, love the one you're with.

"It's not that I don't love you. I just think we should be beyond jealousy."

I don't let up. Abbie Hoffman's *Steal This Book*, Jerry Rubin's panegyric to Yippies, Joni Mitchell's lyrics about how she and her old man don't need a piece of paper from city hall—everywhere people are challenging boundaries, law; sex and drugs are just part of the mix, the letting go, the desire for highs, explorations of the senses. On the one side, there's the puritans and the bad old conformist outlook of our parents, and on the other, the age of Aquarius, of communes, the end of materialism and property.

One night, at a party, she downs seven screwdrivers, ends up in the bathroom in the basement of the dorm, throwing up, moaning for me to leave her, to go away. I hover near her, confused, feeling vaguely guilty. I hear her retching into the toilet. I pretend not to know what's going on.

The next day she agrees. Yes, it will be part of who we are.

• • •

AT THIS POINT, I've never questioned consciously the racial nature of my desires. Sophomore year, after a dance, I ended up making out with a black coed in her room, but nothing more came of that. It seemed no different than a couple of other encounters during my freshman and sophomore years with white women, which hadn't gone anywhere. Later that year, when another black woman began sitting next to me in the student union lounge as I played the piano, our talking never led to anything more than walking one afternoon around campus, holding hands. But these women weren't the focus of my thoughts, my sense of the campus social life. I blended in in ways the black students couldn't and, often, didn't want to. I won't examine these issues for several years. For now, I simply want to pursue my own desires.

It is a freshman I first seek out. Melissa wears short jeans skirts, a man's sport jacket, large-framed glasses. She is small, her body a bit on the heavy side. She looks like a book editor, one of those young women who fill the cubicles of publishing houses, who work for next to nothing, whose speech is quick and literate and whose manner is uncertain, if sometimes masked by New York brashness and bravado. She often studies in the library near my cubicle. We talk about classes, literature, professors. I sense there's an opportunity here, if I want it. It's not that I'm particularly attracted to her; it's more that I know it can happen.

One afternoon, I find her sitting on the steps of the library, reading Auden. Our talk drifts into sexual matters; the open nature of my relationship with Susie is casually revealed. I talk of how I make love, the time it takes. I talk like this as if I were discussing the intricacies of a poem, symbolism in a novel. She shows no reaction. It is already happening.

An hour later, we are in the dorm room I share with Susie. Susie is across campus, visiting a friend. I lean Melissa back against the bed. In a moment, my hand is up her skirt. She responds with a slight moan.

We kiss for a long time, then stop. Not here. It will have to be later, Thursday perhaps. Yes, Thursday is good.

There are others. It is not always as easy as with Melissa. Sometimes I'm nervous, afraid. In part it's the fear of failure; in part it's what I must tell them about my relationship with Susie, the couple I am already part of. They are almost all brief flings, a few nights at most. I fall in love with one of these women, and, even more, love the feeling of having two women love me. She's an actress, with flaming red hair, who loves the poetry of Eliot and played in *The Madwoman of Chaillot*. She ends it with a letter saying she doesn't want to feel like a character in a novel or a poem by Anne Sexton, that she knows I will always go back to Susie.

As for Susie, my passion for her increases after each transgression. It's as if we both sense I've tried to break something between us, and when it doesn't break, that binds us even tighter. Of course, something is damaged, something of her slipped away every time I returned, she tells me years later. But there's a fierceness now to our togetherness. We need each other in ways we can't begin to articulate.

3.

In 1974, I moved to Minneapolis to go to graduate school at the University of Minnesota to study English. For the next couple of years, Susie and I commuted back and forth between Grinnell, Iowa, and the Twin Cities to see each other; a couple of years later, we were living together in Minneapolis.

It was around my third year in graduate school when things began to change for us.

I see us on a Saturday morning in the basement apartment just off the campus, behind a singles bar on Seven Corners. It's September, the air is already cool at night. In the West Bank cafés long-haired students sip from their cups, write in a journal, or sift through the paper. It's eleven o'clock and I'm still asleep. My hair, shorter than in college, still flares out across the pillow; it is jet black, a black like ink, the space between the stars. I'm a late and heavy sleeper, a depressive. The cheap shades of the basement apartment whiten in the noon light. Still I don't get up. I'm naked beneath the sheets, a pair of bikini briefs on the carpet by the futon, jeans, a silk blouse. Against the stereo, an album cover shows a black woman's naked torso, Earth, Wind and Fire gathered around a pyramid.

In the one other room, Susie is seated in a battered chair. There's a small hole in the armrest, cigarette stains. She's wearing a white robe. Her long wet hair falls to her shoulders. Books line the walls; there's a card-table desk in the corner. A galley kitchen with piled dishes. The organic chemistry text spilled open before her. She's barely making it through this class. She graduated college with no idea of what she wanted to be, and now must go through all the premed requirements. She's already done with algebra—baby math, she calls it—now it's on to calculus, biology, chemistry. It's a long obstacle course, any moment she could fail. No guarantee she will finish, will be accepted.

She munches an apple as she reads. She is not very hungover, she takes her liquor better than I do. Alcohol dehydrogenase, she explains. Asians and Native Americans lack this enzyme. She's young too, and the night barely shows on her face. Her skin still retains its pale smoothness. Her nose is a bit crooked; she has a deviated septum. Hers is not the perfect face men make fools of themselves over. She's thankful for that. You have more than your fair share, her mother would say. She would never specify what she meant by this—looks, intelligence, their middle-class status—all of these and probably more. Her remarks annoyed Susie. Why should I feel guilty? she thought. But she does.

It now seems almost natural she would follow her father and

become a physician. A physician, she says, not a doctor. Her heroes are Robert Coles, Piaget, Simone de Beauvoir. She was a preschool teacher in college and has a way with children.

My heroes are John Berryman, Robert Lowell, Delmore Schwartz. All manic-depressives, brilliant talkers, hard drinkers, poets who left wrecks and wives in their wake, the hard shimmering detritus of genius.

When I wake and appear in the hall, she won't know what mood I'm in. At times I seem annoyed, as if something were lacking in her. I'm like a child, cajoling, demanding, pleading, for something I can't have, that I must have, that I will die without. My complexion changes then, there's an emptiness to my voice. She has taken on this tension, this anxiety. She fears, deep down, I can't be saved. That is my fear too.

She looks up. My face is pleasant, composed. There's a Zatoichi film at the Cedar, I tell her. Let's have a sandwich at Sgt. Preston's and then go see it.

Coming toward her, I go into my imitation of Zatoichi, the blind samurai. A comic and slobbery man, a master swordsman with a noble heart, Zatoichi captures flies with his chopsticks, scratches his underarms, and leaves bits of food hanging from his mouth. Zatoichi walks with a cane down the road, pecking his way, when out of the ditch swarm six ninja swordsmen. A minute later Zatoichi slips his sword back in his scabbard. Buzzards swoop down on the ninjas. The music starts up.

Susie laughs. Of course. She knows she has to study, but I'm in a good mood. This can't be wasted. I can be charming. There are moments.

GRADUATE SCHOOL is a bit bewildering. In college, I never took my English major seriously. Now I write papers on mythic ritual in Faulkner's "Barn Burning," on Kyd and Marlowe, the early Elizabethans. I feel humiliated when my professor points out I don't know the difference between "quotation" and "quote." "One is a noun, the other is a verb. Don't mix up the two." In my Metaphysical poets seminar, I try using Harold Bloom's theories about nature and transcendence in Romantic poetry. "That has nothing to do with the text or this course," says my professor. "Totally irrelevant." It's clear some of my classmates are better trained than I am. In my second year I take an incomplete in modern American poetry, and this worries me, though perhaps not as much as it ought to.

I want to be a poet, and can't quite fit this desire with the rigors of a scholar. I'm in the raw, incipient stages of my poetic identity. I read about Robert Lowell pitching a tent on Allen Tate's front lawn, how the young, soon to be famous poet went hungering for attention from the famous Fugitive poet. In "For the Union Dead," describing the Boston monument honoring Colonel Robert Shaw and his Negro Civil War regiment, Lowell wrote that the statue "sticks like a fishbone in the city's throat." I want to write poems like that. Though I'm nothing like Lowell, with his Boston Brahmin origins, I identify with Colonel Shaw, his gaunt, greyhound nobility, and not the Negro soldiers under his command.

I take creative writing classes where we're instructed to stare at the lighted candle at the center of the table and spin out whatever images come up. This seems silly to me, contrary to the stern classicism I'm being taught in my literature classes. We read Robert Bly raging against the Vietnam War, roaring out his mythology in the *Tooth Mother Naked at Last*, or his poems on silence and the snowy fields, the outlying farmland of Minnesota, the ghostly prairie. Bly's politics scare me, even though I am vehemently against the war. I've been taught that political poetry leads to rhetoric, to slogans, to agitprop, nothing good can come of it.

In my third year, the one other grad student of color, the black poet Marilyn Waniek, lends me this anthology of Asian American writers, *Aiiieee!!!!!* I don't read more than a couple of pieces—a scene from Momoko Iko's *The Gold Watch*, a play I've seen on television about a Japanese American family just before Pearl Harbor, and a small selection from John Okada's *No-No Boy.* I'm so ignorant, I don't understand what the novel's title refers to, and I have no desire to do anything about my ignorance. I've learned in graduate school that to call myself a minority writer or a Japanese American writer is to designate myself as second-class, to relegate myself to a literary ghetto, to enter the door only as a beneficiary of some poetic affirmative action. I want to be a writer, plain and simple.

Susie and I are still at an age when we're discovering old things. *To Have and Have Not, Philadelphia Story, Yojimbo, I Hiroshima, Mon Amour,* the films of Truffaut. Old blues recordings, Billie Holiday, Nina Simone. We go to two, three movies at a time, eat escargot and salad niçoise at L'Hôtel Sofitel at 3 A.M., the sky as we drive home lightening to a metallic gray. Summer evenings, we swim across Lake Harriet, the lights from the IDS tower downtown blinking above the tree line. Jets pass over us, bound for New York, Europe.

"Well, I know I'm not a genius," Susie said one night in our small galley kitchen.

"Try some of these." I scooped the scallops and pea pods onto her plate. It was a new recipe. "You know, all cooking is alike. You learn a few basic recipes of Chinese, and you can vary them endlessly, make banquet after banquet. Why aren't you a genius?"

"My calculus prof says that he puts one or two questions on each test which are nearly impossible. They're meant to separate the geniuses from those of us who just study hard, the run-of-the-mill A's. I never get those questions. I don't even try."

"Who cares? You don't want to become a mathematician. You want to become a doctor."

"It'd be nice to be a genius too."

"You're smart enough. Besides, as your mother says . . ."

"I've got more than my fair share. Thanks." She took a bite. "These are good."

"Maybe I'll open a restaurant if this poetry thing doesn't work out."

"You might as well start making out your menu then."

"Very funny."

She looked out the window at the bumpers of parked cars. "It's just that there's all this work to even get to the point of applying to medical school. I don't even know if I have it in me."

"You always sell yourself short. Like in high school. Look, if you don't do this, you'll always regret not trying. Maybe not today or tomorrow, but the day after that and for the rest of your life."

"So what you're saying is I should get on that plane with Victor Laszlo."

I told her again what she wanted to hear. It was part of my job, just the way she was with my poems, which seemed far less promising than her prospects of medical school. The room darkened, we kept on talking, didn't bother to turn on the lights, our faces withdrawing into the shadows, becoming only our voices, threading together.

OUR GAY FRIEND Darren was like a neighbor in a sitcom, popping in daily like the mail. His specialty was the nineteenth-century novel and semiotics. He wrote papers on *The Last of the Mohicans*, the codes of desire in *Madame Bovary*. A hypochondriac, he constantly complained of migraines, jet lag, colds and flus, palpitations, anxiety attacks, pains in his joints, muscle spasms. (This was just before AIDS, before such complaints became signs of alarm.) He mixed these complaints with moanings about men, the stupidity of his pickups at the Gay 90's, his intimidation at the gym, where he was trying to build up his rail-thin, rib-showing, six-feet-two frame. He had a mustache, short thinning hair, and wore a black leather motorcycle jacket which always looked too large for him. He chained smoked Marlboros, and his sexual ideal looked like the Marlboro man or Roy Smalley, the shortstop for the Twins.

"I swear I'm going to end up like Bicycle Mary," he said one afternoon as he ducked into our refrigerator and pulled out a beer.

"Who's Bicycle Mary?" I asked.

"He's this old guy with long, stringy gray hair that he wears in a ponytail, and he's always carrying this shopping bag around. He rides his bike to the bars, and then he sits around drinking, until some young punk sitting at a table gets so drunk he can barely keep his head up or passes out. Then Bicycle Mary sneaks in the booth beside him and puts his arm around him and pretends he's with his date for the night. The kid doesn't even know he's there."

"Well, at least he has more hair than you."

"Thanks. I appreciate that. God, I've got friends like Trotsky."

"After all your time in the gym I'm sure you can take out Bicycle Mary anytime you want."

"But that's just it. I'm afraid, with my sex life, he's starting to look attractive to me. I keep drinking in the corner of the bar and nodding my head, but he never comes near me."

"To be rejected by Bicycle Mary," Susie said. "Poor *bubula*."

"Listen, do you have any aspirin? I've got this splitting headache."

Occasionally we'd go with Darren to the baths. *Los Turistas*, he would call us. We'd dance beneath a glittering ball while men in towels sauntered past. In the back were booths where Darren disappeared to from time to time. Susie drank scotch on the rocks. I was drinking Black Russians, sweetness in double shots.

"What's it like back there?" she asked.

"People just wait in the rooms with the doors open, watching you as you pass," said Darren. "If you see someone you like, you just go inside. Sometimes someone else joins you. No one speaks. God forbid you should speak to someone."

"If only they had a place here like that for heteros, where you could swap partners."

"Yeah, you'd like that," she said.

"Actually they do have places like that. In New York." And I talked about a couple we knew from college who had gone to this remodeled health club in Manhattan. Everyone wore towels like in the gay baths. But instead of single assignations, the couples switched partners.

"It's a way of being together and having the freedom of being single, of trying out new things."

"You already have that," she said.

"So what's the objection?"

We left the old warehouse in the blue light of early morning, our faces worn. Some patrons lingered outside, still looking. It had rained, small pools glinted in the alleys. The streets of the downtown were deserted. A cop car swung around the corner. Everyone tensed as it passed. There was still a light from a coffee shop at the end of the block. Susie was shivering, blowing into her hands. I put my arm around her. Darren was humming the last tune. It was late autumn. A cold wind blew the pavement grit into our faces.

A couple of months later, Darren went to England to study. In his minute, precise script, he wrote postcards describing the gay bars of London, the punk rock scene. He met a pair of gay architects, a young waiter with whom he fell in love. The students on the program were younger, awed by his scholarship, his grasp of Barthes and Saussure. He sent back a copy of *Les Guerrilleres* by Monique Wittig, a futuristic lesbian novel. He spent hours in the British Museum, shopping at Harrods. He saw Felicity Kendall in *All's Well* at the Royal Shakespeare, ate afterward at Indian restaurants. England is dying, he said. Long live the English.

When he came back, he wanted to introduce me to Diane, one of the students in the London program. "You'd be perfect for each other," he said. He was like a pimp or sugar daddy, a butch yenta.

There was a craziness in the air at that time; unfettered promiscuity seemed not only accepted but fashionable. At parties we played games like "murder in the dark," where everyone went around groping and feeling each other up under the guise of trying to figure out who was the murderer and who had been murdered. The lights came up and people might be rolling together on the bed or couch. At a party for my creative writing class, various class members spent time in the bedroom making out; at one point, I found myself alternating kisses with one woman on each arm, while Susie was rolling on the living-room floor with Darren. Another couple in our crowd would go down to the gay bars and try to pick up a bisexual partner. In the grad school offices were rumors of adulteries, affairs between professors and students, gossip about the pickups of famous poets and novelists traveling through town. At dinner parties, people talked about their erotic dreams, old lovers, nights when they ended up in bed with someone they hardly knew or someone they wish they'd never met.

We were busy bursting past boundaries, experimenting, abandoning our sense of propriety, the morals of our parents. I told myself this was part of my investigations as a poet, part of some romantic credo imitating Byron, taking inspiration from the legends of Dylan Thomas or John Berryman, poetic and sexual mentors. The truth was: I could not stop.

ONE DAY in a bookstore I picked up a copy of *Marxism and Form* by Fredric Jameson. The book was dense, nearly impenetrable. I read it once and had no idea what it was about. I read it a second time. A third. I was hooked. It entered my thinking like a drug, rearranged my sight. I barreled my way through base and superstructure, suddenly seeing connections everywhere. The structure of Elizabethan tragedies, the sudden appearance of chess masters in Austria, the missile race between the U.S.S.R. and the U.S.—they weren't just random phenomena, they could be explained through dialectics, through seeing the relationship between the economic, the social, and the cultural. I was tired of the New Critical way of reading, which looked at literature solely as a linguistic construction. I wanted to know why things were the way they were. The New Critics didn't care. They simply accepted the way things were; to them literature had no business mucking around in issues of class or politics.

I read Benjamin's essay on how history is the tale of the victors. He talked about the way the readers of history identify with the victors, the tellers of the tale who make themselves the heroes. "That means," I told Susie, "there are other tales to tell. History is a construct and is created by an interested party, and the interested party is always the powerful and the rich."

This was strange to me, disturbing. I knew who the heroes were, I knew the sort of gods and writers I was supposed to worship; I'd learned to love a certain beauty, a certain learning, certain tales. *Pride and Prejudice, The Portrait of a Lady, The Wasteland, The Great Gatsby*.

Now, suddenly, I thought: Who are the losers? I'd always felt the absence of someone like me everywhere I looked, everywhere I read. I began to get inklings of where my writing might start. The absence of Japanese Americans or the internment camps in my high school history books wasn't simply by chance.

But my thoughts weren't that clear yet. The ideas felt murky, like the vague suspicion of a jealous lover, or the unease one feels when a street or road suddenly turns dark. I still wasn't ready. I had no desire to write about myself. That was the last thing I was interested in writing about.

I pleaded with Susie to read the book by Jameson. It was my current bible, my holy text.

She tried. It bored her, she said.

"More than organic chemistry?" I asked. She was well into her premed courses. I had just gotten another incomplete, this time in linguistics. I couldn't stick to the course work. I was too depressed, too interested in other things, Jameson, my writing, drugs, other women.

"Well, at least that's useful," she replied.

"Oh, Phyllis, Phyllis Stein."

"Well, when you read Gray's *Anatomy* . . ."

"I'll be skin and bones."

We were sitting in a small restaurant on the West Bank. The coffee was poured into clear glass cups. When the cream sank in it, the swirls exploded. We shared a pastry of lemon, meringue, and a soft, cakey crust. The waitress who served us was tall and willowy, her blond hair fell in a sheath over the table. She brushed it back. Her earrings were turquoise, her lipstick pale. In the bar below, Bob Dylan had played sets as a college student. Bikers flocked there now, a row of Harleys gleaming on the walk like great steel tigers.

I looked at Susie and suddenly felt it. She seemed totally unsuited to my needs. I thought of the graduate assistant at the desk next to mine on the fourth floor of Lind Hall. I looked across the room at the waitress, at the woman sitting alone in the corner.

And then I thought of the unbridled nature of my desires, what I could not talk about, except with this woman sitting before me, sharing the bill, sipping her tea. Why tea? I thought. I was annoyed at everything. At the thought that I could not leave her, that I had no choice but to stay.

This was too confusing. I pressed on with *Marxism and Form*.

"Jameson's very simple, actually," I said.

"Oh, sure."

"Really. For instance, take his analysis of the advent of chess in Vienna. There's the superior schooling of the Austrians, and the development of a high degree of mathematical proficiency in the population. But, in part because of the location, there's no heavy industry, no place for a cadre of engineers. So, instead, they play chess."

"What has that got to do with anything?"

"It's a way of explaining how history unfolds. How nothing in society takes place randomly. How it all connects at some level to economics."

"I couldn't get past the introduction."

"It's meant to be difficult. Explaining these things isn't supposed to be simple, because the world's not simple."

"Well, maybe I'm simple."

"That's bullshit. You're just lazy."

"Lazy?"

"Okay, not lazy. After all, you are going to medical school." I paused. "Jeez, it's only one book."

"I read every single draft of your poems. Don't you think that counts for something?" Like many poets, I would hand her a draft with a single word changed, and ask her if it was improved. It's a genre for obsessive neurotics, for narcissists engaged in the minutiae of their appearance to the world, their imago.

"Just forget it," I said, and let the conversation lapse into silence.

1978. I'm at a disco. As the glittering ball twirls dots of light across the room, I turn to see a woman staring at me. She looks vaguely like Ann-Margret in *Carnal Knowledge*. Uncertain at first, then flattered, I soon detect something odd in her gaze, as if what she is staring at is not really me. It is a gaze which forms its own field of vision, its own world. But I ignore that. It is enough that she is looking at me. I ask her to dance.

She is even drunker than I am, though I can barely tell that (I've also smoked a couple of joints). Almost immediately she invites me back to her apartment. Her eyes are steel gray. Her hair smells of perfume and smoke. She wears a black dress, very tight, high heels. Her hair is full, brushed and sprayed high off her forehead. I like that.

She tells me I remind her of someone she knew in Paris. She starts speaking in French. I try to respond, but can't remember anything from my college courses. She switches back to English, but keeps lapsing into French phrases, in a way that would seem affected if she and I weren't so drunk. In our separate, inebriated states, the effect is surreal, as if switching back and forth between a dialogue in the original language and then a dubbed version. She asks me if I know the martial arts, if I've ever lived in Paris. I've never been out of the country, I tell her.

I follow her to her apartment. Her car weaves back and forth on the highway, barely making it off the exit. We're in a section of town I've never seen before, a rim of apartment buildings along the highway. She runs a stoplight, then another. I start laughing, half expecting her to wreck her car. I'm worried about losing her and I keep close, running the stoplights like her, twenty miles over the speed limit. A mild adrenaline rush. Part of the chase.

Her apartment is small, one bedroom, nondescript. There's a photograph of a nine-year-old boy on the table at the end of the couch. A dim light in the kitchen. She doesn't bother to turn on anything else. She pours herself a bourbon, offers me a drink.

She talks of her boyfriend in Paris, a Japanese Japanese. He drove a Jaguar, owned a clothing store, was a black belt in judo. He'd take her to Monte Carlo to play baccarat, on drives through the wine country of Burgundy. They'd stay at little châteaus, eat in four-star restaurants at roadside inns, in small out-of-the-way towns. The vineyards sped by, arbor after arbor, then fields of wheat, rippling like the sea. The speedometer over a hundred. Inside, the riders feel nothing, only the roar of the engine, its terrible power.

She was in love with him, though she never states this directly. She talks instead of his glamour, how he was unlike anyone she had ever known. His dark skin, his wealth, his sophistication. He did not want children, never talked about her boy, who was only four then.

Her stories are jumbled, the slurred speech of a drunk. She keeps looking at me, as if by staring, by drinking more, I would become this Japanese, this man she could never forget. She says I look like him, that I am beautiful too.

In the bedroom, for a long time all she lets me do is kiss her. After a while I get up to leave. She pulls me back. I get up to leave again. She pulls me back. She's wearing a black slip, which she never takes off. Something about the way her body changed after her child.

When we make love, she starts to make guttural noises, spouting curses in English and French, shouting at me to shoot her with my jism, to fill her pussy. It startles me, this talk. I feel soiled, alive. I order her to tell me how she loves my cock, she sputters back her response. When I don't come right away, she asks what is wrong. Nothing's wrong, I say. She worries that she's not tight, she has had a child. Nothing's wrong, I repeat.

She does not seem interested in finishing her pleasure, and this bothers me, I who have prided myself on my patience, on bringing women to the end. She seems in a frenzy of her own making, a fit of epithets in her own solitary battle.

Immediately afterward, I want to leave. She's worried again, and talks about her boy. A half hour later, the curtains are pale and translucent. I sit at the edge of the bed, pulling on my underwear. She stubs out a cigarette on the nightstand, and lies back down on the pillow, staring at the ceiling. We do not talk about whether I'll call her again.

I did go back, once or twice. Each time, she talked more about the Japanese in Paris. It was the first time my race had been the main force of attraction, what compelled it to happen. It made me feel odd, as if I were not really there. I wished it would happen more often, though I knew it would not. There was something vaguely disturbing about this woman, as if she were not really present, as if she were some mysterious machine with the shell of a consciousness. And yet, I was thrilled by the sex, how she was so conscious of my color, my otherness. How my race had, with this woman, become a source of power.

SOMETHING WAS CHANGING between Susie and me. The balance between us. In Contemporary Poetry, I chalked up another incomplete. Susie was accepted into medical school. She had a couple of affairs of her own, but she and I knew they meant nothing. I felt they assuaged my guilt. She said she felt depressed. I didn't really think much about that. I was sleeping twelve, fourteen hours a day. The nights drinking, out at the bars, were taking their toll. She started going to a Freudian.

"She says that someone like you can't be cured," Susie said.

"What the hell does she mean by that?"

"It's just the way you are, your obsessions."

"What does she know about my obsessions?"

Susie hadn't told the analyst everything, but what she told was enough. I was furious with her, the analyst, and yet I feared the analyst's diagnosis like a prophecy.

"What do you do there?" I asked.

"I sit and talk. She listens. I keep asking her what she thinks and all she says is 'What do you think?'"

"What good is that?"

"I don't know. I don't know."

That spring, I was drummed out of graduate school for seven incompletes.

"Come back, when you've finished them," said the head of the English graduate students. "Then we'll talk about restoring your teaching associate position."

I knew I was never going to return. I'd failed, the straight-A student. I felt humiliated, as if I'd been branded. I told my parents nothing about this. I said I was taking some time off for my writing.

A month later I won a grant for my poetry. I worked in the Writers-in-the-Schools, and then won another grant. None of it made up for my graduate school failure. Linguistics; Contemporary Poetry; Modern Poetry; Elizabethan Poetry; Feminism, Psychoanalysis, and Shakespeare; the Romantics; Eighteenth-Century Novel—my backlog of incompletes ran the gamut. Despite my grants, we were more and more dependent on Susie's income from the Public Health Department. We drove a car given to her by her parents. My drugs and drinking seemed to be gathering to some crescendo. I told myself I was an artist, not a scholar, that my lack of discipline was part of my nature, a willingness to walk the razor's edge, slipping and cutting his sole, a sheaf of ankle bone, marking the notches of experience. I had no idea where I was going.

4.

THERE WERE BARS in the city where the dresses glittered and the women's eyes were darkened by shadow, their hair smelling of smoke and Ralph Lauren. Young owners of restaurants or hair salons, students from Tehran or Saudi Arabia, football players, salesmen from fashionable shops. In other bars, jeans and long, straight hair abounded, and boots scuffed the sticky, beer-painted floor. Bikers, high school dropouts or runaways, students out for a wild night. "Don't roll your bloodshot eyes at me," shouted the lead singer. There were the massage

parlors, their storefronts without windows, a plain-looking woman behind a counter, greeting customers. There were the lobbies of porno
movie houses with even plainer and older women in the ticket booth.
Or the high-volume disco and lights of a runway at the strip joints in
East St. Paul or on Hennepin, the young women from Fargo or Farm-
ington or Brooklyn Center, who spring down to their haunches, bal-
ancing on high heels, a look of defiance. To these places came all types
of men. Some smiled, at ease, sipping beers. Others were nervous,
furtive, plying themselves with drinks. I was more like the latter.

I was in all those places, at different times. A quick drunk, I'd get
stoned beforehand, with a bong or with brownies laced with marijuana. It was easier to talk to women that way. Or to stare at them
unabashedly. It was easier then to cross line after line, moving into
forbidden zones with a boldness that almost astonished me, an increasing frequency that was fueled by a fury, a rage I was unable to articulate but could only enact.

There was a ritual to my preparations. A bath, a shave. Silk black
pants or jeans, depending on the place, a silk or denim shirt and jacket.
After sifting through the seeds and stems of marijuana, I patted the
leaves down in the small wooden bowl of the bong, watched as the
flakes caught fire and glowed, like red throbbing coals, burning
brighter with each breath, transformed toke by toke into a city of fire.
Slowly, the buildings animated into dancing figures, shadows outlined
against a basin of flames.

The minutes passed, I did not notice. I looked up as if from a
dream, took a sip of beer or vodka, then went back to the bong. And
all the while I was imagining women, white women, preferably blond. I
thought of rejections by them as a curse, born of my skin. I wished my
face were leaner, tauter. Staring in the mirror, getting ready to go out, I
sucked in my cheeks, imagining how I'd look a few pounds thinner,
with a more prominent facial structure.

There is a knowledge which destroys. Each time I went out, I felt

I had to go further, to lose myself. There was something out there, some woman, some image, that would transform me, let me enter that dream I was creating out of dope and booze and the magazines piled in my closet, their glossy pages of copulation and flesh, their world where there is no other reality but sex. *Playboy, Hustler, Swedish Erotica.* Sometimes I went to the bars first, trying my luck, often leaving at closing time for the porno stores.

At other times, I headed straight to the movies in darkened theaters, the damp, acrid smell that wafted up as I sat amid a dozen other anonymous men. The plots of the movies were improbable, at times ludicrous, at times tinged with a strange sense of morality, of sin and damnation. In one of the more famous, a young woman commits suicide; she has remained a virgin all her life, and now, in the afterlife, she begs to go back for what she has missed. She is granted her wish, coupling with men and women, engaging in twosomes, threesomes, orgies, her desires are indefatigable, her eyes shut tight upon her pleasure, her lips quivering. She sucks in breath through flared nostrils, urges her partner on. At the end of the film, she enters a circle in hell and is placed in a room with a middle-aged bearded man who talks on endlessly about the meaninglessness of existence and will not fuck her and has no interest in sex. This is her punishment, her eternity.

I watched this parable of damnation, believing and disbelieving. It was a construct, a fiction. I didn't care.

THE FILM I REMEMBER best from that time is *Behind the Green Door.* In the opening scenes, a young white woman is kidnapped, dragged in through an alley door to a dressing room, stripped, bathed with oil by four handmaidens, who stroke her thighs, her stomach, her nipples, who kiss her lips. One kneels before her, the young woman closes her eyes. She is the woman on the Ivory Snow soap box, smiling her pure, white All-American smile, a baby cooing at her shoulder. Then she is laid upon a table by the attending women on a stage. The audience is in tuxedos and gowns and sits upon couches. The maître d' is a former pro football player. There are midgets, an enormously rotund woman. The atmosphere is of a carnival in a horror film. Then, to a quavering guitar and a strong bass beat, a black man emerges from behind a lighted green door at the back of the stage. His face and chest are painted with streaks of white paint, a necklace of claws encircles his neck. He is naked except for white stretch pants with a large circle cut out at the crotch. He kneels before the young blond woman, and puts his tongue to her. She begins to writhe. The fat woman in the audience begins to touch herself, the dwarves begin to mount her. The black man pulls back, is serviced by one of the handmaidens, then guides himself in. They make love for a long time, you can feel her excitement mounting. From time to time, she opens her eyes and pulls his face down and kisses him. By the end, her head is shaking back and forth violently, as in a seizure. He is riding above her, propped on his arms. She screams again and again, slowly falling into whimpers, as the black man lifts himself off her quivering body and retreats from the stage in the same slow, deliberate motion as he entered. The film cuts to the young blond woman astraddle another black man, while three other men, two white, one black, are suspended before her on gymnastic rings.

Amid this welter of sexual acts, I know the movie has something to do with miscegenation, with what Susie and I represent together. I know this has something to do with the other I am not, the black man, representative of the primitive, of Africa, striding across the screen, larger than life. Other myths, other taboos. The images fuse with my own history. I hear echoes of literary passages, of the glossy pages in my closet, of cheap paperbacks with their rumors of black prowess. I know there is something missing, that I will never find my body, my Asian body, up there on the screen, and this rage erases all other considerations, consumes me. In the twisted logic coagulating in my brain, I am determined to create my own damnation, to uncover the pornographic behind any facade of innocence, to prove that sexuality drives us, or should drive us all, if we were only bold and free enough.

IT'S A WARM SPRING NIGHT. A Saturday. Perhaps I've had a poem accepted somewhere and want to celebrate. It's also a few weeks after I've been let go from graduate school and am still depressed about that. Either way I think I deserve a reward, a hit. This is where my comfort lies, the way I escape from my failures.

I drive to a disco on the 494 strip, the women in glitter dresses or tank tops, high heels, and long polished nails, the men in suits or silk shirts. I start out drinking doubles, quickening my high. Over and over nothing works. Each woman I talk to wears the mask of rejection, each proposal to dance poses a potential shattering. I give up and hit another bar downtown, in an old bank building, the same one in which I met the woman with the Japanese boyfriend in Paris. The music is the same thudding dance beat, the same strobe and glittering globe flash along the walls.

I find no one. They have all rejected me. I do not know why. It's not just my ugliness, my lack of smoothness or confidence or money, my inability to engage in bar banter. In every face I see there, mainly white, a few black men, there's never one of my own, and if there is, she will be with some rich white boy, she will not notice me. She will look at me as some remnant she must shed, a reminder of a world, a people, she wants no part of, she is better than that.

And then I'm on Lake Street, the place John Berryman and Saul Bellow, my literary gods, used to call the land of used cars. Twenty years later, it's the home of porno theaters and massage parlors, all-night pizza parlors. I hurtle my battered Toyota into the parking lot of an X-rated bookstore, rush past the scrawled graffiti toward the lighted doorway, the glass windows of the store around it painted black. Smashed beer bottles crackle beneath my feet on the asphalt.

Back and forth, I shuttle among the dark video booths in the porno store, each hawking their sundry fantasies, each black plywood box with a single stool inside, the reek of stale urine and come sifting up from the floor. Having made my choice, I am as alone in this box as I will ever be; at that moment it is the image of what my life must become, how it will end. I hold myself back, waiting to prolong what I think of as pleasure, the sensation that will spur me on through the night, through booth after booth, quarter after quarter, until my money is exhausted, though not my will to go on. I keep picking up magazines, looking for the right one, going up to the clerk, a young boy with a goatee and a dragon tattoo showing from his sleeveless T-shirt. I drive home, opening the cellophane of the magazines on the way back, paging through them at the stoplights. In my stoned state, time freezes each image, the genitals and faces spilled across the page, the long blond hair of the models. A car honks behind me. I startle awake.

I retreat further, dig down deeper, the images from the videos swirling with images from the dance floor, the newly bought magazines on the seat beside me, the road swerving back and forth, my foot on the gas pedal pressing down harder, and the despair and rage at the world coursing faster and faster through my body like a seizure, a pronouncement of fate. I head back to our apartment unsatisfied, agitated, chemicals and adrenaline venting through my veins.

Susie knows I will come home like this. That her role is to soothe and subdue me. An impossible task. There is an energy in our lovemaking that is not love at all, and it is growing. She begins to lie to me about her pleasure, how she wants it. She feels herself growing smaller and smaller, like the sound of a voice falling down a well. She sits in the old battered chair in the corner and waits for me, reading her textbooks, trying to remember equations and reactions, phyla and physics, worrying about the test next week, what my mood will be like. She tries hard to believe the lies. She tells herself she can't go on any longer like this, and knows this too is a lie.

She runs a Pap smear clinic for indigent women. There are nights I will berate her beauty almost till dawn, when I will punch a wall in fury or smash a window with my fist, when I will lay in the swirling snow of an alley and wail like a wounded animal. There is a play on Mishima beside the typewriter in the living room. It is one-thirty, and she sits in her chair waiting. She knows I will be home soon. She knows me better than anyone else in the world, even better than herself. She is twenty-three, twenty-four, twenty-six. These are the years, in the future, she would like to forget.

"TO WANT A WOMAN LIKE A FIX." That's one way of putting it. But at times a real woman, one I might pick up, was too dangerous, too threatening. There was safety in images, photos or film, in watching others. A detachment born out of control, maintaining control, buying control. The self that watched could not be violated. I could watch and watch and no one would know, no one would see. It was as if those on-screen were to live the actuality of sex, some in their own private hells, yes, but living nonetheless, while I was removed from life, set apart. The haze of hash helped, liquor, poppers. To get fucked up. To obliterate consciousness.

Certainly I felt rage. At women. At Susie. At myself. At my parents. At whites. At Asians, the women for abandoning me, the men for being like me, invisible, laughed at like Hop Sing cooks and messengers, servants groveling before the white mistress and master.

• • •

A FRIEND OF MINE says that many of those in our baby-boom generation who found our life partners early on weren't prepared to be monogamous; we were too young and the times were geared for sexual experimentation. The attitude toward drugs was looser then; even into the late seventies there was an openness about sexual relations, about moving beyond traditional patterns, that was widely prevalent in the culture. Marriage, we thought, was a dead institution. Or at least something that could wait. There was so much else to explore. In short, everybody was screwing around.

"It's not like you and Susie were the only ones with crazy sexual relationships," said another friend. "God, when I think of some of the things I did. We all did." He described an article in *Newsweek* about the sexual life on campuses today. It's still going on there, coed shower parties, multiple partners. And pornography? Things only began to shift in the early eighties, when the feminists began pouring out these critiques, and they were right in a lot of what they said about pornography. But during the seventies, pornography was still seen as a descendant of the free love movements of the sixties, as an attack on the establishment and the puritanical view of sex as sin and damnation. It was part of the effort to free the body, not shackle it. "Maybe we were wrong," he said. "But you weren't the only one who was wrong."

There's so much, though, that my friend's framework fails to explain. It's too generic, too easy a way out.

THERE WERE DIFFERENT POINTS when things between Susie and me plummeted near the bottom. Our battling grew to a ferocity that frightened us, that dulled our senses. There seemed no way out. It's amazing to me now how long we went on like this. Always after such bouts, we'd return to a sense of normalcy, of routine. It's not that we lived a double life; it was more complicated than that. There were layers after layers to our relationship, a convoluted movement that kept spinning from light to dark, increasing over these years to darker and darker. At times, we went to movies, to readings and restaurants, and sat there like any young couple in love, talking about poets or premed students, Susie's job, my class on the Bloomsbury group, calculus tests. This was one layer. Pornography, drunken and stoned despair, an almost clinical depression, formed other layers; other layers involved my affairs, the other women I was with. From this distance in time it feels difficult to meld them together, perhaps because they were never melded; perhaps only by compartmentalizing our actions, our psyches, could we go on like that. There was always something schizophrenic about our lives then, our relationship. We were intelligent, educated, attractive. I was going to be a professor, she a doctor. We had everything going for us. At times, we were happy. At other times, profoundly unhappy, and that was becoming who we were.

There were days I never left my bed, when I lay there in the sheets, my consciousness stirring in and out, the buzz of hash and booze still veering through my veins, and something deeper, heavier, pressing me back in the bed like an invisible wall, a wave of drowsiness washing over me. Susie would come in, look at me on the bed, and then leave. I could feel her presence standing above me, but I couldn't, wouldn't open my eyes. I wanted only to sleep. The late-afternoon shadows floated in the room, signaling another day gone, the sad waste of time before and after. My body curled amid the sheets, twisting them about me. Darkness, silence, enveloped me, the opiate of oblivion. There was no going back. I would never get up.

Jinnosuke's Biwa

I can no more turn back
than can an arrow in flight
shot when a warrior
extends the bow of birchwood
handed down from his forebears.

—*The Tales of the Heike*

JUST AFTER I left graduate school I wrote a poem about my grandfather, "Relocation," the first poem I knew would be a "keeper." The poem alluded to the fact that many of the Japanese marriages in America at the turn of the century were the result of picture brides, and in this process, some men doctored their pictures, sending photos of their younger selves or even someone else. My grandfather, though, was "so handsome, he came in person" to arrange his marriage. The poem describes his nights gambling in Little Tokyo, his tending of mules in the internment camps, and his reaction to his son's conversion to Christianity and changing his name from Katsugi to Tom. It closes with the old man writing a haiku:

> Bonsai tree,
> like me you are useless
> and a little sad.

At the time, I still felt a certain hesitancy about writing on Japanese American subjects. Many of my poems were imitations of American or Spanish surrealists, poems with "dark wings" and "stones" and unattached parts of the body.

There was, though, something in this poem about my paternal grandfather. Not only did it connect me with a past my parents seldom spoke about, but he offered another male figure besides my father, someone beyond the middle-class American dream of assimilation and success he so fervently worked for. My grandfather, in the family lore, was wastrel, a profligate gambler and carouser, and he was interested in art; he wrote haiku and played the *biwa*, a Japanese stringed instrument. "He'd always be out there on the front porch, singing and strumming away," says my Aunt Ruby, "when he should have been working. I don't know sometimes how my mother put up with him."

This grasshopper picture of my grandfather only endeared him to me more. I felt I was more like him than like my father, and since my grandfather wasn't alive, I didn't have to deal with real cultural differences between us or the actuality of his personality. He became for me a friendly figure of fun, a mentor of sorts, someone calling me to a different life.

Perhaps I also sensed that, however distant my father felt from the costs of the camps, my grandfather could not have been so stoic and forgiving, so inclined to forget. My Aunt Ruth had told me about the time she had asked my grandfather to sign the loyalty oath. She felt impassioned about her patriotic duty, the need for Japanese Americans to prove to the country that they were loyal Americans, that a mistake had been made.

My grandfather pulled out his cigar, spat in the dirt, and looked at her. "When they let me out of this place, then I'll sign."

Certainly, he never bought into the dream of America the way my father did. How could he when he was allowed to become a citizen only after the war, when the laws forbidding Japanese from becoming citizens were finally changed?

When my grandfather was studying for his citizenship test, his children coached him, trying to help him remember through mnemonics. "The group that advises the President is called the cabinet. Just think of this piece of furniture," said my Aunt Ruth, and she pointed to a cabinet in her living room. "And whatever you do, don't say any more than you're asked."

In the judge's chambers the day of the test, my grandfather passed question after question. Finally, the judge asked, "Which body advises the President?" My grandfather's confidence already on the rise, he smiled boldly. "The dresser."

The judge passed him anyway. But a few years later, in his late sixties, my grandfather returned to Japan to live out his last years and to remarry someone twenty years younger. Probably it wasn't so much a rejection of America as a return to a setting that was more comfortable, where he knew the language. With the exchange rate, he appeared to his relatives as a rich uncle, buying slabs of bacon, chocolate, fans, and refrigerators for cousins and great-nieces and great-nephews, smoking huge Cuban cigars, living off the money his children sent him, the small retirement fund built up after the war working at the Edgewater Hotel.

In Japan, after he remarried, he suffered a small stroke. Upon his recovery, he sat down again to write. But the brush kept slipping from his grasp. His second wife said he went up the stairs, weeping, entered his bedroom, and shut the door. He stayed there for two days, lying on the futon, not speaking, not eating a thing. Finally, he got up, walked out of the house, and came back with a bottle of sake and a new box of cigars. By the time he returned, she had thrown away all his writing utensils. She may have been his second wife, but she understood that.

His ashes were buried somewhere in the great cemetery on Mount Koya. When my Aunt Ruby went to Japan for the first time, she searched for hours to find his headstone. Up and down the stones of that mountain graveyard she walked. Finally, unable to find it, in the cedar shadows, on the needled stone path, she broke down weeping. She felt she had failed as a daughter, the remnants of her father's bones irrevocably lost.

It seems an emblem of my task: The past lies in this vase. The vase is gone.

For me, my grandfather's return to Japan is connected with the camps, another "relocation." It marks a severing of a tie to America that was never allowed to become permanent. First the laws, then the internment prevented this. The loss of his urn, the loss of the past, that too seems part of our history, our postinternment amnesia.

When I went to Japan in 1985, I began a novel about his life. I saw that only by learning about Japan, the culture he and my other grandparents came from, could I begin to understand not only who he was but also who my father and mother were. It altered the way I looked at everyone in our family. Suddenly, they all seemed both more familiar and more alien, more knowable and further from my life.

Perhaps too much of the cord to the past had been cut. Or perhaps I wasn't up to the task. At any rate, the novel was a failure. All I've kept are a few scattered fragments.

MY AUNT RUBY, the youngest daughter:

"He was old, older than he looked. In his forties when I was born. But he was good-looking, dapper even. There was a voluptuousness to his face, something of the pretty boy that stayed even as he aged. His skin stayed smooth a long while after his prime, especially the rounded planes of his face.

"He was never one to look for work. He liked women, he loved his poetry and his *biwa*. Like a lot of Issei, he gambled too much.

"Looking at his face, you could see that he kept his secrets. There was a period during the twenties when he ran liquor with a Mexican or a Filipino. They'd drive down south and cross the border. He never told my mother. There was some story about a white woman he gave presents to. That was later, almost near the war. Maybe there were others, maybe my mother found out just because she was white. That was something in those days, people did notice.

"He never thought much about *hakujin*, except during the war when they put us in prison. When Ruth asked him to sign the loyalty oath and he refused, I was angry at him for days. He didn't understand how it was for us; we were born in America. It was all we had.

"He was a man who liked to read the papers. He was overeducated really. He should have been a rich man's son. He lived like a rich man's son. Only he had no money. So that meant we all lived poorer than we were. Some days he'd buy my mother a dress and have to return it the next day. His suits were expensive and immaculate, not something he could afford. Sometimes I wondered why my mother put up with it, but not very often. I liked him too much. He had a swagger that was larger than life, he wasn't afraid of *hakujin* or the respectable *Nihonjin*, the big shots in the community. He had style.

"Even if their marriage was arranged, I know they loved each other. After the war, when we were living in Chicago, my Honey and I went to the movies with my parents. We were just married. We were sitting there watching the movie—I think it was *Rodan*, the horror movie—and I looked over and saw my parents were holding hands. Here my Honey and I were just sitting there watching the movie, and we'd barely been married, and my parents were the ones holding hands.

"He seemed courtly with company, coarse with other men. There was a slyness to him, but he never lied, except to my mother, and that wasn't lying really, because she always knew when he was doing it. He was always touching her. When he'd leave the room, he'd brush his hand on her shoulder. That was unusual for a Japanese man.

"When we were in camp he said he felt like a tiger. I didn't understand then what he meant. He asked me if I thought tigers were happier in the zoo since they didn't have to worry about hunters. He laughed. Don't take any wooden nickels, kid. He liked to use expressions like that. To show he knew English.

"I don't think any of us really understood what the camps meant to him and my mother. What they lost. We were too young to notice, too young to be bitter. Some of the older Nisei, they spoke better Japanese, they had a sense of what was being taken away.

"Still it all turned out all right for him, for us. Look at what we've become.

"To tell you the truth, I don't really know anything about whether he had an affair with a white woman. Maybe Ruth is just making that up.

"Women liked him, though. It's not that he tried to change himself to be with them. He had this charm, this ease. He was rough, but he wasn't. Friendly, certainly, but more than that. He just wasn't withdrawn like the other Issei men, he wasn't stiff. He liked to tell jokes, he was literate and yet never went beyond high school.

"I think he was an unusual man. He had—oh, I don't know—he had spunk. That's a funny word. Old-fashioned, I suppose. But that's it. He had spunk."

THE JOURNEY that my grandfather took at the beginning of this century was monstrous and improbable. He came from an island culture, a civilization cut off for centuries from the rest of the world, a country which had managed to escape foreign invaders and the seemingly inexorable advances of European imperialism. An insular, rooted people, the opposite of nomads or explorers.

Of course, there were extenuating circumstances surrounding his departure. Besides poverty and his status as a second son who would inherit nothing of the family's property, he wished to escape being conscripted for the Russo-Japanese War (I like to think of myself as coming from a long line of draft dodgers; my application for a CO during the Vietnam War, which infuriated my father, seemed to echo my grandfather's refusal).

Still, most Japanese of his generation, despite the circumstances, elected to remain. To them going off to America, the land of barbarians, open spaces and ghost-white people, was unthinkable. Better to stick with what you know, with your own people, even if there is a chance you may starve to death or be drilled through the forehead by a Russian bullet.

Why did my grandfather make that journey? What was he seeking? What in his character was so prone to risk and wildness, to the unknown? What did he find here in America? And what part of him lies inside me?

I know I will never make a journey like his. My trip to Japan, supported by a government fellowship, was nothing like his. I risked virtually nothing. His stepping off the boat at Angel Island, walking into that prison filled with Chinese, Japanese, and a few Filipinos, waiting in those cramped cells to be let into America, was nothing like my coming through customs at Narita, astonished that all the people around me looked like me.

LIKE MY PARENTS, my grandfather and grandmother remained together and in love. Does the wholeness I imagine in their sexuality, the combination of sensuality and love, reflect more my own desires for a past not rent by the internment camps or questions of identity? Is it a myth I'm creating in counterpoint to the reality of my own sexuality? In my poems, their lives possess a center I lack. Race doesn't enter their bedroom. They share a common culture. They recall a common past.

My grandmother was a psychic. Near the end of World War II, after having been transferred to the camp at Heart Mountain, she awoke one night screaming. She had seen her sister engulfed in fire, a seething burst of dragon flames swallowing her body. The face of her sister in that moment was more real than my grandfather trying to shake her awake, to still her trembling body. *"Daijōbu, daijōbu,"* he kept muttering as she kept muttering her sister's name.

She never fell back asleep that night, even as my grandfather lay snoring beside her minutes later. She listened to the sounds of the barracks and the mice scurrying beneath the cupboards and the prairie wind whistling through the walls, and tumbled out memory after memory, the future merging, mixing up the past.

Just after the war ended, a letter arrived from Japan. It informed my grandmother that her sister had died during the night of her dream in a firebombing raid on Tokyo.

My grandfather hated my grandmother's dreams. After all, in the family lore, one of those dreams told her he'd been cheating on her with a white mistress. She woke him with a knife at his throat—"If you ever . . ."—leaving a little nick and a drop of blood for remembrance.

He felt she was too superstitious. He feared her powers. She was like the occult figures in folk tales, the blind women shamans at Mount Osore.

Perhaps that's why he kept escaping to his haiku and *biwa*. Not just because he was lazy or playful, but because he too sought his own connections and powers.

The *biwa* is an ancient instrument, a thousand years older than the more popular samisen. Its four or five strings are of twisted silk, rather than the cat or dog hide used for samisens. Traditionally, the *biwa* was played by blind men, *biwa hōshi*, itinerant entertainers who, like blind Homer, strummed and sang tales of ancient battles and huge heroes, of tragic defeats on seashores or fields where ravens picked the bodies of the dead. Sutras and incantations, verses from the tales of the Heike, so distant in time and culture from the L.A. streets and my grandfather's porch, as he closed his eyes and sang, pulling from his throat a warlord's boasts, a mistress's lament, hundreds of lines from a medieval Japanese song.

Sometimes I imagine myself sitting there before him, knowing all I know and yet still a boy, an apprentice, my spine upright, my ears attentive. I'm completely silent, none of the raucous laughter I evinced at eight or nine when I sat with my cousins at his annual memorial service on the North Side of Chicago. I hear the songs over and over and I never tire of them, their music is mournful, slated with soul, quavering like the blues, the notes bent up or down in a delta twist.

My job is not to question but to listen, to repeat in my mind over and over the melodies and words until they form the very fiber of my larynx, the phalanxes of my thought.

> *From far Gion the temple bell*
> *echoes the transience of all things.*
> *The sala blossoms' color*
> *whispers the great must fall,*
> *the mighty will vanish*
> *like dreams on a spring night.*
> *Destroyed at last,*
> *their dust wheels in the wind.*

Like my grandmother, like my grandfather, I'm blessed and cursed with images of the future and the past. I hear the camps in these lines, the edicts of emperors and presidents, of generals and petty officials, of mothers and fathers and wayward sons. I am Atsumori, my thighs burning and twisting in the foam off the beach, my death moments away, I am Yoshitsune, who could leave his mistresses but never his lust, I am Munemori, so unwise in battle, so passionate in his longing for his wife and children, I am part of the Taira clan that vanished, defeated by treachery and folly and pride and the force of fate, our earthly presence reduced to syllables in an old man's mouth. I learn the lessons I need to go out into the world, to take this poetry to the ears of strangers.

Bittersweet

"Illusions about the things of this world do not concern their existence, but their value. The image of the cave refers to values . . . We accept the false values which appear to us, and when we think we are acting, we are in reality motionless, for we are still confined in the same system of values."

—SIMONE WEIL,
GRAVITY AND GRACE

1.

I HAVE A LESBIAN FRIEND who writes so explicitly about sex it embarrasses many readers. Of course, there's an element of homophobia in this. But there's also a difference in time. She says the way she writes comes from what she and her friends will talk about at a dinner party—eating pussy, making love that afternoon, the smells or tastes or techniques of a new lover, and then the conversation will roll on to something else, k. d. lang, the Middle East, buying a new jacket, whatever.

"Jane's a queer," says another friend. "I'm a lesbian. There's a generation between us. I don't care what my photo looks like on the back of my book. She does."

We are creatures of community, grouped together, whether we like it or not, even in the bedroom.

To me, the idea of an erotic Japanese American novel seems an oxymoron. Perhaps much of my writing is doomed to fail from the start. What of my writing is bound by my generation's sensibility, unable to imagine other ways of speaking about sex?

A FRIEND WHO'S A THERAPIST tells me of this phenomenon she's noticed with several young Asian American women clients. Each of these women says that the thought of going out with another Asian fills them with revulsion. It would be, say these women, like going out with their brother. Indeed these women find this feeling so strong that when they think of making love with an Asian man, they feel nauseous. They want to vomit.

I asked my therapist friend about the specific ethnic background of these women and where they grew up.

My friend said that now that she thought about it, all were Japanese Americans. All but one had grown up in the Midwest.

When my sister dated a Chinese American medical student from Yale, she said it felt incestuous to her. She didn't say if she felt like vomiting.

She has never dated another Asian American. She married a Jewish medical student. Now she dates a WASP bond trader.

What, I wonder, is natural? What is sexual attraction? How is it formed? When an Asian American falls in love with someone of another race—almost always a white person—how are we to interpret their explanation that they were attracted to an individual, that race wasn't a factor?

If the Japanese women in Japan felt like the clients of my therapist friend, there would be no Japanese race.

Yet when I questioned my friend, she said she never really examined this phenomenon very deeply in her sessions with these clients. They had other, more pressing problems.

I should add that my friend is Jewish and is married to a Chinese American man. These things are more complicated than they first appear.

We were discussing all this at dinner, my wife and I, my friend and her husband. My wife asked my friend how this made her feel about her children's sexuality, the nature of their desires and how others might look at them. Somehow my friend never quite answered that question.

Her husband and I both agreed it was, in part, race, and, in part, the condition of growing up in the Midwest, where most of the Asian community consisted of relatives. Neither of us talked about the fact that we both had married a white woman.

•   •   •

IN *THE RAVISHING OF LOL STEIN* by Marguerite Duras, a young woman watches her husband dance with another woman. Gradually, the young woman realizes her husband is becoming attracted to this woman. Instead of finding this painful, instead of rushing in to prevent any liaison from occurring, she feels herself strangely in accord with her husband's move away from her toward this other woman. She identifies with his decision, his desires. It is as if she were canceling not only her own desires but her very being. She forgets to suffer the pain of losing her husband, her rage at his betrayal. This, says the author, is why she becomes mad, why she loses her mind. She forgets to suffer. It is like the phenomenon that occurs when the air is still and the weather is cold, at the temperature of freezing, but the water in a river or lake or pond forgets to freeze. The temperature must descend further for the icing to occur.

The long, slow movement into oblivion. Of course, I see this in Susie's response to my infidelities. But I also see it in the Asian American clients of my friend. I see it in my lack of desire for Asian women as a young man, in my desire for my wife, in my secret fear that my wife would betray me with a white man, my secret desire that the man will not be white, but black. It is part of the pervasive nature of my sexual desires. It sings at the very heart of my lust.

2.

THE OTHER DAY I received a letter from an old lover.

She has two children now and lives in Boston. One of the children has a disease which she does not specify. It is, she says, the tragedy of her life. Nothing in her life now seems what she expected. She has lost contact with all her former friends in the city where she used to live and where we met. At times, she sits in her kitchen, at some quiet hour, the children at day care or asleep, her husband at work or asleep, and she stares at the swing set which only one of the children can use, at the long, drooping branches of the weeping willow in her yard, and she thinks about her life and wonders how she got to this point. I don't know if her marriage is happy or not. I know tragedies like spina bifida or autism or Down's syndrome can place such strains on a couple, and for some couples this is too much. What would have been a satisfactory marriage if nothing untoward had ever happened becomes a marriage whose very foundation seems to be disappointment and depression.

She writes that of all the people she knew before she moved, I was the one she remembered. She quotes from some poem: "They come, they go. They change you more than they know." Or maybe it's "you know." She sent that on a card to me nearly twenty years ago, when she was nineteen and I was twenty-three.

In the letter, Michelle says that she saw *The Lover* a week ago, the film of the Marguerite Duras novel about an affair between a young Chinese banker and a French schoolgirl in colonial Vietnam. Although the script wasn't written by Duras, it retains enough of the book to become the vibrant-hued echo of the black-and-white film, *Hiroshima, Mon Amour*, a film written by Duras about an affair between a Japanese architect and a French actress in the city of Hiroshima. For me these films, as well as the novel *The Lover*, are talismans, the only echoes in a media-saturated world where I find anything resembling the sexual relationships I have had. It seems a rather generic connection, but in the vague desperation of the Chinese banker or the Japanese architect, in the way they seem to pursue their French lovers, in the ways the issues of race and colonialism filter the vision of their affair, as if peering upon figures grappling in a bed through the cover of netting, in all these slippages I feel something in my own psyche responding. I know those men, they are inside me. I know that bed.

Michelle writes that she thought of me after seeing that movie.

Not in a romantic way, she says, but in some sentimental, nostalgic way, in some past where she was free from the burdens or responsibilities or trappings of her present life, where all was possibility, where there was this young graduate student who read Shakespeare with her and helped her with her papers, who took her to the best restaurants he could afford and then dancing, who changed her in ways he did not know. Reading this, I felt that for her our affair somehow retained a nobility, a purity of emotion I did not share, and that my interpretation of what our affair had been was only half of the story, only my interpretation.

She ended by remarking that I had not answered a couple of cards she had written periodically in the last few years. She assumed that my not writing said more about the business of my life than my feelings about her. On the surface, she was right in this. I am a poor correspondent in regard to personal letters. They are just something I do not do. Perhaps this is the male inability to retain connections, to keep contact with the past, but I think it's more complicated than that. Often, the emotions I feel are too confused and shameful, too difficult to reconcile in a single letter.

I HAD A LINGUISTICS CLASS just before Michelle's. After the tedious task of diagramming sentences or the structural semantics of Chomsky, I'd see her smiling at me as I left the classroom. She wore cutoffs that showed tanned legs, toned by lengths and lengths of swimming. Despite this lean muscularity, there was a fleshiness to her body that would have hinted of something more zaftig if she hadn't been in such great shape. That was what attracted me to her. That and her hair, which was carefully curled and flipped off her face in generous waves. As my wife has often said, "You like women with big hair."

My wife, I should point out, has never had big hair. Or what would be called a classically voluptuous body. Can you choose what excites you sexually, what elicits your desires? I see these women in the light of my sexual fantasies, in the role of an affair. In appearance, they seem to have bought into a certain feminine ideal that smacks of fifties foldouts or country-and-western singers or actresses in grade B sorority flicks.

Not women you take to poetry readings. Not intellectuals. Not my wife.

The way this demarcation works is quite familiar. Yet it's not simply the difference between the women you fuck and the one you love. In my case, I felt a particular sexual charge with those women who looked as if they would never imagine having an Asian lover. I was excited by what I thought would deny me, what was most forbidden.

And the fact that Michelle was attracted to me?

That was a sign that I was special. I was not like other Asian men. I possessed a sexual power most of them lacked.

Yet the fact was I didn't know many Asian or Asian American men. What I was fighting against was the stereotype of the asexual Asian man, the eunuch gook. Nothing I did could prevent such images from cropping up in the media. Nor could I change what I imagined was the way most whites looked at me. Throughout my twenties, I constantly suspected those women who found me attractive were exceptions. I almost never saw an Asian man with a white woman, though I'd certainly seen examples of a white man with an Asian woman.

Deep down, I knew that if I was different from other Asian men, I wasn't that different. In the hierarchy of American sexuality, we were all relegated to the bottom. I was just more enraged than most at finding myself there.

Instead of constantly pursuing white women, there were other reactions I could have had. I've come to see the falseness in the ways I measured myself against the grid of racial sexuality, how much I was searching for some validation that was simply not there. I could have chosen to ignore the stereotype; I could have dated only women of color or Asian women; I could have tried to be less self-conscious about my sexuality. But I was for the most part unconscious of what was driving my behavior. I did not let myself see I had a choice.

I TAKE HER TO MAGIC PAN or Chez Colette, the North Star Inn, a young man's images of sophistication. I spend as much as I can given my stipend as a graduate assistant. Crêpes biegnet, beef Wellington, coq au vin. The waiter is elderly, suspicious. I pay in cash.

We go dancing at discos, the awful and tasteless music of the times. I wear a three-piece suit and am a good dancer. My hair stylishly long, I look like a Hong Kong punk.

She lives in a sorority and this excites me. When I visit her, there are always other attractive women around. I play piano for her in the lounge. She asks if there is nothing I cannot do. I smile and say nothing.

We make love on our second date. She comes back with me to the apartment I share with Susie. It is in the basement of a three-story complex, the bedroom window faces the parking lot. White plaster walls, used furniture. Cheap student housing. I have arranged for Susie to be elsewhere. Michelle knows about her, I have hidden nothing. It is almost like dating a married man. She doesn't care. Later she told me she had forced herself to wait for our second date.

In the bedroom, we smoke from a bong. Disco music again on the stereo, Donna Summer. A dense cloud begins to hover above the bed. My movements are slow, deliberate. Tense. I don't always perform well the first time, and this worries me. After I kiss her, she pulls back, asks me to wait. She goes to the washroom. When the door opens again, she stands before me naked. Her body blinds me, moves me with its power. I take a long time preparing her, my tongue patient, probing. I love the smell of her, of women; it intoxicates me, a rush of adrenaline, an instant high.

I am floating above her. Her legs are powerful, a counterweight to my motions. It is as if I were rowing in violent oceanic waters, the current strong and deep. I am afraid she will thrust me off of her. I push down. We sprawl about the futon, turning in a circle, tangled amid the sheets. We spill out onto the floor, in a slipstream of movement. Back onto the bed. She is moaning beneath me. I want it to go on forever. I am weakening, I cannot stop.

It will get even better than this. Always I will recall the tremendous push of her thighs, the way our bodies circle the bed. The blue panties I uncover when she allows me to undress her. How she tells me there is no one like me, the other men she has been with are nothing.

We do not talk of the woman I live with. That is a zone of silence. A place we pretend does not exist. This is one of the lies I use to satisfy my desires, and if there's a sense of shame in this lie, there's also a sense of power, a feeling that I'm getting away with something, that I'm entitled to do this.

SHE TALKS of her high school years, how she ran away from home often. Hitched from her small town to the city. To Colorado and ski country. She took acid, smoked dope, drank herself into a stupor. Was absent from school for weeks at a time. Her father died when she was fourteen. She warred with her mother. Her boyfriends were drug dealers, petty thieves, ski bums. Older than her. Her father had been an insurance salesman, had left the family enough money when he died. Her mother remarried. A car dealer, her stepfather was a stranger, someone she had no attachment to, not even anger or resentment. She hated her small town, its quaint ways. Had she made it all the way to

California as she had planned one summer hitching, who knows what would have happened.

Then in the last semester of her senior year, something changed. She started attending school, quit the boyfriends, the running away from home. While the other kids circled the main street in their cars and pickups, she spent her weekends writing in her diary. She read fashion magazines, *Jane Eyre, Pride and Prejudice.* She still said nothing to her mother, but they had stopped their war. She even regretted the trouble she had given her. She stopped the drugs except for the marijuana. She was going to college next year, she would join a sorority.

At first I think she is not intelligent. She asks me for help on her papers, which ramble and then trail off into confusion. I sit with her at a desk in the basement of the sorority, the complete works of Shakespeare open before us. *Othello.* The attributes of the tragic hero. I explain to her Eliot's essay on Shakespeare and Seneca, on the self-dramatics of Othello as he makes his last confession, as he tries to put the mess he has made of things in the best light. I do not note the line about the "black sheep tupping the white ewe," the issues of miscegenation that hover within the text. What I know are the classic readings, the criticism of Harbage and A. C. Bradley. That is what I am trying to teach her.

Gradually, she starts to get A's on her papers. I tell myself I am responsible for her success. It keeps me from thinking about other aspects of our relationship. Occasionally she makes remarks about blacks, how she cannot imagine making love to one. I am different from them, though she doesn't say exactly how. I'd like to chastise her for her prejudice, but keep silent. It's useless, what good would it do? Besides I like the fact that she thinks of me as different from blacks and yet, at the same time, somehow more romantic, more exotic, more of a lover than the white men she's known. She admires my intelligence, or what she takes for my intelligence, my knowledge of literature, which is not vast yet larger than hers. I show her my poems, brief bits of fashionable surrealism, influenced by Merwin, Wright, and Bly.

She gives me a record of John Klemmer, a jazz saxophonist. It is the music we make love to. Each time we put it on the stereo, it works like a Pavlovian bell. That and the bong we smoke. More than our conversations, what I will remember is our lovemaking. How she straddled me once, how it felt inside her, how her long dark hair hung down over me and then whipped back with a fling of her head.

I will think of her as the perfect body. I will remember how she preferred to appear before me that first time, suddenly undressed. Her delight in that. My utter delight.

IT ENDS several times. The first time I am late picking her up. We are going to a play, *The Misanthrope*. She barely speaks to me in the car. Lips pursed, she sighs in disgust. "It's so inconsiderate." I try to placate her, to apologize. It does no good.

At the theater, I look across the aisle and see Susie, who's attending the play with a friend of mine, a poet. Miles is supercilious, with thinning red hair and black glasses; he dresses poorly, is not a threat. He has remarked casually how unfair it seems that Susie is going to be alone that evening. Miles's way of silently criticizing my affair is to bring Susie to the same play. At a certain point, Michelle sees Susie in the lobby, which seems to increase her anger, though she will not refer directly to Susie's presence.

In the car, on the way home, I continue to apologize for my lateness. I am irritated at her anger, bewildered, afraid. I have the patience of a married man with the complaints of his mistresses, though Michelle is not quite a mistress and I am not married. Still, it is the same patience, the ability and desire to woo and please, to cajole, to place before her a visage of infinite understanding and goodwill, of endless charm. But no charm seems to do the trick tonight.

Back at my apartment, she announces she does not want to make love. She announces this like a weapon. I continue to apologize, thinking I can change her mind, put her in a different mood.

And then she breaks down crying. Earlier that day she had run into a friend of her brother's. In a rather cold and casual way, this friend let her know that her brother had found out he had a tumor. She hadn't spoken to her brother in weeks. A bitter, angry young man, her brother had said he liked his privacy and proclaimed he didn't need others, that people were a bother, that solitude was what nourished him. Still, she loves him, feels she understands his anger, that somehow it was related to the anger she felt in high school, that desire to turn and run, to keep the world, with its pack of restless dogs and cheap comforts, at bay. She's afraid he's going to die alone, that no one will be with him at the end. He'd never tell anyone in the family, she'd found out merely by chance and a friend's cruelty.

"He was such an asshole," she says of the friend. "It was as if he knew I didn't know and was pushing it in my face."

I feel relieved. It's not me she's really angry at. A few minutes later she excuses herself, goes to the washroom. Then I hear her calling me in the hall. She is standing in the shadow of the doorway without her clothes. A tentative smile. I move toward her uneasily, wary of her mood. It doesn't matter. She is upon me, I am upon her, it doesn't matter.

Only later, a day or two, a week, two weeks pass, and I don't call her. If you asked me I wouldn't have been able to say why. Perhaps I resented her display of anger that night, was frightened by it. I have seen in her a coldness I don't want to get near, an ability to wound that is too much like my mother's, a rancor which turns me helpless, and I will not be helpless before her. She hates black men, the way they call out to her on the street, the effrontery of their desires. She bears still the solid, rigid middle-class values of the small town she rebelled against in high school, the belief that the poor do not work hard enough, that anyone can pull themselves up by their bootstraps; after all, that is what she did. She feels she knows what it's like to want to destroy yourself, to run away from responsibility, to break whatever rule seems to get in your way, and she feels she knows how useless all that was and how to get out of it. She has little patience for excuses, for slovenliness or whatever she sees as lack of taste, an inability to keep decorum—the working-class crowd at a blues bar, students who don't study, welfare mothers. How little she shares my values, my automatic liberal responses, my tendencies to explain and sympathize with outcasts, since I know, deep inside, despite her praises of me, I too am an outcast.

It bewilders and delights me that she does not think of me like this. It is too much of a contradiction.

LATER we break up for good. Her new boyfriend will go to business school out East. She will get her degree in library science and move with him to Connecticut. They will get married, have two daughters. Then, when she sees my name in *The New York Times* for winning a grant, she will call me. She sends a Christmas card a year later with a photo of her daughters. Another card the next year. The cards stop. And then, upon seeing the film *The Lover,* her letter.

In me the letter evokes sadness and sympathy, a bewilderment at how my own vision of our affair does not coincide with hers. The events were the same, but what we were feeling, what we remember is different. That we see things differently is not in itself odd. What seems odd to me is that I somehow come out better in her mind than I do in my own. Part of me wants to attribute this to her being taken in by my facade, the wonderful mask I put on for her. But rarely do others view us exactly as we view ourselves, and there is truth in each of those views, including our own; they exist, they are real, and we don't necessarily get any closer to the truth by finding some median between conflicting views or some point where they merge. That divergence is our reality.

I have no idea what she made of my being Japanese American. At the time I made little of it myself. My brief consciousness of my ethnicity was restricted to a few poems and a generalized resentment which I never vocalized.

When I first met her, I was beginning my descent into pornography. I felt I was living double, triple lives of degradation and deceit. At times, I kept searching for what I thought were pleasures I could not live without, could not get enough of; at others, I'd focus on what seemed most normal, most acceptable. I saw my affair with Michelle mostly in this way. Compared to the pornography or the casual one-night stands, it was not so shameful. Only I did not love her, and she loved me.

What did she see in me? There were obvious limits to what I could offer her, limits I don't think in retrospect she should have accepted. Affairs with men like the man I was are doomed to failure. I feel now that they echo some need in the woman for her own self-loathing, a wish to be abandoned.

But this is not how she chooses to see our affair in her letter. In her letter we are something other than what I have remembered.

IN *THE NORTH CHINA LOVER*, her film treatment of *The Lover*, Duras writes the following notes to the first meeting of the two lovers, the Chinese banker and the French colonial schoolgirl:

The man who gets out of the black limousine is other than the one in the book, but still Manchurian. He is a little different from the one in the book: he's a little more solid than the other, less frightened than the other, bolder. He is better-looking, more robust. He is more "cinematic" than the one in the book. And he's also less timid facing the child.

Am I the lover in the book or in the movie version in Michelle's eyes? Both are like me. It depends on the angle of vision.

Michelle, of course, is nothing like the young Duras, except perhaps for a certain sense of abandonment and defiance.

She, she has stayed the way she was in the book, small, skinny, tough, hard to get a sense of, hard to label, less pretty than she looks, poor, the daughter of poor people, poor ancestors, farmers, cobblers, always first in French at all her schools, yet disgusted by France, and mourning the country of her birth and youth, spitting out the red meat of Western steaks, with a taste for weak men, and sexy like you've never seen before. Wild about reading, seeing—fresh, free.

What I constantly forget in this recounting is that Michelle did love me, said so openly, and what she loved in me was something I did not see in myself. Or she saw in me some specialness I wanted to project but did not believe in, the lover who was like no other, that would leave his print indelibly etched in her psyche.

And still for her there is this connection. In some ways her life is not very different from my own (so domestic and child-centered these days). She emerges from the movie theater with her husband, the images of the young Chinese lover and the lithe French schoolgirl reverberating in her mind's eye, the undulating motion of their bodies, the contrast of the darker skin against the lighter, his face vibrant and unretractably sad. And this mother, this wife, thinks of herself as a young girl, in bed with a man who did not resemble this Chinese lover, so sleek and slight, yet who is brought to mind by the appearance of the Chinese lover on the screen, rolling about the floor, making love to a white woman. Such a thin and obvious connection. In the parking lot, she enters their Lexus quietly, saying nothing, absorbed in her thoughts. Or perhaps this reflects the distance she and her husband have come to feel between them, a distance that has grown since the birth of their second daughter, since the onset of unfamiliar burdens, too numerous to mention. They drive home through the summer suburban streets where sprinklers jet through the darkness and air conditioners hum in between the houses, where the streetlight catches a few moths fluttering about but no pedestrians. It is like a ghost town they are driving through, some pneumatic tube, encased within the air conditioning of the car, the soft rock on the stereo, singing a song about old Mexico. She turns to look at her husband, a broker who loves his children and is good to them, though hampered by his distance as a man, as the one who must work to support them. He is still good-looking, attractive to the secretaries at work. She wonders what it would have been like if she had made other choices. She resolves to write a letter, breaking a long silence. All her husband knows is that she once dated a Japanese American writer when she was in college. She has not spoken of him more than that. She thinks of how they are approaching forty, of the years of child raising she has ahead. She thinks of the paper on *Othello*, of a spinning ball of lights above a dance floor, of someone playing piano in a darkened room. She closes her eyes, falls briefly asleep, only to waken as they come up the drive. She tries to recall if she has change for the babysitter. She looks at her husband as he gets out of the car, his hair thinning, his neck reddened by last weekend on the golf course. He tells her he'll wait in the car for the babysitter. She opens the garage door into the house, hears the hum of the refrigerator, the sounds of the television in the living room. She feels blinded by the ordinariness of her life, she feels an acceptance that is by now as familiar to her as this sadness that sits within her chest, and moves almost like breath, rising and falling moment after moment, day after day. Then she remembers the lover on the screen, recalls herself standing naked in a doorway, approaching a man who does not love her, whom she will never forget. The babysitter looks up, bleary-eyed. She has fallen asleep. On the television screen the audience titters and the host smirks. Michelle turns the television off and opens her purse.

Two days later, she will write a letter. When she is finished, she will stare out the back window of the house for a long time. The letter bears a faint hint of her perfume. She doesn't expect an answer.

3.

IN 1978, just before I was drummed out of graduate school, I taught a series of composition classes for Southeast Asian refugees.

All of the students spoke English, but their abilities ranged widely. Some had been in America since Saigon collapsed and had gone to American high schools; others had come in the recent waves of boat people. Their papers were so different from those I normally encountered in freshman composition, they often left me at a loss. Considering the students were writing in their second language, the compositions were quite good, but, of course, there were mistakes in grammar, punctuation, spelling. When I made my inevitable red marks, I always felt a bit dense, as if I were missing the point.

One man, Minh, was forty-two, with graying hair and a sweet gentle smile. In one paper, he wrote about hunting the Vietcong; the paper seemed to make little distinction between hunting a human and hunting an animal, except that hunting a human was perhaps more dangerous and more satisfying. He described the methods of tracking, the waiting in the underbrush, the patience required, the need not only to outwit the enemy but to outlast him, the cold steady application of both mind and body. In person, though, Minh's demeanor was quite placid; he smiled politely at my corrections, accepted them with a resigned air. He mentioned once a desire to sleep with a white woman (he was married).

Other students wrote about leaving Vietnam, Laos, or Cambodia. The elaborate escape schemes some had had to make were the stuff of novels. With the Vietnamese, a plan would be set to leave on a certain day, and those involved had to make sure that they would not be missed from work. One student's brother, who was a doctor, sliced off part of his finger in order to be absent the next day from work. Even if they were not missed at work, the boat they were in still had to weave its way through the marshes and inlets of the Mekong Delta, constantly aware that at the next bend there might be a patrol boat.

When I went over the papers of Huy, one of the older, more sophisticated students, he'd talk of Bergson and the use of time in Faulkner as models he'd like to follow. These older students responded heatedly to a book I'd assigned them, *The Pursuit of Loneliness*, a sociological critique of American society written during the time of the Vietnam War. A liberal tome, the book came out against the Vietnam War, using arguments which hardly sat well with those who'd fought for South Vietnam and who had been forced to flee their homeland by the Vietcong and the North Vietnamese.

As I listened to their arguments, not all of which I disagreed with, the war took on a complexity missing from my student days, when I marched in idealistic solemnity, through our small college town, carrying a candle in my hands, and singing with a hundred other students, "Someone's dying, Lord, Kumbaiya . . ." It was one thing to protest against the dour abstract pusses of Johnson, Nixon, Westmoreland, or Kissinger, or even the seemingly corrupt South Vietnamese leaders; it was another thing to listen to these Vietnamese standing before me, people whose presence I enjoyed, whose intelligence I admired and whose suffering I sympathized with, people who made real to me in paper after paper how crazy, contradictory, and confusing their lives had been from the moment Saigon fell.

Naturally, these students knew many things about the North Vietnamese that I did not. When the North Vietnamese first entered Saigon they placed bags of rice in the squares and offered them to the people in a show of affection and goodwill. But when the people picked up the bags and left the square, a block later a soldier would stop them, saying, "Brother, comrade, do you think you really need all that rice?" Gradually, mysteriously, things began to disappear, goods from the market, houses, personal possessions, people. One student wrote how the Communists had buried hundreds of dead outside the city of Hue; the paper ended by saying, "My cousin lived in Hue."

I knew that the writers, or at least their families and the government they supported, were perhaps not guiltless; a lot of my students came from the upper classes or the bourgeoisie. In the view of many of the American left, their families had been picking the fat off the land for years, ignoring the repercussions, taking as their due what had been stolen from the labor of others. What they received was their just punishment, the retribution of fate and the oppressed, a late justice. All the while, even now, I can hear these students asking, "What right have you to judge?"

Besides complicating my picture of the war, my Southeast Asian students changed my awareness of myself. The classes marked the first time in my life I felt being an Asian American was an advantage. The students were obviously more comfortable with me because of the way I looked, and some even said so. Several remarked that they were surprised when I entered the first day of class and walked to the front of the room. For some I served as proof that entry into English and writing compositions weren't impossible for people who were Asian.

At the same time, my white TA later told me that when I walked into class that first day, she thought: Oh God, here I am in this class where I have to teach students English as a second language, and now the teacher is going to have an accent too? After she told me this, I corrected every single grammatical mistake she ever made, as if to prove I had the same right to the language that she did.

One day, when I was in the cafeteria with my class, an administrator called the cashier and asked to speak to the teacher. The cashier immediately went over to my white TA.

It would take years for such incidents to effect any real sea change in the way I thought of myself and my identity. Still, something was shifting inside me. I was writing more and more poems about my Japanese American background, and I began to write a series of poems dealing with my students' stories, seeing in their experiences a vast difference from my own and yet, at the same time, some sense of kinship. After all, their struggles with the language, with America, the trials of their immigration, echoed certain Japanese American experiences.

Somehow my seeing such connections was related to what happened with Thuy. Or perhaps being with Thuy made me see such connections. Probably both.

THUY was in the second or third class of Vietnamese refugees that I taught. I was twenty-six. She was nineteen, and the age difference seemed large then, forbidding.

She had long jet-black hair, longer than that of any of the other females in the class. It was a summer school session, the students in shorts, jeans, T-shirts, flowered cotton prints. Vietnamese mainly, a few Cambodians, a Hmong. She was Vietnamese, but had grown up in Laos.

There was a picnic the first week of class for all the minority students in the summer session. We went to a lake outside the city. It started when we got up from the blankets to go swimming, and I looked at her in a black tank suit. We joined a group of students playing catch in the water. We'd dive at the ball at the same time, and our bodies touched, or we'd stand together, waiting for someone to throw us the ball, our toes barely touching, but touching nonetheless, underwater. I was aware she was my student, that such things shouldn't be done, but I was always pressing sexual boundaries in those days, trying to see how far I could go.

Then there were the conferences I scheduled with each student. As I went over her papers, she'd be shy, self-deprecating, nervous, giggly. I tried to continue in a professorial manner I hardly felt capable of assuming. In that steaming office, on the top floor of the building, there was no one else around, and I could sense her flesh beneath the soft cotton garments of summer. Our knees kept touching as I bent over her paper, marking a missing article, the wrong verb tense, a misspelled word.

In 1978, long after the last protest fury of the Vietnam War, Thuy seemed untouched by questions of politics or memories of violence. In a comparison-and-contrast paper, she chose to describe the differences between Vietnamese food and American food. She had escaped seeing any warfare, and only when the Vietnamese invaded Laos was her family forced to flee Vientiane. Her family's leave-taking, compared with that of the other students, had been fairly easy.

It was her innocence that attracted me. No doubt if she had been more worldly, coarser even, and still as beautiful, I would have been attracted to her, but not in the same way. Her innocence manifested itself partially in her refusal to participate in the gossip that so permeated the small community of Vietnamese students. As in Little Tokyo a half century before, their small population and immigrant status created the relationships of a village where everything is known, where nothing can be hidden—a fact which I was not to appreciate until it was too late. But perhaps to say Thuy refused to gossip makes her seem too self-conscious. She did not have, within her, that sense of maliciousness and spite, that envy and suspicion, that seems to propel all gossip, even the most innocuous. She also seemed incapable of anger, something that made her all that much more attractive to me.

But there was another side to her innocence, and that was her slowness to acknowledge the messages that passed between us, in her writing conferences, at picnics, at the beach, beneath the water, the slight, but hardly accidental touchings, accompanied by smiles, glances held a moment too long, just stepping over a boundary without either of us saying, "Yes, now." From time to time, in her notebook, there were little crossed-out scribblings, which she quickly hid from me, at the same time letting her actions tell me of their presence. This went on throughout the summer session.

Near the end of the class, when I showed up one afternoon at the bank where she worked and offered to drive her home, she could hardly have been surprised. Yet my offer was made under the pretense of simple courtesy. I enjoyed this in-between time, when things were still at a platonic level, because it seemed so much less strained, less knowing, less worn than any of the other affairs I was having in those years. At her home, we set up our own form of courtship. We'd practice reading, trading off pages, going through the stories of Flannery O'Connor, "A Good Man Is Hard to Find," "Everything That Rises Must Converge." I sometimes wondered what Thuy did with those pure products of America gone crazy, the Georgia rural bumpkins, the peasants of America, the unmistakable demotic dialect that runs through those stories. Did she see herself in O'Connor's story of the displaced people, where the farmhand's wife, helping the owner of the farm prepare curtains for the soon to arrive European refugees, asks, "Do you suppose they even know what color is?" Reading about the machinations of the slick Bible salesman who steals the gullible, prideful crippled girl's crutch, did she see some resemblance to me?

No, in all probability, it was simply my kindness she and her family saw. I was someone willing to teach their daughter English after hours, to introduce her to this strange, newfound homeland and its culture. After we finished reading, her seven siblings would appear, some of the older ones bringing their families over. With her father and mother, we'd sit down to great bowls of rice noodles, slices of pork floating on the surface, and the pepper and coriander pungent in the steamy broth. As I ate, the spice and steam brought beads of sweat to my forehead, and I felt somehow that I was accepting something I did not deserve, a reward for false pretenses.

On weekends, when the adult siblings and their children descended on the modest three-bedroom apartment, the rooms were crammed with relatives, mothers cooing to their babies, men talking to each other about . . . what? politics? the war they lost? new job prospects? business deals? I was closest to Thuy's two younger sisters. One of them, Duyen, was sixteen, a junior in high school; her face was fuller, more sensual than Thuy's, though not as pretty. She'd learned English at a younger age than Thuy and we often talked about the Top 40 hits she liked. I think she was Americanized enough to accept someone non-Vietnamese as her sister's boyfriend and still Vietnamese enough to appreciate the fact that I was still Asian. An even younger sister, Hien, at fourteen was completely bilingual and bore the traits of a second-generation child even though she had been born in Vietnam. She seemed quicker than her sisters, brighter, though this was helped along by her fluency. Hien would make sarcastic remarks about the Vietnamese boys at school or her brother's friends, and I could tell she would enter America in a way her other siblings would not.

In those afternoons with Thuy's family, as the grandchildren ran through the halls, shouting American curses, wearing Hulk T-shirts, I felt I was witnessing a repetition of the assimilation that took place fifty, sixty years ago in my own family, in tiny apartments or houses in

L.A. or Seattle. Like Thuy's tailor father, my gardener and grocer grandfathers came home to find strange English syllables drifting through the halls, pattering across the dinner table, salting the dinner hour with tastes and sounds other than those of *shōyu* and rice, *rāmen* and barbecued pork, the world of Asia draining from their plates. Perhaps that sense of being in the presence of what I had missed, of what I had longed to see, also kept me there, drew me closer. Certainly, I knew I was accepted by Thuy's family in ways a white person would not have been.

Thuy's brother, Tran, was two years older and seemed to have a harder transition than the others. His English was worse than hers, he did badly in school, he had little interest in work or getting ahead. He seemed ill suited to the steady work his brothers-in-law had already plunged into, seeking modest lower-middle-class livings, gaining a toehold in America through sweat, steadiness, and brains—that and an enduring acceptance of what chance had bequeathed them.

Tran would tell me of the fights he used to have with the white kids in high school, how at first the Vietnamese kids just accepted the taunts of gook and Chink, the standard "Why don't you go back where you came from?" and perhaps even an occasional "My brother was killed by you people. . . . I hate your guts."

One day, Tran and his friends came to school with num chucks, two sticks tied together with a rope, and challenged the white kids to a fight. They beat the shit out of them. Of course, that didn't stop anything. It simply meant the white kids were never going to fight them at even odds again; instead they'd gang up on one or two Vietnamese kids, gaining their revenge in parcels, fueling a cycle that didn't stop until graduation.

A pacifist by nature, I talked to Tran about peaceful assimilation, as I did with a number of other male students, one or two of whom carried switchblades with them. All the while, I knew there was little chance I would get through to them. I could not help but admire their tenacity, their willingness to spring and fight back, and I never mentioned how, listening to their stories of getting the whites back, some part of me responded with unpacified glee.

IT HAPPENED SWIFTLY, with the quickness of some steamy noir movie. At a party following the end of the summer session, we were taking a walk around the block. Late August, the light of evening drawing up shadows from the ground, a moist heat that left our clothes sticky, our faces dripping, providing an easy excuse to leave the heat of the dancers, strutting and bumping to the Average White Band.

Slowly we strolled down an alley, past a streetlamp, garages, bushes tinted with the smells of mint. She was wearing a white cotton blouse, a simple skirt. Perhaps she was telling me about the city where she grew up, its French buildings and names, the shop where her father made suits and sold them to diplomats; how later he ceased making the suits himself, a dozen people working in his shop. Listening, I tried to picture her as a small child, going to the Catholic school, returning home along the river, the sound of bicycles wobbling on the cobbles, a dream of peace.

Then she stopped, or I stopped, or we both stopped, five thousand miles away from that city, all our hesitations over, and what surprised me was not that we were kissing but that, almost automatically, my hand was thrust up her skirt, and she was parting her thighs, letting me into some knowledge I did not think she possessed. And there, feeling myself guilty for what I was taking and taking it anyway, I listened to her say my name, barely audible, and saw her eyes close in a look that might have been anguish and would always look to me like anguish but which hid whatever she was feeling, an acknowledgment of what had been hinted at that whole summer long.

· · ·

OUR AFFAIR ended a few months later. Her parents had set down certain rules—only one night out a week, the rest of the time she could only see me in group settings—and we kept breaking them. Rumors came back to her parents that I was living with someone. Her parents told her she could no longer see me. I protested, but I could see it would do no good. It was probably better for her if we ended it.

Still, it took me years to see how little I had offered her, how the affair was wrong from the start. I wrote a poem addressed to her, which ended like this:

> And what it all adds up to I can't tell.
> An accident of history? Something sordid, brief, betrayed?
> You were beautiful. The only Asian woman I've ever touched, reaching
> beyond the mirror of my own self-hatred, propelled by my lust.
> And there was this night, at the top of the tallest building in town,
> looking down at the lights and car beams shuttling towards the horizon,
> when you bent by a candle-flame, said you would never forget this night.
>
> But somehow I suspect that for you, as for me, that memory now means little.
> You're probably indifferent. Which is just as well.

When a friend showed this poem to his class, the young women argued that, with the ending, I was trying to get off too easily, to minimize the effect of the affair on her. It's difficult to decide about such things. For me, the lines say simply that, with time, she probably saw me, my actions, in a less romantic light; she probably understood that the memories I'd given her weren't, in the end, worth much. Still, the force behind the criticism is true. I abused the power of my position as her teacher and did not keep the boundaries between us.

The Internment of Desire

"What is identity? What is an Asian American? What is a chink?
What is a jap? a slant? a gook? a yellow peril? What is an immigrant?
a refugee? a lazy son? a bad student? a misguided youth?
a constant embarrassment? a surrealist? an uptight . . . banana?
a person who doesn't write about his or her feelings? a person who
doesn't meet the approval of others? If I am—as has been said with
authority—one of them, why should I try to prove you wrong?

"Am I the names you have given me? Should I listen to you
in order to find out what I should do in order to correct
your mistaken impression? If I learn to answer correctly, will I be allowed
to enter the Hall of Poetry and climb on my little pedestal?
Who are you to have said these things? Who are you to make up the rules?
Should I tell you the story of my life in sentences that you will accept
in order to convince you that I too am a poet, a human?"

—JON YAU,
"BETWEEN THE FOREST AND ITS TREES"

1.

IN THE YEARS OF MY DESCENT, I'd often hit a local blues bar, the Cabooze, which was fabulously crowded on weekend nights. I was always the only Asian in the place.

One Saturday night, the only place to park near the Cabooze was a vacant lot filled with a few patches of grass, gravel, and garbage. I drove my battered graduate student Toyota into the lot. I'd already been smoking dope for a couple of hours, had had a couple of beers. My thinking was moving along the lines of some Nazca etching, some elaborate sand drawing which I couldn't decipher. The moment the car got to the edge of the lot I feared I'd made a mistake; a few feet later, I was certain. I could feel the car sinking into something soft beneath it, and the wheels started to spin. I gunned the engine, sinking deeper and deeper. I got out of the car and looked at the wheels. I got into the car and put it in neutral. I got out of the car and tried to push it out. Nothing happened. So I got into the car, and gunned it again. And again. And again. With each blast from my foot the car sank deeper and deeper.

Was that the night I picked up the woman so overweight it embarrassed me even as I was doing it? Susie was out of town. I was desperate for something, someone, I just wanted to get laid. But what did that woman see in me? What inside her was so desperate, or so drunk—how do you separate the two—that she would go off with someone who couldn't remember her name? When she asked afterward if she could call a cab, she knew I didn't want her to stay. I drove her home to assuage my conscience. I think I cried afterward, for me, for her, for the money I spent to get my car towed, for the anger I felt that I'd been reduced to this, how I deserved this.

Or was that the night at the porno store, after the bars had closed, when I first tried poppers? At one o'clock, I'd stood milling around at the entrance of the bar, desperate for some woman to acknowledge my look, knowing all the while how futile it was, I didn't have a chance. Somehow I had to make it up to myself, reward myself for what I'd been through that night—why was this happening to me, what have I done, why are these tires stuck like this, why doesn't that bitch see me, why am I invisible, how can I rip this face from myself? I drove straight to the porno store, entered the video booth, full of rage that I picked up no one. I sucked the poppers up my nose, the smell like the airplane glue I used in childhood, the first brief blast a rush of disorientation, like an explosion somewhere far up in my sinuses, between my eyes, while the image on the screen of the woman writhing on the bed, servicing two men, one white, one black, served to tell me who would always be left out.

There were so many nights. It's hard to decide which was the worst.

MY CIRCADIAN RHYTHMS for years were that of a depressive. Staying up till the small hours of the morning or till dawn and beyond; nights of restless sexual prowlings and cravings, or the obsessive working over and over a poem; or I'd drive the streets, cherishing the emptiness, eager for the glamour of an after-hours restaurant or bar. My sleeping was endless, unavoidable, often past noon, into the afternoon, losing contact with the sunlight. The hours of a vampire. There seemed fewer and fewer moments of lucidity, when my consciousness was not cluttered with an awareness of my own self-loathing and failures or my failed desires or the fantasies which grew more and more lurid and left me unsatiated, constantly clamoring for more. When I was stoned, when I was engaged in some sexual act, there was another sort of oblivion, like that of sleep. It was as if consciousness was to be avoided at all costs, its pain hounding me everywhere my thoughts went, every route of escape. I'd lie on the bed, like a man in a fever, half awake, for days. I'd prolong my states of sexual tension, masturbating for hours. My jaw muscles would ache from clenching. I felt I had done something terribly wrong, but could not name it. Or else I named it as pleasure, something I deserved, something I craved.

In that state I understood the reclusiveness of Howard Hughes, that addiction to darkness and solitude, to closed shutters and sealed rooms, I understood the abandon of the dictator in *The Autumn of the Patriarch*, I understood the icy coolness of giving in to whatever darkness your own demons could devise, of never saying no to a fantasy or desire, I understood what Satan meant in *Paradise Lost*, the much repeated line: "I myself am hell." I felt proud of how far I had gone over the edge, how the emptiness kept coming back. I wanted to be delinquent, mad. I still possessed the adolescent fantasies of a Chatterton's death, his streaming red hair laid out by laudanum, the opium dreams of Coleridge, Byron's year in Venice with four hundred women. The poets I read saw madness as a message to the soul, as the soul's shout back to the world, mirroring all it sees. I could talk the talk, recite the lines, the essential texts. Camus on suicide, Lowell and Plath, Lautréamont and Baudelaire and the whores of Paris, *The Story of O.*

Susie was the first to opt out of this. Initially, she had tried a Freudian but it was expensive and the woman said so little, nothing seemed to be happening. After a few months, the insurance ran out.

Several months later, Susie visited a woman's therapy collective. The therapist wore long skirts, a shawl, a necklace of shells. She looked like a weaver, a clerk in a health-food store. After Susie talked for forty minutes, the woman asked her about alcoholism in her family. Afterward, Susie wondered at her presumption. A week later, her father entered the hospital with liver failure. A few weeks after that he was in AA.

Suddenly, she was moving, moving away from her past, seeing

with the edges of clarity, moving away from me, starting to name the essential abuse I was part of. I sensed something was changing when Susie entered medical school, and I felt frightened. I kept insisting my SATs were higher than her fellow students'. I sounded ridiculous and pathetic, even to myself. One evening before the auditorium on her campus I ranted about the worth of poetry in the modern world, the nature and merit of my work. She and a friend who was with us laughed.

The next week I entered therapy.

A MAN WISHES to believe there is a beautiful body with no soul attached. Because of this wish he takes the surface for truth. There are no depths. Because of this wish, he begins to worship an image. But when this image enters the future, it loses what the man has given it— momentary devotion. The man wishes for another body, another face, another moment. He discards the image like a painting. It is no longer to his taste. Only the surface can be known and loved, and this is why the image is so easily exhausted, why there must be another.

What is this danger that lies beneath the surface? How can it hurt him? It reminds him of the depths he has lost in himself.

Over and over, with my therapist, I would talk of the ache I felt looking at the women I could never have, who would never acknowledge me. He often said he understood how I felt. Later, when I found out he was gay, I asked him how could he have said that to me. "I said I understood," he said. "I just didn't say what sex."

His office was in a suburban medical building. It was antiseptic, like a dentist's. In my first session, he asked me whether I thought therapy might damage my creativity. I said I assumed we were going to ask questions. That's what I do as a writer, I said. I don't think there's a problem.

The problem was what I believed about my sexuality, what I thought I needed. It was nearly a year before he mentioned this. Up until then we talked about my family, how I viewed myself. How thoroughly I hated myself.

There were times during the sessions when he asked me not to speak. The silences made me feel uncomfortable. What did they mean?

He had a lean face, his hair was thinning. His skin was pale. He wore soft plaid shirts, jeans. I suppose his voice fit a certain stereotype. Empathic, soft, concerned. Later, though, it grew harsher, when he knew he could confront me, when he knew I wouldn't leave. I have this image of an animal trainer and a beast fresh from the wilds, the distance of trust that needs to be breached. The patience. The timing. It took a long time before I was reconciled.

What is the family system like where the seed of abuse grows into addiction? It is one where abuse is denied. The child knows that if he or she tells about the abuse, no one will believe it. Or the parents will tell the child not to tell anyone else, to forget it ever happened. The feelings the child has concerning the abuse will not be acknowledged. The child will be told, verbally or nonverbally, that feelings are to be repressed.

The rules of such a system do not have to be stated out loud. Facial expression or body posture can tell the child what not to express. Or the child discerns tabooed areas of speech by observing what the family fails to talk about, and how the family acts as if what is not talked about does not exist. This silence is a common occurrence in alcoholic families. Since no one admits the existence of alcoholism, no one can express his or her feelings over the damage done by the alcoholic.

I know there was silence in my family. We lived inside of silence after silence.

There was no past, there was no Buddhism, no Japanese language, no camps, no racial prejudice, no insults, no feelings of exclusion, no doubts about our right to be wherever we were. We were like every other family around us in our suburban block of Morton Grove, like the Jewish students in my high school. Some of them had parents who had escaped from the Nazi camps, had relatives who had died in the camps; we read about that in our English classes, copying passages from Elie Wiesel, discussing Anne Frank.

Our family? There was no story to tell.

So: there were secrets in my family. But where was there abuse? Did my father hit me? Yes. Even into high school, when he slugged my arm after I banged up the car in a parking lot. It was a huge boat of a Buick. I wasn't being reckless. I just didn't judge the distance to get out of that spot. It didn't matter. He was furious.

But he hit me only occasionally. Besides, that's what parents did in that generation. Mr. Thompson next door hit Herbie, and Mr. Thompson had played a season for the Packers, a monster of a man, who every summer when the carnival came to town rang the bell with the blow of his hammer time after time. Imagine him coming after you, whacking your ass. And what of my father's father, Jinnosuke, who chased my father around the yard with a two-by-four? My father might have threatened to use a two-by-four on me, but he never actually did.

Let's face it, there were far worse childhoods than mine. I can't really say I suffered any significant abuse. Wasn't there something inside me that was like that from the beginning—alone, alienated, unable to connect? Wasn't I always just a little too sensitive? I was a problem in school, anyone could see that. Look at all the checks on my report cards, the F's in deportment.

As for the *Playboy*s in my father's closet—I found one there only three or four times. A few issues. Not stacks of them, not the *Gents* and *Nuggets* and series of back issues that were there in Terry Steinberg's bathroom. I don't think my father ever cheated on my mother.

Did he ever go to a prostitute, say, when he was in Europe, in the service? No. He was engaged and then married to my mother. He was a young Republican, a new convert to Christ, with a puritan's sense of duty. When my aunt asked him if he was ever tempted to stray on business trips, he told her, "Yes. But then I think about what I would lose." He was a faithful man. Why blame him for having such a licentious son? Isn't there something here of my own nature? Didn't I make myself, what I have become?

My father wanted me to work hard and make something of myself. Isn't that every parent's dream, isn't that what America is all about?

Look at the times, the delusions of the counterculture, the invasion of drugs and pornography into American society, look at all this as a broad social change that was sweeping through the psyche of this country, that no one could stop, least of all my parents. There are other ways of viewing this mess.

My therapist might detect in what I've just written strains of resistance and denial. Even now things still aren't clear.

Start with the premise that a person—generally a male—may be addicted to pornography, and that this addiction may be part of a larger addiction to any number of other sexual "highs"—affairs, visits to prostitutes, anonymous sex, exhibitionism, voyeurism, etc. See where this premise leads.

Compulsive sexual behavior is different in nature from substance abuse. Picturing yourself shooting up or drinking will not produce a high, even if it may produce a longing to get high again. But picturing sexual acts or images in your mind does produce a sexual high. Since it can be argued that sexuality is part of our biological nature in a way that drinking alcohol or shooting up heroin is not, some question the metaphor of addiction when applied to sexual experience.

Certainly one's sexual desires lie at a deeper core of a person's identity than the desire to drink. You can cut back or even eliminate acting on your sexual desire, but does that affect what it is you desire? Surely, the desire for a particular person or even type of person or a particular sexual practice says more about a person than what liquor they like to drink. For this reason, one could argue that it's much harder to heal from compulsive sexual behavior than from substance abuse: such recovery entails a more radical altering of your essential self.

"You need to give this up," my therapist said.

"Why? It doesn't do any harm."

"You have a problem with sexuality. An addiction."

"What do you mean? I don't have a problem."

"If that's the case, fine. But let's see."

"I don't have a problem."

"Do you really believe that?" Pause. "If you can't give this up, I don't see how much farther we can go. It's the next step."

I was terrified at what he was saying. How could I let it in?

What does the devourer of pornography seek? He fills an emptiness in himself through creating emptiness elsewhere. But where is that elsewhere? In his wish to see others suffer exactly what he suffers, he finds a face, a body, a blank moan, a woman who must remain mute so his pleasure can exist. And in that muteness his pleasure, his power, hides. . . .

I remember the afternoon I poured my pornography into the Dumpster, the glossy pages unfolding, spilling like liquid dreams. I doused them with gas, the match popped, and the faces and naked bodies flamed, curled to ash, smoke sifting through my lungs, blood, brain. Something caved inside me, some long, slow unrepentant sigh.

I knew, even if I went back, it would never be the same. Something inside me had changed.

AT A CERTAIN POINT, Susie's therapist moved to Alaska, where she wanted to work the wilderness. Susie saw someone else from the collective; she began to read feminist texts. Sitting on the floor against cushions, they talked of family systems; she recited her past, detail after detail. Boundaries began to be laid down. She could not do this, I could not do that. Certainly the other women had to stop.

We met with our therapists in couples counseling. There was no getting around how abusive I'd become, no way of denying the stories. We both wept. She grew slowly into her rage. I tried to brush it aside, divert it. I let it wash over me, it was what I needed to hear, what she needed to say. It grew more and more painful. It felt as if we were peeling this onion, layer after layer, not knowing if there would be anything left at the end. We separated, she moved to another apartment. I called a friend that night and burst into tears. It was over, she was never going to return. I sat in the battered chair in our living room, alone in a way I'd never been for years. I went to the piano, started this free improvisation that went on for hours, waiting for sleep to descend. There was an endless interregnum of a few months. I could not believe she was gone. I kept telling myself it was only temporary. The bars, the pornography, the women, moved further and further away. I saw the person who moved through that world, and it was no longer me. I felt this peace descending.

And then she came back. And we started again.

Our apartment then was in a converted old schoolhouse. Pink paint cracked from the weathered walls of the building. We said it looked like an old farmhouse in Italy. The bathroom was down the hall, European style. In the building were a glue addict on welfare, students, a rock musician, a couple from Nigeria. Susie was in med school, I was working in the Writers-in-the-Schools program, traveling to East Grant Forks and Little Falls to teach fourth-graders to imitate the odes of Neruda, Lorca's songs. I was trying to be respectable, to see myself as a legitimate poet.

"Do you want to go to a movie tonight?" I asked one evening.

"No."

"What's the matter with you?"

"Nothing."

"Okay." Pause. "What's bothering you?"

"You never do the dishes." She began to clear the table. "You think I'm just your maid?"

"I'll do them. Why don't you want to go to a movie?"

"I have a test tomorrow."

"Then why didn't you say so?"

I went to the sink. She brushed past me. "I'll do the dishes later," I said to her back.

"You think I can go out to the movies anytime I want?"

She was looking out the window at our aging Toyota. Its sides were peeling great blue swaths. The heartbreak of psoriasis, we said. I started washing the dishes.

"You don't understand what it's like," she said.

"Okay, okay. Study. I'll go out to a movie by myself."

"Oh, sure."

"C'mon. It's not like that anymore."

"That's easy for you to say."

I put a dish in the rack and turned to her. My hands were dripping. I felt something tighten in my stomach. I wanted to lash out.

"So say it. Say why you're angry."

"You know."

The room darkened, night began to enter. We didn't notice. The argument moved into the living room. Eventually, she said it was everything, all I had done, the years of affairs, the pornography, the depression, the rage. I didn't want to hear what she was saying, her anger. Yet I had to listen. There was nothing I could say back. That was part of the pact. I'd already agreed to it. I relented, let her go on.

I recalled all we had gone through, all I wanted to take back. Part of me wanted to still be there, but I knew I could never go back. What we were doing here was something we had to learn, we were still learning.

In a building one step from a slum, we lay together and did not make love. Night after night, we talked, endless talk. I thought of stories of women who stayed with men long after the time to leave had passed. I thought of men in my therapy and 12-step groups who had been arrested, who had lost thousands of dollars, who had been divorced, had lost their children, their jobs, who fought each day the desire to go back, to enter the ease of that destruction, the call of the vertigo sucking you down. I thought about how long it seemed she had been angry at me, how much longer that anger would stay. I thought I could not live with that anger, though I knew I was. Living with it. With her. That we would go on. I could heal, I could help her heal. There were new possibilities, we began to create another life. Slowly, she began to forgive me. That was the miracle.

OVER AND OVER, in the next couple of years, I tried to write about my sexuality, my descent during my twenties. At first, I wrote about it in a neutral voice, essays on male sexuality and pornography that made no reference to race, that pretended race did not exist. It was easier to write that way, clearer. At first, the writing came in short, hard bursts, epigrams of a new consciousness. I was reading feminist texts at the time, like Susan Griffin's *Pornography and Silence*, Adrienne Rich's *On Lies, Secrets and Silence*. I was learning about the damage pornography does to women, its ties to the structures of the patriarchy. I was reading 12-step and therapy books, pushing myself past the crudeness of the prose, my hypercritical literary tics. I felt I needed to start all over again, to write, if obliquely, something that related more directly to the life I had been living, what I was trying to escape. I was trying to find more accurate ways of describing my life, the harm pornography does to men. I collected these writings in a chapbook, *A Male Grief: Notes on Pornography and Addiction.* It was my first published book.

1994. It is nearly fifteen years. I have gone past the movies, the affairs. I have since given over to some higher power what I could not control, that image, that urge, that sense of damnation. I have confessed before others, not just my therapist but men with their own stories to tell. These stories were filled with images of saunas, bookstores, movie houses, trysts in cars and hotels, a litany of act after act, crossing lines we thought we'd never cross and did. Some stories told of boyhoods far more gruesome than mine—yet those stories too helped me make sense of my past. The men around me listened with the empathy of one who knows what it's like to be there, in that world apart.

Telling is a form of healing; the Catholics with their confession, Freud with his couch, both acknowledge this. To be shriven, to be understood, to be purged. To find the buried, the necessary emotion, and release it. What comes forth at first is fragmented, inchoate. Or feels distant, perhaps intellectual, as if you are speaking of someone else's life. In therapy, there is always someone before you, urging you past denial, past evasion, past thinking. Only gradually do the feelings come through; only gradually do the events become linked together into a narrative. This narrative changes over time, at first harsh and necessary, something arrived at through a struggle, then gaining clarity and acceptance, familiarity even, and then it gradually begins to recede in intensity, becoming part of the backdrop of your life, who you are.

It is like the act of writing, it is writing. It is what you tell yourself so that you may begin anew, with a different set of imperatives, an altered sense of what you must do.

And so, I have stopped. I do not go there anymore, though the wish, the images remain. And if I choose to write about it, it is in part because those images still come to me, still need to be described accurately, showing the truth they hide. There are days I'd rather let this process go, stuff it in some file cabinet, to be pulled out decades from now, when it doesn't matter, when I don't fear exposure or exposing anyone I love. When it will take on the shimmer of someone else's life, someone I no longer know.

ONE OF MY LAST THERAPY SESSIONS was a joint session with my parents. It was something I'd been dreading, something my group therapists had urged. They told me I was almost ready to terminate but I was still stuck in certain ways around my parents. "I don't understand what you mean." That's why you need to bring in your parents, they said.

This was not something I wanted to do.

The session took place in a small well-lit room. My parents sat on a couch together; my therapists and I sat in front of them on chairs. My parents had dressed formally for the occasion, my father in a dark blue Hart Shaeffner & Marx suit, my mother in a green dress. They were obviously nervous. Dick was intense, serious, his gaze unblinking and sure; his body was wiry and angular, his hair was receding. He was the son of a Montana rancher, had fled early to the city. Ron wore a work shirt and jeans. His hair was long and blond; he had a mustache and the jocular manner of a former bar hound.

The session started slowly, my therapists assuring my parents the purpose was to foster communication, not to hurl accusations.

I was aware nothing like this had ever occurred in my family.

After a stammering start, I brought up the time Susie had called them and told them I was suicidal. This was near the end of grad school, when I was sleeping sixteen, seventeen hours a day. She thought my depression had something to do with them. She was calling them while I was in the shower, and wanted them to call me. She thought it might help. After she hung up, she waited several minutes. I came out of the shower. An hour passed, two.

They never called back.

Susie and I came to view their silence as emblematic, though Susie's call for help was likewise emblematic of the pain I'd caused her. I didn't say any of this, though, to my parents. I simply recounted the incident.

My mother said that they thought the situation couldn't be as serious as Susie had described.

That was it? That was all she was going to say? Her response left me incredulous. At the same time, I wasn't surprised. What good is this? I wondered. Why go on?

I then brought up an earlier incident after my freshman year in college. My father was driving me home from Iowa at the end of the school year, and as we neared the Chicago area, he informed me we weren't going home first, we were going to a barbershop to get my hair cut. I objected. We argued. My brother, who was sitting between us, remembers my father grabbing me across the front seat and shouting, "You kids have been a chain around my neck for years."

I was stunned by his ultimatum about my hair, his determination to mold me, to shear what I had patiently grown for several months, gaining a hipness I had wanted so desperately all through high school and now, perhaps, was on the edge of obtaining. My hair was a symbol of my belonging, of being a "freak" like the other "freaks" who dominated my college, of somehow getting around whatever deficits I lived with because of the way I looked, my Asian face. My father had no idea of what my hair meant to me, the struggles I had gone through over my appearance.

I submitted to the haircut, I couldn't fight my father. I was afraid of him physically, there was no way I could refuse. After the barber finished, I bolted from my seat out into the street. Halfway down the block, I stopped, my heart pumping like a quarter horse's, and tried hard to hold back my tears. I heard my father calling me. As in a trance, I trudged back to the car, not looking at him. I wouldn't speak as we drove home. As we passed my high school, I thought of how lonely I had been before college, how out of it I'd felt, how all my newfound knowledge of hipness was now for naught. And then I was standing in the living room, shouting to both my parents that I didn't want to be depressed this summer like I was all through high school.

"I didn't know you were depressed," said my father.

"Oh, Tom," said my mother, "you knew."

But when I told this story in the therapy session ten years later, and described my father's denial, he said he didn't remember. His face was completely blank.

My father, I thought, blind to what's before his eyes, the man who gets on with his life through selective amnesia. My mother, seeing everything but unable to give it voice.

Sensing a dead end, Ron tried to get my father to talk about how hard he had worked as a young man to support his family, to become a success. I didn't understand why Ron was taking this tack; where was he going?

"Sure, it was hard. I had to work two jobs, I had two kids and a wife. Nobody handed me anything on a silver platter."

Slowly, fractionally, as my father mapped his climb from a young GI to a cub reporter to his work in the communications division at the AMA, his voice started to tighten, a small quiver moving up his neck to his cheeks, a brief sliver of red venting in his eyes. What was he recalling? The deadlines at INS, the nights he'd pored over projects with Joe Stetler at the AMA, long after everyone had gone? Or was there some other pain, some exhaustion or failure or submission he'd long ago cut loose and buried in oblivion?

Then, as if an alarm had gone off, he pulled his head back, away from some unseen fire, and shrugged. "No, no, that was just what you were supposed to do. It wasn't anything at all."

When I saw this, I realized I could let go, I didn't have to convince my parents of what had happened. It was impossible. If my father couldn't admit his own pain, what was stirring inside him—even as I saw it stirring for a brief moment and so knew it was there—how could he admit what I had felt, how could he acknowledge that? Somehow I knew the same was true with my mother. I could shout from the rooftops about my childhood, and they were never going to believe it. If I had slit my wrists with a razor blade in high school, if I had bled all over my mother's white living-room carpet, my father would have said, "David must have tripped, it must have been an accident. He's getting A's, he's on the basketball team." And my mother would have said nothing.

But even as Dick was talking to my father, Ron was whispering that I should tell my mother how much I needed her.

"I can't do that," I hissed, "I just can't."

But he kept at me. What I felt was beyond discomfort or embarrassment, a jab of shame so penetrating, I wanted to pretend I hadn't heard him or, much worse, that my mother wasn't sitting there, listening. I was not going to do this, there was no way I'd let down my armor or shunt aside the distance between us. That was my zone of comfort, what made my being in the room there with her possible. It was ridiculous, what he was asking, some sentimental touchy-feely bullshit. This was the woman who had always felt I didn't appreciate them, who constantly harped on how I was too big for my britches, how I was too self-centered, lost in a fog of my own making, my own little world. Who was proper and distant, perfect in her housekeeping, perfect in her attire, who never let anything untoward or messy near her. What Ron was asking was impossible in her presence. We just didn't do such things in our family.

Finally, I blurted out, in words to this day I can hardly believe I pronounced, "I need you, I love you, I need you so much," and burst into tears.

My mother sat there stunned. And then, to my surprise, she rose, stepped forward, and hugged me. It was not a typical gesture. I was rippling with sobs. I felt embarrassed at my need, naked.

It was an experience I wouldn't want to go through again. My mother had given me, in that instant, a gift.

The next thing I recall is standing outside my therapists' office building in the early-autumn sunlight, feeling awkward in the presence of my parents, over dressed for the urban neighborhood we were in. The rush-hour traffic streamed by; in the park some Native American kids were playing basketball. My father, ever the optimist, remarked that he thought things had gone well, better than expected. "You could see they're well trained. They weren't trying to stir things up simply to stir things up."

"Yes," said my mother. "I could see they wanted us to be at ease."

I didn't know what to say. I had had my epiphany, if I could call it that, but I couldn't tell my parents what I'd learned, for what I had learned was I could own my sense of the past without their approval or understanding or even hearing. I still felt angry at them, but also vaguely embarrassed, saddened by what they'd just gone through, sensing how alien it was for them, so out of place in the culture of therapy through which I'd begun to heal. Mostly, I was relieved it was over. We walked to my father's silver Seville—they'd driven up from Chicago—and I told them Susie and I would meet them later at the hotel for dinner. I can't recall if I hugged them goodbye.

And then things went back to the way they were before.

Well, not quite. After our session, my anger toward my parents slowly began to dissipate. They seemed less and less an obstacle in my life. I came to accept with greater conviction that I couldn't change them, that they were who they were. They, for their part, began to pull back, not emotionally, we were never that open with each other, but in terms of control—they seemed less inclined to make critical comments about me or my life, to offer advice, to tell me what they thought I should do. I think they started to worry less about me, about my being a writer; they no longer made remarks about my lack of responsibility, my impracticality and head-in-the-clouds character, my immaturity. When my brother left his job at a bank to pursue his dream of becoming a rock-and-roll star, my mother constantly asked him whether he could return to his job at the bank or get a similar job. My father wondered when he would give the whole thing up. When my sister wanted to quit her job and go back to school, my parents both advised against doing so; they were so persistent that she consciously avoided talking to them about the subject and asked everyone else in the family to do the same. Within a couple of years after this session, I knew my parents would never act like that with me. They had let go. Some cord had been cut.

2.

MY FRIEND ALEXS, who's black, thinks that I'm reckless in my willingness to share secrets. "You write about sleeping with all sorts of women and pornography, about the ways race has affected your personal life. Me, I reveal as little as possible." He laughs. "Every moment I am not being pursued by some governmental authority is a blessed moment. . . . The less you know about me, the better. The longer I live.

"The thing I worry about is this: Do you give people too much ammunition to condemn you? You give very little counterbalancing information. I'm talking about the contrast between your craziness early in your life and your balance and security now and how openly you talk about the changes you've gone through. You run the risk of demonizing yourself."

I tell him that I'm trying to explore what my life says about the issues of sexuality and race. The ways I hurt Susie and others in my early life are part of that exploration. I know people will criticize me not only for what I've done but also for writing about it. It goes with the territory. But what's the alternative? Pretending it didn't happen, that such issues don't exist?

Alexs and I met a few years ago when we were both giving a reading at a local college. It was his invitation that led me to do my first performance piece in a series he was curating. Eventually, we ended up doing a show together about our friendship and Asian American–African American relations. He's taught me a lot about race, how much I don't know about the lives of African Americans. We talk constantly about how our attitudes toward writing are shaped by our racial backgrounds. For instance, there's our relationship with our fathers.

"To talk about my father and how hard he worked and how strong my family was and how that has led to my success—all that balances what is automatically the demonology that's associated with African American men," Alexs said recently.

His words made me feel I needed to think more about my father in relationship to the issues of race, that perhaps I've not been as generous with my father as I could be.

Alexs said this may be so, but he thought our jobs were different. "What I want to do is to say, 'No, there is a gentle spirit in African America.' Humanizing the African American male. For you, your work is about exposing the madness that is in the civilized caricature of Asian America."

• • •

IN HIS GREAT *BLACK SKIN, WHITE MASKS,* Frantz Fanon examines a black neurotic, Jean Veneuse, who uses his blackness as the sole explanation of his psychic condition. For Veneuse, there is no inner solution to his lack of concrete contact with others. The causes are all external. Such a person, says Fanon, isn't interested in health or psychological equilibrium. If the social difference between blacks and whites did not exist, Veneuse "would have manufactured it out of nothing" in order to remain entrenched in his own self-hatred.

Trapped in feelings of inferiority, Veneuse clings to the sense that his skin color is a flaw; a loner, he accepts the separation imposed on him by the color line. At the same time, he wants "to elevate himself to the white man's level," and his "quest for white flesh"—he constantly seeks out white women—is part of that attempt. Veneuse's acceptance of the color line dooms him, says Fanon. It keeps Veneuse from seeing that the world must be restructured and, with it, his own psyche.

I first read Fanon around 1985. It was a couple of years after Susie and I had finally gotten married and just before I was to leave for Japan. I was in New York, studying Japanese at Columbia, and finding it more difficult than I could have imagined. At times I retreated into other reading. I had some vague sense that Fanon had written a book about revolutions called *The Wretched of the Earth.* But for some reason I started with *Black Skin, White Masks.*

I was riding the subway home from class, still new enough to New York to be captivated by the advertisements in Spanish and the mixture of languages on the train, two old women conversing in Russian, a Hasid reading a Hebraic text, two Chinese girls with their schoolbooks, not to mention the various dialects coming from the black and brown mouths around me. I had a long train ride to Brooklyn Heights, and I settled into my book. I came to the passages on the black man who constantly sleeps with white women, how he has the illusion that his sense of inferiority will be erased by doing so. Somehow crossing the color line sexually will prove himself as good as a white man.

In an instant I understood what I'd been doing all those years.

What had long been unconscious had suddenly become conscious. Fanon had laid it all out before me. I'd elevated whiteness, I'd inculcated its standards of beauty, I'd believed on some deep level in the myth of white superiority. That was part of my sickness, part of the colonizing of my sexuality. I felt that every white woman who rejected me somehow reaffirmed both my sense of a color line and my sense of debasement.

Here, I realized, was a truth that neither therapy nor my work on family systems nor addiction had ever addressed. None of that psychological thinking had ever considered very deeply the context of race.

As the years have passed, I've come to feel both liberated and entrapped, penetrated and critiqued by Fanon. For in his dissection of Veneuse, I see a counterpart to my lifelong perception of myself as a 'loser," an outsider unable to make "concrete contact with his fellow man." Veneuse's wish to blame each flaw and defeat on skin color seems to echo my explanations of my sexual insecurity: I was a Japanese in a white world. It was as if I sometimes could see no other cause for my neuroses, the flaws in my psyche.

In recent years, as I've grown further and further away from the madness of my twenties, as I've come to see how lucky I've been in my life, I've finally stopped looking at myself as someone who's always going to get the short end, as someone whose identity must be based on being a victim. I'm happily married, with a wonderful family. The young man who went out haunting the bars, searching for sexual trysts, for some confirmation from women, particularly white women—that's simply not me anymore.

Still, I don't think the original imprinting, this colonizing, ever completely leaves. You just learn to choose other ways, you learn another response.

When I traveled to Japan in 1985, I realized that my reading of Fanon helped deepen my experience there, my questioning of identity. It wasn't just that I was encountering various aspects of Japanese culture or that my experience there enabled me to imagine more deeply the lives of my grandparents and therefore the lives of my parents. The presence of Japanese faces and media images made me much more aware of how culture shapes how we see our bodies and the bodies of those around us. A telling instance occurred one afternoon in the Seibu Theater in the Ginza, when I was watching *Out of Africa*. Buoyed by months of living in a culture where everyone looked like me, where my racial and cultural background was not neglected, I suddenly found myself looking at Meryl Streep, Klaus Maria Brandauer, and Robert Redford and the characters they play—Karen Blixen (a.k.a. the writer Isak Dinesen), her husband, and her lover—in an entirely different light. The moment occurred when Blixen is taken by her husband for the first time to their farm in Kenya and all the African servants come out to greet them. It's night, and the movie tries to impart a sense of the heroine traveling into an unknown space. Always the focus is on what the Meryl Streep character is going through; her face and form were blown up at the center of the frame.

Despite this, I realized I felt bored with her character. I'd seen the great white bwana story and the romance of Europeans in Africa a hundred times before. What I wanted to know about, what I knew little about, were the minds of the Africans around Blixen, the Kenyans who, two decades later, would organize the Mau Maus and the revolt which gained independence for Kenya. What was the interior life behind those black faces? I found I couldn't keep both the Meryl Streep character and the black faces at the center of my attention at the same time. I had to choose. Indeed, I had been choosing all my life. Only now I was withdrawing attention, affection, curiosity, from the white face at the center of the picture and giving it to the black faces. I was striking a new balance. And the world looked differently. I saw that this was a form of cultural and political power, the almost unconscious and instantaneous granting of priority to faces of one skin color over another.

After I came back from Japan, on a visit to Boston, I happened to attend an African American literary conference. It was the first time I had ever been surrounded by a group of black writers. I was pleasantly surprised at how everyone embraced the aesthetic "Art is political." At the time, I had been arguing with white Minnesota writers about this issue, and I was relieved to be in a place where this was not a question. But more importantly, it also forced me to ask questions about why there seemed such a discrepancy between the white Minnesota writers I knew and the black writers at this conference.

Slowly, I began writing work that was more and more explicit about my sexuality, trying to articulate connections between sexuality and race. One of these poems, "The Colors of Desire," opened with a section entitled "Photography of a Lynching, circa 19__ " The poem began with a photograph of a lynching, which it then connected with my viewing of the pornographic film *Behind the Green Door*, where a black man makes love to a white woman, and the way that image focused on the taboo of miscegenation. The poem was one of my first attempts to move beyond Japanese American issues and history into a broader racial context. The initial section ended with me leaving the porno movie theater in a hash-laced haze:

> I left that theater, bolted from a dream into a dream.
> I stared at the cars whizzing by, watched the light change,
> red, yellow, green, and the haze in my head from the hash,
> and the haze in my head from the image, melded together,
>   reverberating.
> I don't know what I did afterwards. Only, night after night,

I will see those bodies, black and white (and where am I,
the missing third?), like a talisman, a rageful, unrelenting release.

I showed a version of this poem to an all-white workshop I was attending in Vermont. Some of the members of the workshop were confused as to what I meant by the phrase "the missing third." I conceded that perhaps there were some technical problems and that the poem could be clearer, but I also argued that their response brought up certain racial issues. The poet teaching the workshop disagreed.

After class, I pressed my point again. I wasn't bothered by the fact that I'd received criticism about my poem; I'd been in enough workshops to be used to that. I was bothered by the unexamined racial assumptions the teacher had made.

"After all," I said, "if you tell a white person that there's a man sitting in an X-rated movie theater, they'll probably think it's a white man. If you tell a black person, they'll probably think it might be either a white man or a black man. But if you tell that to an Asian person, they'll at least entertain the possibility that the man might be Asian, and therefore the figure which might be missing from the binary opposition of black and white would be an Asian."

He finally admitted I might have a point.

Still, I could tell he wasn't happy. He'd decided that I was difficult, someone bent on making my own power play. A pain in the ass.

A few weeks after the Vermont workshop, I read the same version of "The Colors of Desire" to an Asian American studies conference. None of the Asian Americans I asked seemed confused about the phrase "the missing third."

A couple of years after this, in 1989, when I first began traveling around the country, I noticed the reception to my poems differed depending on the racial mixtures of the audience. A poem which sometimes seemed difficult or extreme to white audiences did not seem so to audiences of color. I was forced to confront the fact that I could not write for both audiences at once. And I had to ask what were the differences in the lives of people of color that could explain their responses. I realized the deeper I went into my own life and into the lives of my community, the farther away I traveled from the preconceptions of a white audience. I would not exclude the lives of whites from my writings; but I also would not write for their approval or in fear of their responses.

In a later version of "The Colors of Desire," I added an image of my father stepping onto a segregated bus in Jerome, Arkansas, confronting the line between the white and black passengers. "How did he know," the poem asks, "where to sit?"

These lines were written in response to Bill Hosokawa's *Nisei: The Quiet Americans* and a passage where he describes the Japanese Americans getting onto segregated buses in the South during World War II. Over and over I thought about this passage, which describes a telling point in American history:

> The evacuees who were sent to Arkansas had been astonished to find they were regarded as white by the whites and colored by the blacks. The whites insisted the Japanese Americans sit in the front of the bus, drink from the white man's fountain and use the white man's rest rooms even though suspecting their loyalty to the nation. And the blacks embarrassed many a Nisei when they urged: "Us colored folks has got to stick together."
>
> If there was no middle ground in the South's polarized society of black and white, in the rest of the country after the war, a Nisei could live as a yellow-skinned American without upsetting too many people, and he also discovered it was not

particularly difficult to be accepted into the white man's world.

Most Japanese Americans of my father's generation decided to sit in the front of the bus. And many are guilty of the same racist attitudes toward blacks as white Americans. But whatever their attitudes toward blacks, Japanese Americans made an understandable choice when confronted with the segregated buses: Sit where the power is. Don't associate yourself with those who are more oppressed than you; don't become partners with the powerless if you can avoid it.

Of course, blacks and other people of color in this country know when Japanese Americans and other Asian Americans are assenting to an honorary white status. When we play that card. And as long as we do that, there's little reason for other people of color to trust us.

But there is a paradox in this choice, a paradox many Japanese Americans wish to avoid. In making their choice, the Japanese Americans are no less connected to blacks than to whites. The racial identity of Japanese Americans was formed not just by the internment camps or by their dealings with whites, but also against the backdrop of race relations involving blacks and other people of color. There was an unspoken message all about them in the camps, especially in the South: Things are bad now, but they could be worse. We aren't lynching your kind. Yet.

Do I overdramatize? A threat doesn't have to be carried out to be effective.

What were the charges that prompted the lynchings in the South where my father was interned? They were that a black man had raped, or had sex with, a white woman or even that he had simply "recklessly eyeballed" her. Behind this grotesque violence was the fear of the black man's sexuality. But there was also the fear of the white woman's sexuality, the need to rein in her desires. There was also the couplings, many of them rapes, between white men and black women, which occurred in the past and left most American blacks with some white blood. This was part of a history everyone knew about, but no one talked about publicly. What was talked about was the hatred of black men, of what they represented as sexual beings.

The body tells us we are human, one species. We can copulate and procreate across color lines. This is a horrible unspeakable truth in a society where the sexual segregation of the races is still the norm. It brings up the suspicion that we all may be, after all, only human. That some are not destined by God or nature to be inferior, to have less of society's power and bounty.

Amidst this immense desire by whites to suppress blacks, the Japanese American did not call up the same vehement fears. Of course, during the war fears about Japanese Americans were certainly exacerbated. But these fears didn't carry the same sexual charge that the fear of blacks did; there was the fear of the "sneakiness" of the "Japs," the seeming insanity of their "banzai" methods of fighting. This is not to say, though, that white America was prepared then to entertain the thought of interracial coupling with Japanese Americans.

Did my father think of such issues when he looked across the floor at a Nisei dance in 1949 and saw my mother and said to his friend, "That's the girl I'm going to marry"? I don't think so. It would have seemed natural as rain to my father that he would marry another Nisei.

3.

IN MANY WAYS my experience with therapy was a lucky one. Ironically, I went through my period of recovery before I began to question my identity, before tensions and differences began to arise between my white friends and me, before I started to question my honorary whiteness. It was a time when I felt a trust toward whites, and so could enter into the process of individual and group therapy without certain reservations I now feel with them. Now it would be difficult for me to open myself to them and that process in the same way.

In 1989, after my first book of poetry came out, many of my readings and conferences took me to the West Coast, moving me out of my white midwestern surroundings. Suddenly I was visiting places where Asian Americans were an expected presence and not the anomaly I felt myself to be. It was a heady time, filled with self-discoveries about myself, about Asian America. As I met Japanese American and Asian American writers, scholars, and critics, I could feel my self shifting, slowly becoming someone else, gaining a history and a sense of Asian American culture I hadn't even known existed.

I started to think of myself not just as a Japanese American or an Asian American but as a person of color. I began to see that there was a wider gulf between my experiences and those of my white friends than I had wanted to think. I began to see how much they were mired in a conception of their own identities which put blinders on them, which kept them from seeing how their experiences related to mine. I became someone I—or they—never expected myself to be. This process was not without its pain or costs, but it felt like part of a process I had been undergoing for quite some time.

Another healing had begun.

SAN FRANCISCO, SEPTEMBER 1989. Talked with Philip Gotanda, a Sansei playwright, in a small café in San Francisco. One of Philip's plays, *The Wash*, was recently made into a PBS movie. I sense the opportunities coming his way are part of a wave of interest, a change in the ways America views Japanese Americans.

At the same time, the increasing presence of Asians in America, the recent waves of immigration, and the economic success of Asian countries have all increased xenophobic and racist fears.

"There's a section of San Francisco, just near Jap Town, and lately, when I'm walking there," says Philip, "guys will yell out, 'Hey, Jap' or 'Hey, Chink.' Ten years ago, things like that never happened."

Philip and I started talking about Sansei males, wondering about how our sexuality has been affected by the legacy of the camps. He told me about the new play he's working on. It's about a Sansei whose car is found in the river; people think he's committed suicide. This Sansei is a golden boy, gets A's in school, is popular, has a lot of white friends, does sports. As Philip described him, I couldn't help thinking about myself, how this is the way my parents would have described me in high school and college. In the play, the Sansei is an actor, and when he reappears after an absence of several years, his suicide a hoax, he informs his parents he's been to Japan and starred in a movie; only later it's revealed this was a porno movie.

"Let me ask you something," said Philip. "When I was younger and I got depressed, I'd think about suicide. But when I went to Japan, I sometimes got depressed, but I'd never think of suicide. Did you feel anything like that there?"

"I know I felt easier there," I said. "My sexuality didn't seem to be tied up with some wound. It seemed—I don't know—more natural. It wasn't just being in a culture where Asian men weren't looked at as geeks or just bucktoothed slant-eyes. I realized that if I had grown up there, I wouldn't have had to keep guessing about why a woman might not be interested in me, if it had anything to do with race. After all, they couldn't reject me because I was Japanese."

Philip and I began discussing the film about the relocation camps that Alan Parker is directing. The film's star is Dennis Quaid, a bit of casting which ought to seem odd, but isn't. Quaid plays an Irish American who falls in love with a Nisei woman in one of the camps. Parker had asked Philip if he wanted to work on the film's script. But when Philip found out the plot, he wanted nothing to do with it.

Of course, both Philip and I are well acquainted with the feelings of anger and frustration such casting arouses in us. Indeed, Philip has written a play about two Asian American actors who struggle with the dominant culture's casting of white heroes and Asian houseboys and gooks, and the decision on the part of Asian American actors about whether or not to accept demeaning roles in order to practice their profession.

Philip told me that his brother helped start the protests against the film's plot and its resultant casting. Curiously, Alan Parker went to see Philip's play *Yankee Dawg You Die*, and decided to cast the two actors in his movie as the father and brother of the heroine.

"Of course, he missed the whole point of the play," I remarked.

Even though Philip didn't want to work on the film, he ended up meeting with Parker anyway. Parker's defense of the casting and plot of his film had a slight twist to it. Parker might have said he couldn't get the film made without casting a white male star, but with the success of *Mississippi Burning*, it was more and more difficult for him to say that. By the time Parker met with Philip, his standard explanation of the film's plot was "That's simply the story I want to tell."

"Parker likes to portray himself as a working-class bloke," said Philip. "He'll make a point of letting you know that he's not part of the British middle class, much less the upper class. So I told Alan, 'Let's say I'm going to make a film, and it's going to be this great film about working-class blokes, and it's going to have all these strong handsome working-class blokes in it, and we'll make it about your family, and get this actress for your mother, and someone to play you, but let's say that instead of an English or American actor for your father, I'm going to cast an Asian American or a Japanese actor. Because that's really the story I want to tell.' "

"So what did Parker say?" I asked.

" 'That's not anything like what I'm doing, that's not what I'm doing at all.' "

SAN FRANCISCO, JANUARY 1990. Met with a political science professor named Roger Matsuo. He's an older Sansei, eight years older than me. He's been divorced for several years and has a son of six.

Rough-hewn and handsome, with a salt-and-pepper beard, his hair still black, he wears tortoiseshell glasses. His nose is prominent. Big-boned, lanky. Back in Japan they might say he has some Ainu blood in him. Cigarettes have burned a permanent yellow in the tips of his index finger and thumb.

We talked in a place down the street from the City Lights bookstore. A block away from the strip joints and porno clubs. I tried to concentrate on the former rather than the latter.

Roger talked about how most other Nisei parents didn't talk to their children about the camps. They didn't want their kids to end up being bitter and confused. Given the fate of many of the Kibei and No-No Boys, it made sense simply to say, *"Shō ga nai."*

I thought of my father's saying, "I never wanted you to have a chip on your shoulder. To always be on the lookout for racism." I felt like I needed to look at it in a different light, that I had not understood what he had needed to do in order to survive, to go on with his life after the camps.

UNIVERSITY OF MINNESOTA, MAY 1990. Talked today to a group of students at the college about the internment camps. Came up with the following analogy: If you are a shoplifter and you are put in prison, when you are released you show you are a reformed shoplifter by not shoplifting again. But what happens if you are put in prison for being of Japanese ancestry?

The answer, of course, is you try to hide that ancestry. You try to break your ties to it. You assimilate.

There's one big problem, though: That ancestry is visible in your body. Criminality is written into the way you look.

During World War II, some whites believed that simply by being genetically connected to the enemy, the Japanese Americans would naturally side with the enemy. They were the enemy, spies, a fifth column. They were guilty; there was no question of their innocence.

In the logic which propelled the internment camps, there was no way to acquit yourself, either before or after the internment.

No wonder my parents never spoke about the camps.

SAN FRANCISCO, JUNE 1990. Met with Roger again on this trip. Our conversations are getting more involved. I'm learning more and more about the camps.

"My parents were imprisoned in the camps merely because of their color and race; it wasn't for anything they did," I said.

"So?"

"The point is, they didn't do anything. So what they felt couldn't have been guilt, which comes from a sense of responsibility for one's actions. They couldn't feel as if any action they had taken on their part put them there."

"What did they feel, then?"

"They felt shame."

"Shame? What's that? Some sort of psychobabble?"

"Jesus, Roger, don't be so uptight." He smiled. I continued. "Shame says that the very core of your being, your whole self is wrong, inferior, tainted."

"And you think your parents felt that?"

"Not consciously. They couldn't speak of this. The nature of shame is silence. Besides, they were still partially Japanese by culture, they shared with their parents strong impulses toward leaving things unspoken. At the end of the war, my parents left the camps wanting to prove to America that they were 'true' Americans, whiter than the whites. Any mention of color would have spoiled that illusion, challenged their sense of acceptance."

"How do you connect this with your father's class desires?" I could see Roger's Marxist bent coming out. "And his desires for you?"

"Well, of course, being upwardly mobile was part of that. It was part of outwhiting the whites."

"But they went farther than the other Nisei. They were more upwardly mobile. How do you explain that?"

"Perhaps it's a measure of how far they wanted to distance themselves from their past and their race. 'White is better, we are inferior. There's a color line in America—don't speak of it and perhaps it will vanish'—no one ever said this out loud in my family. But I know that message was there."

"How do you know? If no one spoke about it."

"I guess I don't for sure. But I'm certain all those messages were there in my sexuality. My whole discovery of sexuality was tied up with finding a *Playboy* foldout in my father's closet, a picture of a naked white woman. I knew her whiteness served as a marker for both my desire and inferiority. Of course, I wouldn't have put it that way at the time."

"I don't know if I buy that. It's not like every Asian American boy who picks up a *Playboy* thinks about race. That's not what they get all hot and bothered about."

"I'm not so sure, Roger. How can you separate the two?"

• • •

NORTHFIELD, MINNESOTA, SEPTEMBER 1990. Gordon Hirabayashi came to the college where I'm teaching. He's one of the four Japanese Americans who took the case of the internment to the Supreme Court during World War II.

At lunch, I peppered him with questions about his case and the internment. How, for instance, had the Japanese American Citizens League reacted to his suit?

"They were against it," he replied. The JACL didn't want to upset the authorities and were worried about the reaction of the white public to such suits.

What made him take the case to the courts?

"I was a Quaker, and that was a part of it. And then my mother was always very forthright. She always stood up for her beliefs. She encouraged me in my suit."

He talked of walking all night in Seattle and breaking the curfew for Japanese Americans. He kept waiting for someone to stop him but no one did. Finally he burst into the police station and demanded that they arrest him.

When the courts finally decided against his case and sent him to the camps, it was long after all the other Japanese Americans had been transported. The authorities said he had to be interned, but provided no transportation. He had to hitchhike to the camp where he was assigned.

The irony of this still seemed to amuse him.

It was an odd experience listening to Hirabayashi. He's slightly older than my father. A small, solidly built man, with salt-and-pepper hair and gold-rimmed glasses, like my father. I suppose he looks nothing like my father really, it's just I've known so few Nisei, and have rarely had conversations with them as an adult.

I was struck by how relatively unassuming he seemed, given the fact that he played such a heroic role in Japanese American history. On the other hand, his anger was still clear and present, and he spoke strongly against the treatment of the Japanese Americans during World War II. He goes all over the country speaking about his case. I could see the energy that fueled his protest not just against the internment orders or the government but also against the JACL and other members of his own community.

I realized I'd never heard a Nisei adult talk so openly about the camps. I'd never heard a Nisei declare so forthrightly that the camps were a blatant injustice, a trampling of the Constitution.

Certainly my parents have never talked about the camps or the past like this.

And then I felt a sudden shudder of recognition. It was something I felt intuitively, not rationally, and yet I knew for certain it was true:

If Gordon Hirabayashi had been my father, if my father had talked like this, I would have felt differently about my body, about my sexuality. I would not have seen them as a source of wounding and shame. Then the thought crossed my mind: Would I have ended up with Susie then?

Of course, had Hirabayashi been my father I would know more about the camps and its history, and I would have grown up with different political beliefs. But what I felt listening to him in that moment wasn't intellectual. There was something in his energy, his anger, his freedom, that went beyond intellectual awareness or knowledge. I felt something physical in his presence, something palpable about the way he was in his body, the way his words allowed me to be in my body.

My identity, the most intimate of feelings about my own sexuality, were directly tied to what had happened nearly fifty years ago—the signing of Executive Order No. 9066 and the internment of the Japanese American community. And the different political responses to the camps—the 442 boys, the No-No Boys, Hirabayashi and the three others who took the camps to court, the Kibei and Issei, my father and mother? They were all connected to my deepest obsessions.

• • •

San Francisco, January 1991. Today Roger showed me this Bay Area magazine which purported to examine the issue of interracial dating among Asian Americans.

"Look at this," I said after I'd read it. "All the couples in interracial relationships go around proclaiming that race doesn't matter in their relationships. Love is color-blind, they say."

"What's wrong with that?"

"Well, why is it that Asian American women are outdating the men at a rate of three to one?"

"I don't know. A lot of the men may be geeks," said Roger. "I've never had trouble getting women."

"You must be the exception. Besides, if they're color-blind, why is it that the Asian Americans are all dating whites, not Latinos, not blacks, not Native Americans."

"You forgot Inuits." He smiled.

"I'm serious."

"Well, my wife was Chicano. So what does that prove? And what about you? You're married to a white woman."

"When I look at my own marriage, I can't say that my love for my wife and my sexual desire for her aren't influenced by the white standards of beauty I grew up with. Of course, I love her, and she loves me, but I can't say that love is color-blind. It's not that simple."

"What about her love for you?"

"I don't know. That's harder to articulate, isn't it? But I know race is there."

"You're getting into dangerous waters here, man."

"What do you mean?"

"Why do you think no one writes about that shit? Maxine Hong Kingston or Frank Chin, neither of them will touch it. And they're both married to whites."

"What about Amy Tan?"

"Amy Tan? Come on. Do we ever get into the bedroom with her? It's only at the dinner table, the white-guy-who-can't-use-his-chopsticks routine."

"So?"

"So you better watch out, my friend. They're going to come at you with knives."

"For what?"

"Are you really that naive? Or are you being disingenuous? You know what you're doing, you just like to pretend that you don't."

ST. PAUL, JANUARY 1991. I was reading through a sociological book on Japanese Americans and came upon this statistic: Over fifty percent of the third-generation Japanese Americans marry out, mainly with whites.

For almost all Japanese Americans of my parents' generation, you married another Japanese American. Not a white person. Certainly not a black person. Not even a Chinese American. No, you married another Nisei, and there was no question about it.

I have had to ask questions about my sexuality my parents never asked.

My own sexual history certainly isn't a common Sansei experience, but it does point to zones of silence within our culture. Questions about how our desires are formed or where they came from are somehow too troubling to many, including many Asian Americans in interracial relationships. Such questions bring up too many doubts about the "natural" process of assimilation.

EUGENE, NOVEMBER 1991. Last week, Garrett Hongo said he was talking with a Sansei academic about my book, *Turning Japanese*.

"It's an interesting book," said the academic. "But all that sexual stuff. It's kind of weird, don't you think? He talks about being unfaithful to his wife. Is that the kind of role model we want for young Asian Americans?"

This isn't the first of such reactions. I've heard that some other Japanese Americans also felt this way. In a way, I don't blame them. When I reread certain passages of *Turning Japanese*, I share their sense of unease. Part of me would rather write your standard barbed-wire-camp poem or some paean to Japanese food and a wonderful Obaa-chan, skipping all the sexual stuff, but that's not how I see things. I know a man of color writing about his relationship with white women is a lightning rod, runs the risk of indelibly branding me. Sometimes I feel this palpable force at my side telling me to shut up.

Are Japanese Americans less willing than other Americans to talk about their sex lives? Perhaps, as in any community that feels itself to be marginalized, there's a reluctance to reveal ourselves, our inner thoughts and feelings. Perhaps it makes us feel naked, as if our lives were exposed to those with power over us. We don't want whites to see who we are, what we feel. There's safety in remaining hidden. Even from ourselves.

In the camps, with their communal toilets and showers and barracks, there was little privacy; in an effort to work around such close quarters, the fulfilling of sexual urges entered into a zone of muffling. Did this engender a further silencing around sexuality?

A Sansei woman friend recently talked to me of how her mother was sexually molested in the camps. She mentioned that the Sansei poet Janice Mirkikitani was beginning to write about the issues of sexual abuse. "It's not something the Nisei or some of the Sansei want to hear about," she said. "And it's certainly not part of any picture most of us have of Japanese America."

• • •

ST. PAUL, JANUARY 1992. In policy discussions on race, whom you desire is considered a private matter and whom you hire is not. There's a separation between the bedroom and the boardroom. You don't want the government or its laws meddling in your private life, what you do behind closed doors is your own personal matter, etc.

Is there a relationship between whom I desire and whom I hire, or between whom I want my children to desire and whom I hire? Why are we so reluctant to ask this question? Is it that the lines of race run deeper than we want to acknowledge and occupy a more intractable area of psyche than we're able, at this point, to deal with? Certainly, I can change whom I hire more easily and more quickly than whom I desire.

Would a society without racism be one in which sexual desire is not configured along racial lines? I don't know. Is it desirable that all sexual desire ignore racial features? That seems an impossibility. What I do know is that an examination of sexual desire in relationship to race tells us a lot about each subject and who we are.

SAN FRANCISCO, MARCH 1992. Met with the Sansei actor Marc Hayashi. I'd just had a play workshopped at the Asian American Theater Company, and I told him that I was excited about the sexuality that Kelvin Han Yee brought to the reading.

"I suddenly realized there was more I could do with the character after seeing what Kelvin could put into him."

I asked Marc if he thought there were many Asian American male actors who could do that.

"No, there aren't," he said. "You can't portray what's not there in the culture."

I don't think he meant this as a cut against Asian American male sexuality. I think it has more to do with the place Asian American men find themselves in in this culture.

"I've always felt I had to be more extroverted, to put myself out more, in order to be heard," I said. "I didn't feel that way in Japan. Maybe that has something to do with it."

"It's more than that," Marc said. "It's the roles the culture gives us. The culture is incapable of seeing who we are. Our reality hasn't penetrated their psyche. That's why mainstream culture can't create roles for us that aren't demeaning."

Marc spent several years in Hollywood, until he finally tired of gook roles. He started doing regional theater, getting good roles, white roles, in plays by Williams, O'Neill, Albee.

"Here I was making it as an actor, but there was something about those roles. I kept feeling crazier and crazier doing them. It wasn't that I wasn't cutting it. I was. It's just that those white roles were just as bad as the gook roles."

"If playing a white man onstage made you feel crazy," I said, "just think about what it does if you do that in real life."

LOS ANGELES, APRIL 1992. Met this young Sansei writer today who seemed disgusted with the established Japanese American and Asian American writers. To him, we are all too tame.

"Don't you see, we're all too nice. That's what the problem is. We're all such good solid citizens. Where's our Genet? Our William Burroughs? Our wasted addicts? Sometimes I think we're all numb. Nisei, Sansei, Yonsei, you, me, the whole shitload of us."

"I agree with you in a way, but there are other writers who . . ."

He wouldn't hear of it. Later on in the conversation he suddenly revealed why he was so agitated.

"You know what happened to me on the way over here? You know what happened?"

He lit up a cigarette, blew out the smoke as if spitting it.

"Okay, I'm stopped at this light, and the light changes, and this guy behind me honks. So I give him the bird. Casual, no big deal. The next thing I know he's there beside me, screaming his head off. He doesn't know what he's saying. He's just screaming. And I just know this guy's going to pull out a gun and blow my brains out. So I gun it, and he follows me, and I'm racing through stoplights, and he's following, and finally, at the last minute, I do a U and get onto 405, and as I do, I'm thinking: You idiot. You mealy-mouthed son of a bitch. Why don't you just get a gun and blow away a guy like that. Or just have one, so you can pull it out, just in emergencies. Just to show him who's boss. That guys like that can't get away with the shit they pull off. Because it can't happen again. You've got to fight back. But all the while, I know I won't do it. Because I'm sane, I'm a good JA boy, I'm a model citizen. It's fucking crazy. And you know, somehow, I think it's all because of the camps, that it goes back to that. It's what we've inherited. We're just a bunch of toadies, little Boy Scouts and Girl Scouts, always toeing the line."

ST. PAUL, MAY 1992. How does the rage latent in any shame break the surface? When the sources of the rage aren't identified, the person directs the rage at any number of objects—intimate relationships, chance encounters on the street, daily life. The destruction such unexamined rage can wreak is enormous. I know. I've lived through that and made Susie suffer as well.

I do not think my parents could admit their rage: it was stamped down in the camps, in the Japanese concept of *gaman*—enduring, preserving; it was muted by their belief that by fitting in, by forgetting their cultural past, by becoming the model minority, they could assimilate. Their rage would have destroyed this belief. Their silence also spoke of a need to put that defeat in the past. Did they choose a certain level of repression to maintain their sanity?

Yet I know the rage was there, shaping their lives, the world of my childhood. I need only look to my father's rage to succeed; I need only to consider his need to keep me so tightly under his reins, his quick punishment of any errant move on my part. For years I looked at his rage merely as a dysfunction, part of an aberrant family system. I failed to consider the public history, to ask how deeply the events of the internment or the forces of assimilation shaped him.

Mirroring his desires, I looked at him and my mother as deracinated subjects, outside the forces of race. This too was part of my sickness.

4.

IT'S 1970. I'm sitting in a chair in our rec room in Morton Grove. There's a sheet draped around my torso, safety-pinned around my neck. I'm eighteen. My father takes the scissors to my hair, cutting off black strand after black strand.

"I know what you're thinking. You think you're going to go away to college and grow your hair long. Well, there's no way you're going to do that."

I don't say a word to him, don't look up. I'm furious, paralyzed with rage. With each clip, I feel myself getting uglier and uglier, geekier and geekier. I can't believe this is happening, there's nothing I can do. I have no control over my body, the way I look, the way others are going to look at me. Everything was going to be different at college, I was going to have a second chance. Now what will girls think? How can I even talk to them?

My skin is tingling, there's this boiling, run-amok energy inside my body that's got nowhere to go. I keep thinking of bolting from this chair, but I know I can't. I've got this sickening feeling in the pit of my stomach, an ache; my nerves feel alerted, as if from an electrical shock.

I cannot say anything to make him stop, there's not even a chance of his listening. He knows best, he knows what I should be. There are rules, I will have to learn this, there are rules in life. I have to look the way he wants, have to think the way he wants, have to work the way he wants. I must toe the line, I have to do as I'm told.

"Move your chair," he says.

Suddenly, he shouts. "Damnit. You did that on purpose." He slaps me on the side of my head. My ears are ringing, my cheek burns.

I have plopped the chair on his foot.

"You did that on purpose."

"I did not."

Did I do it on purpose? Did I want to hurt him?

He is furious. I'm terrified, outraged at his charge. A few moments later he shoves me over. Then he asks me to get up. I stand, not saying a word. He tells me to sit back down. I do.

I fall on the floor, my buttocks bang against the linoleum.

He's pulled back the chair.

Minutes later, it is done, the black strands littered about me on the floor. I stare at them, wishing I could take time backward, undo what's been done.

I run up the stairs and go to my bedroom. In the second-floor hallway, I hesitate. I can't bear to think about it, yet I must go look. In the bathroom I stare at myself. I keep looking and looking, as if by looking it will somehow change. I feel ashamed, exposed, as if I were standing naked in a crowd of people. I hate my face, how round it looks now. I'm almost in tears. I can't stop. It's no use. It's done. It's done. I go to my room.

Suddenly, inside me, something snaps. I'm leaving. This is it.

I go down to the kitchen to get a paper bag, go back upstairs and begin to pack. I'm trembling with fear, spurred by what I'm going to do. I'm going to get him back. It's like when I was a young boy and I'd lie in my bed at night and pound my stomach in the dark, enraged at my father, my mother, thinking with each blow I was hurting them, making them feel sorry for what they'd done. I want him to feel sorry for what he's done. With each second I feel myself growing younger, older than I've ever been before.

I run downstairs, out the door, shouting, "I'm leaving," before he can answer, before he knows what I'm doing, before—I'm afraid of his prowess, I can't fight him, there's no way I could win in a physical fight —before he can stop me.

Or I do not shout, but simply mutter the words "I'm leaving," mutter them so he doesn't hear me, mutter them because I'm so afraid of what I'm doing. I know it's only now that I'm defying him, only after he's had his way, his will, after he's done what he wanted, only now, after the moment when I might have been able to stop him, when my defiance would have meant something.

I start walking, I have no idea where I'm going. I've heard from a couple of girls at school that there are hippie pads in the city where I could hang out. I have no idea where they are. I don't know how I'm going to make this work, I don't think I can. I'm not a scrapper, I don't have the courage, the steeliness, to make it on the street. I lack cunning, a warrior's will.

Three blocks from my house, near my high school, my father pulls up the Buick alongside of me.

"Get in."

"No."

"Get in."

I keep on walking. I can tell from the tone of his voice that he's not going to hit me again. I can tell my mother has told him to come and fetch me, I know she hasn't said what he did was wrong, but her tone will have implied he's gone too far.

"You can at least get in and talk about it."

I feel a sense of triumph that he's come to get me, I've gotten him back, it doesn't matter. I stop, the car stops.

I get in. I return home. On the way back neither of us says a word. There's nowhere else I can go. This is the only world I know, a cycle of eruptions neither of us understands, the rage returning from some source we can't name, transformed into the Oedipal battles of the time—hair, Vietnam, God, my future career.

DURING WORLD WAR II, white Americans saw the bodies of Japanese Americans as evidence of an invasion, a foreign threat. The internment camps rid the West Coast of that evidence by making those bodies of Japanese Americans invisible, silent. The camps were proof that the government and the white majority could accomplish such banishment, proof how deeply the private lives of the Japanese Americans could be invaded.

Did any of this affect my father? What were the things he feared? What anxieties beset him? How did he make his way in the world? Who gave him advice for rising in America? Was it Professor Bigelow or Joe Stetler, his boss at the AMA? Was it his Christian God? Or Dale Carnegie? Was it *Father Knows Best* or Arnold Palmer? Or was it his father, of whom he rarely speaks?

My father lived once in a forgotten house, a foreign house, a house that vanished beneath a freeway. He rode a bus once to a racetrack, where he lived in stables for a few weeks, and then to a camp in the swamps of Arkansas. He lived there so briefly, a mere breath in history and probably not even that. He imbibed the dreams of his suburban generation. He was never a race man, though he had a race.

Why didn't the Nisei fight back? Some did, some didn't. That's probably the wrong question. Were they afraid? Yes, but fear forms so many answers, that too is probably the wrong question. What angered my father? That question may be useful, but the answer is lost, forgotten, he could never tell you. Why did his son turn out so strange? My father would probably tell you his son isn't so strange or even troubled, though of course he disagrees with much of what his son writes.

Violence is change, terror is change, but healing also is change. So is forgiveness. So is sorrow. And there are wounds so sweet and sticky, we hover about them like flies, we can never quite leave.

And yet we are leaving all the same. I left his home so long ago. My hair has grown long over the years. My father says nothing of it. And I am still his son.

AFTER *TURNING JAPANESE* came out, a Sansei colleague told my dad that she'd read his son's book.

"Then you know what a bad father I was."

"I don't think that. You know, my brother and my father had the same sorts of battles, over hair, over Vietnam. It was the times."

They talked a bit more, then my father asked, "But what about hitting him? Do you think I was wrong to hit him?"

"That was a generation thing. That was how the Nisei punished their children. The Sansei don't do that anymore. You weren't any different."

Talking on the phone, my father mentioned this conversation to me in passing; he didn't make a big deal of it.

A few months later, he was talking to another Sansei he'd met on a business trip. The Sansei said that he always felt his father didn't love him because he never said the words.

"But that's just the way the Nisei were raised. Some people just can't express what they feel, but they feel it," my father replied.

My father told me about this incident too. I'm not sure how conscious he was that he was speaking about himself, that he was speaking to me what he couldn't say directly.

• • •

A FEW NIGHTS AGO IN BED, I was rereading the last section of Philip Roth's *The Facts*. There Roth's alter ego and fictional creation Nathan Zuckerman criticizes Roth's autobiography, saying that Roth has left out his dissatisfactions, even treating his conflict with his father peripherally. In contrast, it's the note of grievance and criticism, of disgust, satire, and estrangement, which so characterizes the power in Roth's fiction. "Which am I to believe is the posturing," says Zuckerman, "the fiction or . . . this manuscript . . . steeped in the nice-guy side?"

I read Susie this passage.

"That's hardly your problem," she said. "You're a master at making yourself look bad. It's your good sides you have trouble writing about."

"Do I have any good sides?"

"You do, dear."

I read her the passage where Zuckerman describes how Roth revolted against his tribal identity: "I could be wrong, but you've got to prove it, to convince me that early on you didn't find something insipid about the Jewish experience as you knew it, insipid about the middle class as you experienced it, insipid about marriage and domesticity, insipid even about love . . ."

I closed the book, sat up a bit.

"So what was I trying to escape?" I asked Susie. "What was I rebelling against?"

"Well, I see two sets of figures you were going against." First, she said, there was my father and the Japanese American community. In the beginning, I bought into the model-minority myth, it was what was driving me. Then I reacted against it. I hated how my father wanted me to be caught up in it, to be the steady and industrious Japanese American.

"You decided you weren't going to be a lawyer, the good Sansei son. You weren't going to be like Bob Hoshizaki and become a doctor."

"But I also revolted against the tribe of whiteness."

"Yes, that was your second rebellion. You became pissed off at

258

whiteness, and you became particularly pissed off at white writers. And you became pissed off for sitting at the knees of the white father writers. You kept on saying, I'm going to grow up and be just like you. But then you found no matter how you grew up, no matter how hard you tried, you'd never be like them. So you left them. Otherwise, you'd always be one down, you'd always be second-class. It's only when you went off on your own that you really had any possibility of being successful."

"But my father took up with the white fathers." He had chosen Professor Bigelow and Joe Stetler as mentors. He'd rebelled against his father and took to them instead. His rebellion and hard work garnered his entry into middle-class America, and he accepted whatever caveats came with the bargain.

I picked up Roth's *The Facts*. I pointed out that as much as I identify with Roth, there's a difference between us. He can pay homage to the white fathers, Jewish and goyim, and still become a major player.

"Here's the way I see it," Susie said. She felt the camps had emasculated the Issei fathers, at least in the eyes of their sons. After the camps my grandfather ceased to be a father figure to my father, he was no longer that frightening authority that chased my father around the yard with a two-by-four. He had nothing for himself, he was completely irrelevant to the choices my father was making in that he had no power to stop them, no power to voice his opposition in a way my father might have had to heed. So after the camps, my father went off in search of new father figures, and it couldn't be another Issei, because he saw them as being like his father.

"Now your feelings about *your* father were so tortured and raw," Susie continued, "you couldn't accept any father figure no matter what color. You don't want to have to pay the price of accepting authority from someone else."

"Why?"

"You can't stand to have anyone have authority over you. You can't have a boss, a mentor."

I got up from the bed and put *The Facts* in the bookshelf. "But that's just begging the question," I said, pacing about. "I think I revolted because I saw that submission would be deadly. It wasn't just some Oedipal struggle."

"Why would it be deadly?"

"I would not be able to survive. I'd have to kill something inside myself. Not let it grow. Because if I accepted my father's way, I knew I would not be a legitimate heir. I'd be the bastard son."

"The usurper to the throne."

"Yes. Like Edmund in *Lear*." But was my father like Edmund? My father wanted to be the good son to the white fathers. He never expected the throne. So I don't think he thought of himself as a bastard. He never expected to be acknowledged at all, even as a bastard. He was grateful to submit himself for their approval, even if he would never rise as high as the white sons.

I smiled at Susie. Something was becoming clear. "It's interesting, this bastard position."

I pointed out that it's one where you're filled with fury, absolute rage. You know you're as good as the legitimate heir, it's simply an accident of birth that keeps you from the throne. You want recognition from your father—in this case, not a real father, but the white fathers —and yet you hate him because he can never give you recognition, he can never truly acknowledge you or allow you to have what you think you deserve.

I stopped pacing and sat back down on the bed.

"Let me go out on a limb here," said Susie. "As you were growing up, you sensed your father would always be a vice president, he would never get to the top, he would never be president. If you followed his route you saw that would happen to you, even though he kept saying you can do better than me. He was never going to be the top man and he was offering you the same thing. You could never be in the line of succession; at most you could be lord chamberlain. So you had the son's rage at your father for his not being more successful, for not realizing he was being a dupe. But you were also enraged that he hadn't given you the bloodline to be king. It is his fault after all that you're not white. And you hated his naiveté, his belief that just by dint of hard work you could make it."

"Did I know this?"

"Of course not. Of course yes."

"You know that's not the way I think of him. What I hated was . . ."

"You don't hate hard work."

"No. What I felt was that his world was incredibly boring. I knew I'd die of boredom working for some corporation or as a lawyer." Pause. "But the thing was, it wasn't boring to him." Given the world my father grew up in, what he moved up into probably seemed quite exotic and rewarding. He was traveling in a world he never could have aspired to as a child.

"This is a bit much," replied Susie. "But while you didn't fear they would put you in a concentration camp, he was still trapped in a prisonlike state. And if you followed him you'd be in the same camp."

"That's interesting. The holdover of the camp mentality."

"Yes, the internment camp as a metaphor for the glass ceiling," she said.

But there was another level to that. There was also the internment camp as inducing the mentality to accept the glass ceiling. The internalized internment camp. Perhaps I had to kill the internment camp within me, to free myself of its bonds. My father dealt with it by pretending the walls weren't there, the internment camps didn't exist.

"I had to say those walls are there, let's destroy them. The walls are real, and I'm absolutely furious they're there."

"And you're furious at him for not seeing them, and for not be-

261

lieving you," said Susie. "And that's part of your role. You always anger some Asian Americans when you talk about yourself and them as people of color. Because what you're saying to them is that the walls are there for you and for them, just like they're there for other people of color. You're not that different, that special, that much of a model case. You're telling them they need to believe the walls are real."

"I'm furious at him for trying to blind me." Pause. I started to laugh. "And, as every Freudian knows, to blind is to castrate. To repeat: We're expected to serve as the eunuchs of America."

"Here they are." Susie raised her hand, swaying it back and forth, with her forefinger and thumb pinched together. *"Los cajones."*

"This is the piece I was waiting for. I kept thinking we're going over this as a psychological Oedipal struggle and as a political thing, but where's the sex?"

"But there's a difference between a eunuch and a bastard. A eunuch doesn't have rage. He has no testosterone. A bastard does, he's highly sexed. And part of his rage is he won't get the princess."

"The white princess."

"Obviously."

"Amazing, isn't it?"

"I can be brilliant, you know. Now, let me go to sleep."

"Good night, princess."

"Good night."

5.

I AM THINKING OF DESIRE—why I desire you, why you desire me. We have been together so long, have delved into each other so thoroughly we no longer dazzle, no longer elicit delirium from each other. We are the long, thoroughly married; our arousals are expected, squeezed in between work and children, your schedule and mine, the crammed hours of our days.

Yet we are, certainly, the type of couple that intrigues me. I like the disorder we represent, the anomaly. I love what we have written on each other's bodies and where that writing has led us. There's a constant surprise there, an unwieldiness.

What do people see when we walk down the street? Last week we went shopping with my sister, Linda, and our children. Several people mistook Linda for the wife, the mother.

I sometimes wonder: Do your colleagues, your patients and their parents look at you differently after they've met me?

Most people—even Asian Americans, even you and I—are less articulate about why you were attracted to me than vice versa. There's a zone of silence there, an absence of thought and observation. A couple like us isn't really a taboo anymore; we're just odd, unremarked.

In the books, in movies, there's always the white man with the Asian woman, *The Joy Luck Club*, *When Heaven and Earth Change Places*, *The Teahouse of the August Moon*, *Shogun*, dozens of Vietnam or kung fu flicks. The images, the stories so characteristic of the West meets East, the white male's seemingly natural prerogative. But the other way around, there are only a few examples, Marguerite Duras— *The Lover; Hiroshima, Mon Amour*—the BBC's *The Ginger Tree*, or that long-forgotten film *The Crimson Kimono*, where the white woman actually chooses James Shigeta over the white man. I keep those works, those films, in my head like talismans. I feel the need of precedent. It's part of my obsession, my sickness. It's nothing my father or mother would know, though they must have dreamt it. After all, my brother and my sister also married white. It would have been strange, to all of us, if they had done otherwise, though I don't think my siblings or my parents could express why.

Do either of my siblings go on about this like I do? No. It doesn't matter to them.

Or as my sister once said to me, "You talk about things I would rather sweep under the rug."

WHAT OF MY MOTHER AND FATHER entered my desire for you?

I think of my father's homecoming from Germany, six months after I was born. How my mother was so young then, barely twenty. My father seemed so much older and worldly at twenty-three. If I were to see them today, I would think of them as children.

They lie together naked in a bed that is rickety, on a mattress as thin as a futon, its edges snarled by wear. It's the South Side of Chicago, a street near Cottage Grove. There's the high-pitched wail of a siren, which fades in the distance. The rumbling of the El. A cold, palpable wind passes through the window, over their bodies. My mother's sisters and her father sleep down the hall. I am sleeping in the crib in the corner. It's been so long since my father and mother have seen each other, they are pained by their desire, frightened a bit, I think. He's surprised again at how small her body is, how delicate. He reaches for her over and over, they are rolling together, their skin shivering in a cold room, the moistness of their breathing dripping at the windows.

All of a sudden I start to cry. The wail comes out of nowhere, it is the kind of despair only an infant can reach, so needful, so mournful, it pierces to the bone.

My mother rises from the bed, scoops me up in her arms. I don't think she sings to me. That isn't her way. There, there, she repeats over and over, like a mantra. She lays me down beside my father, whose body is still half caught in the motions, the statement of love.

He laughs, though, at this wailing body, suddenly simmering down to a whimper. He's not frightened, as he thought he might be. He smells the skin of my mother, my skin, and the aroma is so strong, like smelling salts, it knocks his head backward, brings him bolt upright.

He closes his eyes and listens to our breathing, then the sound of my suckling at her breast. My mother is still murmuring to me, the warmth of her body fastening around me, the milk from her breasts drowning my tongue. How this baby suckles with toothless gums. How this gurgle spills upward from his throat. My mother breathes heavily, once, twice, three times, and suddenly she's so tired she can barely keep awake, there is nothing she wants more than to sleep. She lays me down beside her, between her body and my father, my head still fastened to her breast, still suckling. She seems to have forgotten the desire that was in her moments before.

At first, my father is disappointed at her exhaustion. Then his disappointment passes, and he too feels this desire for sleep washing over him. Is it morning or night in Europe now, where he has traveled from? His body is still shuttling past time zones, wondering where it is. He can't believe what night has washed up between them. He can't believe what he feels now, this infinite love. The knowledge is tinged with a sadness at his distance from this sleeping couple, this mother and child. He tastes something like iron on his tongue, iron and salt. He falls back against the pillow, as if shot. He closes his eyes.

He wakes hours later. Beside him on the bed there's only this expanse of wrinkled whiteness, the ghosts of their bodies, and a wash of cold sunlight, sifting through the frost at the window.

My father rubs his chin, scratches his ear, and looks at himself in the mirror above the bureau. His body is lean, muscled, dark. He has so many dreams, he doesn't know where to start, ambitions for himself, his son, the seriousness of a young man who does not think of himself as young.

A young Nisei soldier, his recent bride, his first son. 1952. Halfway across the globe, in the hills north of Seoul, the fighting has grown fiercer than anyone predicted. It will never touch him, never even get near him. He knows he is one of the lucky ones.

He hears whispering in the hall. I'm awake, he calls. And then this sound, unmistakably human and odd. The cooings of his son. Who appears in the doorway in the arms of his wife, hauled in like a sack of fruit, like a small pillow, knees, elbows, skull, all rounded with dimpling fat.

My father thinks how they will soon rent an apartment, they cannot live much longer with her sisters, her father. He barely knows what to say to the old man, his Japanese is so rusty, it's virtually nonexistent. He will try to talk to the family about Europe, but no one will be interested.

He gets up, goes to his wife, and kisses her. He can hardly believe he is here.

I can hardly believe he was ever that young. Or what I feel for him, for my mother, now could be so particular with love.

I KNOW I speak against their extinction. My parents. They are in retirement; they moved this past year to Las Vegas, after nearly half a century in Chicago. I feel totally estranged from this move, it seems so odd to me. And perfectly right for them. The houses are cheaper there, the air warmer, the days open year-round for the fairways, a morning jog.

Once I suckled on my mother's breast. I think of that now as my wife is pregnant with our third child, as Nikko has made a habit of touching her nipples, my nipples, his own nipples, the way another child might suckle his thumb for solace, to calm and reassure himself. Long ago, I lay with my cheek against my mother's shoulder, smelling her hair, the faint scent of smoke perhaps, the smell of her milk. I'm looking at the window behind her, the sun. There's a book on the sill, its pages open. No one now remembers what that book was about. I close my eyes, I fall asleep.

When I waken it is more than forty years later, and I hear my own son knocking at my study door, wailing to be let in, as I write these words. I pick up a green, battered Modern Library edition, Joyce's *Portrait of the Artist as a Young Man*. I open the cover and there's my mother's signature in flowing precise lines. I'd always assumed the book belonged to my father.

My image of my mother alters ever so slightly.

I DON'T UNDERSTAND this love of ours, how rich it is, how abundant. There are so many stories to tell. The present wants to crowd out the past, and usually it succeeds. All that history ebbing in a touch, an errant phrase, the thought we can't quite put our finger on and quickly forget. We live now by a river, our house is a large colonial. Morning sunlight slips freely through the branches now the leaves have gone. The collie next door circles and circles the lawn, tied to its stake. It calls to the Labrador two doors down. A bus clatters down the street to a cluster of children, each with a backpack propped on her shoulder blades.

A teddy bear, a pack of cards, crayons, and paper lie scattered on the rug. Evidence of what our bodies have produced. I know these children, their characters and quirks, I am learning their lives. Each night we lay in our bed piecing together stories of their days, their sayings, the various gestures they make, Nikko's bobbing-head yes, Sam's plethora of adverbs beginning each sentence—"Obviously . . . Actually . . . Hopefully . . ."—the punctuations of a precocious child. I couldn't have foreseen we would come to this spot, that the trees out back would be bird-thronged, the roof slate, the gables and windows so many and differently shaped. For years I kept trying to move away from you. For years I never left. I missed the mark so often. How did I ever find it?

I thought I was in love with pain. It was this open window through which I could view the sea, the dissolution I sought. I think of the two of us, how long we have lived in this city, half our lives, the half of our lives we have lived together. I had so many ideas about us, so many of them wrong.

There's so much I didn't know about us, so much I don't know about the others I've written about here. I know they continue to live and contradict me, that they are nothing like my words. They are braver than I thought, more noble. I could never pretend to be invisible to them, even if they didn't know I was watching. I peered in through windows, entered rooms without knocking, listened to their talk at night. Still, something escaped me. Just as we have escaped.

We could have split apart. Someone might have predicted it. Might say you should have left me. I might have continued on toward decimation. The course is never certain. I never thought my parents would move to Las Vegas. Or that my sister would get divorced. Or that I would have two children and one more on the way. Or that I would one day help found an Asian American arts organization in, of all places, Minnesota. It's all so complicated. The more I tell the stories, the falser they get. That's because I see more complications, not less; other layers crop up, unexpected voices. My view isn't the final one, even if here I get the last say.

LATE AT NIGHT is for love. All the sheets on our bed are thrown off, an amorous disarray. Our chests are still heaving, our breathing still hard. You are lying on top of me, collapsed as if shot. Our eyes are closed, we're barely conscious. There's only this murmuring that gurgles up from one of us, then the other, though never at the same time. My flesh feels flush with blood. Your breathing rolls like a wave through my ear. I feel myself slipping from inside you. One of us sighs. The beat of the CD continues, heavy and intense, as if we still haven't stopped.

Suddenly the last song dies off, there's the soft whirring of the disk. I think I hear Nikko crying. It's only a cat. Or the creaking of the house. A faint light from the street enters at the gables.

ACKNOWLEDGMENTS

This book is the result of the efforts of many people.

I want to thank my parents for their love and support and for the strength they have brought to their lives and the life of our family. My thanks to my Aunt Ruth, Aunt Baye, Aunt Ruby, and Aunt Miwako for their talk of the past. My sister Linda's support of my work and my family has meant a lot to me. Many relatives, including my parents, have helped out with child care during the last stages of revision: my in-laws, David and Jane Sencer, my sisters Linda and Susan, my Aunt Miwako, my sister-in-law Ann Sencer. I am very grateful to those who have helped take care of my children over the years, Diane Natrop and Merodie Nelson, and a special thanks goes to Molly Weiss, who has become part of our family and has blessed us and our children with her love.

I want to thank Jay White, Garrett Hongo, and Alexs Pate for reading through the manuscript and offering helpful criticism, as well as buoying my spirit and availing me of their intellectual acumen. The friendship of Valerie Lee, Li-Young Lee, Kelvin Han Yee, Sheila Murphy, Jon Jang, Cynthia Gehrig, Peggy McIntosh, Cathy Nelson, Alan Soldofsky, Arthur Jafa, and Marilyn Chin helped sustain me in my work. Philip Gotanda and Marc Hayashi provided useful insights and dialogue that spurred my thinking. N'kaulis Lyfong and Michelle Colbeth provided needed assistance. I also want to thank the numerous people who have supported the Asian American Renaissance and the spirit of the Asian American community in Minnesota, both of which have made my work less lonely.

My agent, Amanda Urban, helped usher this book into existence and gave me encouragement at crucial times. My thanks to Martha Levin and Charlie Conrad for believing in my proposal. Betsy Lerner went out of her way to read a late draft and provided many helpful comments. My editor, Charles Flowers, was a true treasure and read through numerous drafts of the manuscript, guiding and supporting me beyond the call of duty. I am extremely grateful for his efforts and for his friendship. May every writer be so lucky.

For publishing portions of this book, I want to thank the editors of the journals *Conjunction, Mother Jones,* and the *New England Review,* and the editors of the anthologies *Under Western Eyes: Personal Essays from Asian America* and *On a Bed of Rice: An Asian American Erotic Feast.* Thanks also to Milkweed Editions, which published *A Male Grief.*

Very real support came from an NEA Literature Fellowship and a Lila Wallace–Reader's Digest Writers' Award. A Jerome Travel and Study Grant supported a trip to the West Coast that became a starting point for a portion of this book.

Finally, I want to thank my family, the center of my life, the anchor of my soul. The presence of my children, Samantha, Nikko, and Tomo, has given me hope and energy for this work, and their love is the light I live by. My wife, Susan Sencer, has done more for me than I can say. She has loved and supported me and our children, and together we have gone the long hard way. She has read the drafts of this book with patience and care, and her criticisms and suggestions have been of immense importance. She has put up with much with great understanding; this book would not be possible without her. She has, as she knows, my enduring gratitude and love.

ABOUT THE AUTHOR

David Mura is also the author of *After We Lost Our Way* and *The Colors of Desire* (poetry), *Turning Japanese* (memoir), and *A Male Grief* (nonfiction). His poetry has appeared in *The New Republic*, *The Nation*, and *The New England Review*, among other journals. He has been awarded two NEA grants, the Discovery/*The Nation* Award, a U.S./Japan Creative Artist Fellowship, and, most recently, a 1995 Lila Wallace–Reader's Digest Writers' Award. He is also a performance artist and, with African American writer Alexs Pate, has created and performed in "Secret Colors" and a movie, *Slowly, This,* for the PBS series "Alive TV." He lives in Minneapolis with his wife and three children.

Printed in the United States
by Baker & Taylor Publisher Services